*As a result of the overwhelming, countrywide
popularity of the first edition, we are publishing this
new and considerably enlarged edition of*

BOBBY JONES on
GOLF

*With a brief introduction by that much-loved
and well-known sports authority,*

GRANTLAND RICE

Revised in 1997 by
Sidney L. Matthew

*In this edition is contained everything of importance
that Bobby Jones has ever written on the game of
golf. Detailed and thorough study of every
phase of the game is complemented with
action and posed photographs of the
author and others much in the
golfing limelight.*

THE "ESSENTIAL" BOBBY JONES .... A Foreword by Sidney L. Matthew v

"BOBBY JONES" .... An Introduction by Grantland Rice vii

GOLF CONCENTRATION 1
*The two forms of concentration – What to think of when making a golf shot – Developing
the right kind of confidence – The virtue of patience, a valuable essential*

ON PUTTING 5
*Necessity for relaxation and concentration – Putting as a game within itself – Training the
eye – Should putts be conceded?*

PUTTING PSYCHOLOGY 11
*Emphasizing the necessity of eliminating fear and worry in putting – Discussion of restrained
left hand, keeping the head still, the pendulum stroke*

ON STANCE AND SWING 16
*Advantages on both wide and narrow stances – Good footwork foundation of swing – The
straight left arm – The upright and flat swing*

THE SOUND GOLF SWING 24
*The simplicity of the golf swing – Controlling the right hand – Keeping on line after impact –
Freedom vs. compactness*

A FEW FAULTS AND HOW TO CORRECT THEM 28
Temporary remedies for golfers off form – Eradicating faults after the winter layoff

TIMING THE GOLF STROKE 32
*Containing some unusual spark photographs on the actual timing of the golf stroke from the
moment the club strikes the ball to the instant the ball leaves the tee*

ON WOODEN PLAY 34
*Some cures for hooks and slices – Advantages of the high tee – Difficulties caused by pressing
– The intentional hook – The intentional slice*

THE BACKSWING — A MOST IMPORTANT PART OF THE GAME 39
*One of the most important phases of the game is here discussed in full detail – Types of backswing
– Mechanics of swing – The hip motion in the backswing – Hazards of abbreviated backswing –
The right hand complex*

ON IRON PLAY 42
Dealing particularly with long iron shots – A cure for shanking

JUDGING DISTANCE DIFFICULT 47
*Letting the eye judge – The inadvisability of relying on card distances –
The necessity for being observant*

PLAYING SHORT! 49
*On pitch, run-up, blast, chip, and other short iron shots – The three types of bunker shots
– The chip shot and its relation to the putt*

BRAINS AND IMAGINATION IN GOLF 56
Several instances where headwork is more important than skill

"WARMING UP" 58
    Dealing with necessity for practice on drives, putts and pitches

ON THE CORRECT GRIP 60
    Where golf club should be grasped – How grip affects the swing

NERVES IN GOLF 64
    The necessity for mental composure – Tips for the nervous golfer – Worry and hurry detrimental
    to the game – The strain of competitive golf

FEAR OF WHAT MIGHT HAPPEN LEADS GOLFERS INTO TROUBLE 68

THOSE HOODOO HOLES... 69

THE PART LUCK PLAYS IN GOLF 72

FIGHTING THE WIND!... 74
    Dealing with the effects of wind and rain during play –Playing in wind a test of temperament

YOUNGSTERS SHOULD PLAY GOLF ALONG WITH OTHER SPORTS 77

THE DIFFERENCE BETWEEN ENGLISH AND AMERICAN COURSES 79

ON THE GREEN! 83
    Discussion of the putting greens on the various American championship courses

SOME RANDOM THOUGHTS ON THE GAME................ 86
    Winter tournaments, a means of stimulating golf interest – Golf resolution to remember in
    spring practice – Miniature course golfers and the longer game – Advantages and disadvantages
    of large galleries

MORE ABOUT THE NEW GOLF BALL........................... 90
    Preference for steel or hickory shafts – Freak clubs seldom practical – Rust on clubs sometimes
    helps – Advantages of retaining old favorites

ON GOLF CLUBS... 92

HANDICAP IN GOLF MAKES GAME POPULAR................. 98

THE UNFAIRNESS OF FURROWED BUNKERS................. 99
    A few opinions on a type of bunker that is rapidly becoming the vogue on a number of
    championship courses

IF GOLF IS WORTH PLAYING, IT IS WORTH PLAYING RIGHT................. 100
    On adhering to the rules of the game – Interpretation of Winter Rules

SPORTSMANSHIP AND GOLF....................................... 103

ON FUTURE GOLF ACTIVITIES 105
    A brief discussion of the writer's future participation in golfing activites – Some views on
    the strain of golf competition

First published in 1929 by One Time Publications, Inc., Copyright 1931 by Bell Syndicate, Inc.
Revised in 1997 by Sidney L. Matthew, copyright 1997, and published by Sleeping Bear Press, Chelsea, Michigan.
Photos not noted specially are courtesy Emory University Special Collection and Sidney L. Matthew Collection.
Prepress by GrandAd Graphics. Printed in Canada by Friesens, Altona, Manitoba.

In 1931 Bob Jones teamed up with Lambert Pharmacal Company to broadcast twenty-six weekly radio programs nationwide on NBC. Jones talked about many of the golfing lessons in this book.
(Wide World Photo)

The "Essential" Bobby Jones

A number of years ago, the curators of the Royal and Ancient Golf Club of St. Andrews noticed that the radiant beauty of its stately and historic clubhouse had become dimmed by centuries of environmental endurance. They embarked upon the ambitious task of sandblasting away the darkness and bringing to light perhaps the most famous shrine in golf. Sometimes a little spring cleaning can go a long way. Like polishing the silver or knocking the rust off your clubs. After 68 years, it's probably time that this work by Bob Jones be dusted off too.

This volume, first published in 1929, was immediately greeted with unbridled enthusiasm by the golfing world because it contained the "essential" Bobby Jones. There was then a great need for all of Bob's "essential" thoughts on golf to be collected in one place. After all, Jones had staked his claim to the mantle of the greatest player ever in 1930 when this volume was last revised and reprinted. Achieving the Grand Slam petrified the Jones legend into a granite fortress which O.B. Keeler accurately predicted would be attacked by others in vain forever. In six decades little has changed. If anything, Jones' stature in golf has grown and is indeed experiencing renaissance.

Jones collected these lessons in golf and life while traveling 120,000 miles over 14 years during both lean and fat times. They were published in bi-weekly columns for Jack Wheeler's Bell Syndicate under by-lines, "Bobby Jones on Golf," "Bobby Jones Says," "My Theory of Golf," and "Secrets of Golf." With one college degree in mechanical engineering and another in English literature, Bob could have written his golf thoughts so that only physicists and psychiatrists would get the gist. Instead, Bob focused on Everyman: the "weekend dub" and the "hickory hacker."

Jones knew that the average player wasn't interested in winning championships. But, because golf is a rare game that requires you to call penalties on yourself and even play foul balls, its enjoyment hinges on a handful of fundamentals. Jones felt that if golf was worth playing, it was best to make some effort to play "correctly." Take notice Jones didn't say "perfectly." Bob never insists that you copy his perfect style. He only opens your eyes to the "whys and wherefores" of hooks and slices. His method acknowledges what God gave you while focusing on what you do with it.

O.B. Keeler, Jones' biographer, extolled the resulting benefits of following Bob's advice:

> You do a thing often enough the same way and the muscles remember; this takes a tremendous load off the mind so far as details are concerned and leaves the pithy and momentous enterprise – that is, where you want that ball to go – sticking out like a dog-fight at a Wednesday evening prayer meeting.

In reintroducing these classic golf lessons of Bob Jones, an effort has been made only to improve the photographs and make the text easier to read. The rest and the best is all "essential Jones."

SIDNEY L. MATTHEW

Grantland Rice, admirer and great friend of Bobby Jones. Mr. Rice's
record in the past few years at the annual Writers & Artists Tournament
in Florida leads us to believe that, despite his interests in other
sports, golf is his favorite game. At left is Johnny Farrell. (Frank Christian Photo)

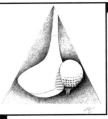

"Bobby Jones"

While Bobby Jones has retired, at least for some time, from tournament golf, his swing, his method and his skill will go on indefinitely.

It might be interesting to know that in the last year or so the Georgia star has taken up the study of his own swing, and other swings, in a far more serious way than he ever did in the earlier stages of his play. At that time he was a carefree, natural golfer with no other particular thought except hitting the ball. But his work in writing, motion pictures and radio performances led him to a deeper study of each important detail.

In addition to having a swing good enough to win four major golf championships in one year, Bobby also happens to have the capacity for intelligent research, hard study and close concentration. He is one of the few who have been able to take the intricate golf swing apart, study it all along the line, and still let this research have no effect upon his own game.

Bobby Jones has now had 22 years of golf at the age of 29. This must be a record. He has a long memory that goes back to his earlier methods and to the changes necessary to bring his game up to the remarkable record of 1930, when he swept the four main battlefields of the ancient game against the best in the world. In the last few months he has been able to make an even more careful study of all the phases of sound golf, with all thought of tournament preparation removed from his mind. His main ambition has been to give to all who play golf the benefit of his study and his observations, to do all he can to make golf an easier and simpler game to play and to give the average golfer a clearer understanding of what it is all about.

This is something the average golfer has lacked in too many cases. His viewpoint has been obscured and blurred too often by too many contradicting and too many puzzling types of advice and suggestion.

Bobby Jones has set out to clear up as much of the fog as possible and to show the shortest cut one can take to a better game.

His first series of golf lessons have now come to the more advanced stage. This does not mean they are more complicated and harder to follow. It simply means that through so many tests made for the purpose of instruction Jones has been able to improve upon his former outline.

He has gone into every detail of the swing, both the mental and the physical side of the game, with his complete concentration put upon the broad subject he has tackled. He has felt in a way that the proper exposition of the golf swing has been a challenge that must be met. Recently he has become more the student and less the player, but he has done enough to combine both forms that will help him to find the proper expression for his thoughts and beliefs. His game is as good as it ever was. In fact he will still be a great golfer at fifty, because he combines so much in the way of skill, power and mental control. The study of the golf swing seems to become more and more interesting to all who follow this game as the years go by. It is an untiring subject, since it contains so much in the way of variety and at times seems to wander through the mists where there is no final answer to any problem.

If any one can come close to the solution that so many have sought, Bobby Jones should be the answer. He is now the student as well as the star, with a philosophy that has grown in stature through the years. He can look today with a clearer eye than ever before, and his observations upon the game he loves so well should be among the most interesting and most important contributions made to sport.

GRANTLAND RICE.

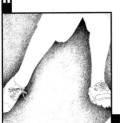
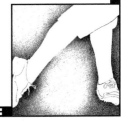

Bobby Jones
The "Emperor" of Golf.

"Emperor" Jones teeing off in the practice round before the U.S. Open at Winged Foot.

Golf Concentration

There can be very little question that concentration is the big thing in golf, and this is true whether we are concerned with winning championships or merely with holding up our own end in a week-end fourball. There is a lot of truth in the "slogan" - as Andy would call it- that golf is played more between the ears than on the golf course. This does not mean that anything like a superior mentality is required; but it does mean that there must be no mental daisy-picking while a shot is being played.

From the angle of the semi-serious week-end golfer there is a lot to be gained by devoting a little energy to train himself to concentrate on the game. I admit, however, that his problem is far more difficult than that of the professional who seldom has to bother his head with things outside the game. It is sometimes practically impossible to shed the thought of business as one would discard a cloak when the office door closes behind. Therein lies one reason that I always leave home far in advance of any important competition. I find that after spending the morning at my desk my golf in the afternoon is never as good as it ought to be. I try always to give myself at least a week away from everything but golf so that I shall have nothing else to think about.

Two Forms of Concentration

The most effective tournament player is the one whose concentration upon the game is least affected by the strain and importance of the event. I am convinced that two classes of players react to the strain in two entirely different ways. It breaks the one class, and enables the other to play. To the one, the need of a fine shot is ruinous because he cannot stop thinking about how badly he needs it long enough to give his attention to playing it; to the other, the consciousness of the importance of the stroke causes him to lose himself in concentration upon the execution to a point where he forgets what it will mean if he should miss.

I do not believe there is another sport that requires the uninterrupted intense concentration of the mind which is demanded of a golfer in competition with others of anything like equal skill. In all other games it is possible to take breathing spells without risking too much. But in golf the unexpected can, and usually does, happen with such startling suddenness that the unwary person may be caught before he knows it. One lapse of concentration, one bit of carelessness, is more disastrous than a number of mechanical mistakes, mainly because it is harder to bring the mind back to the business in hand than it is to correct or guard against a physical mistake recognized as soon as it appears.

Nothing could be farther from the fact than the fond notion that an expert golfer plays entirely subconsciously, without having to resort at all to conscious control. The habit of correct swinging causes a great many of the movements of the swing to be instinctive. But there are always two or three things that have to be looked after actively all the time. When this is appreciated it is possible to understand what it means, when playing a first-class championship round, to concentrate upon the execution of seventy-two golf shots in a space of eighteen holes and over a stretch of upwards of three hours' time.

And by concentration I mean the kind that not only excludes everything foreign to the game, but also takes account of all that the player knows should be provided for. We find numbers of players with fine form who hit the shots as well as anyone, yet fail to win because of imperfect concentration. It is so easy to walk up and hit the ball without thinking much about anything, and the player never realizes until the damage is done that he has not had his mind on the shot.

The men who are capable of complete concentration throughout an eighteen hole round can be counted upon the fingers of one hand.

1

GOLF CONCENTRATION

The others go to sleep on any number of shots. Sometimes they never realize even afterwards that they did take a nap, and a lot of times they mistake fear and anxiety for concentration. It is possible to worry a great deal over the result of a stroke without really thinking of the way to play it successfully, and there are several different angles that may need consideration in trying to determine the correct way.

This is one of the ways that mental staleness is manifested when a player is "overgolfed." The lack of mental alertness which results renders it impossible for him to maintain complete concentration on the details necessary to be considered for the different shots he is called on to play. He is trying to the best of his ability, but the thing is just beyond him, and he pays for it in the form of extra strokes on his score, or holes lost which might have been saved or even won with the right kind of keen mental application.

It might be asked again just what is concentration. I think that is very simple. There are certain fundamentals that go with every stroke. The right sort of concentration must take these into account. For example, the golfer should know that he should let the weight go with the swing. He should know also that he should let the left side come well around. These are two things he should think about in advance of the swing especially if he is troubled with a fault of overlooking these two points. He cannot take them for granted; they must be thought out before he starts his swing, and he must think through the swing to see that they are carried out, or at least concentrate enough to see that they are started on their way. These are just two examples out of several.

What To Think of
When Making a Golf Shot

One eminent professional instructor once told me that he found that most of the men who came to him for instruction when playing a golf shot concerned themselves with every detail except hitting the ball. His first job, he says, was to redirect their attention to what they had started out to do–to fix their concentration only upon hitting the ball in an effort to develop a sense of timing. Once they had acquired the habit of hitting he was able to begin to work out for each a sound and reliable swing.

There appears to me to be a great deal of good common sense in this method of attack. It is possible, of course, to build up a swing part by part, as an automobile is assembled, and indeed, with a rank beginner, some start must be made in this way before the pupil has anything to work upon. He must certainly be given some idea of how he is to swing the club before he can begin to cultivate what my friend has called the "habit of hitting." But a good many of us entirely submerge the thought of the ball in a flood of "do's" and "don'ts" which engulfs our minds from the moment we take the club in hand.

I think this is one reason that the tide of golf swings up and down with such startling suddenness. The game itself is one where form is fleeting, and the very best go stumbling blindly when a moment before everything was rosy.

Hit the Ball

My friend is certainly right in saying that the thing of first importance is hitting the ball, and that the habit of hitting it must be cultivated to an extent which makes the act subconscious. When one has reached this stage, it becomes a question of how much more can be thought of without disturbing this habit.

I find this phase of the game to be a very real difficulty, entirely beyond any matter of mere theorizing; and I think that a large percentage of shots missed by a good player are missed because he cannot each time remember all that he knows about his stroke. I am certain that I have now a far more accurate idea of a correct stroke than I have

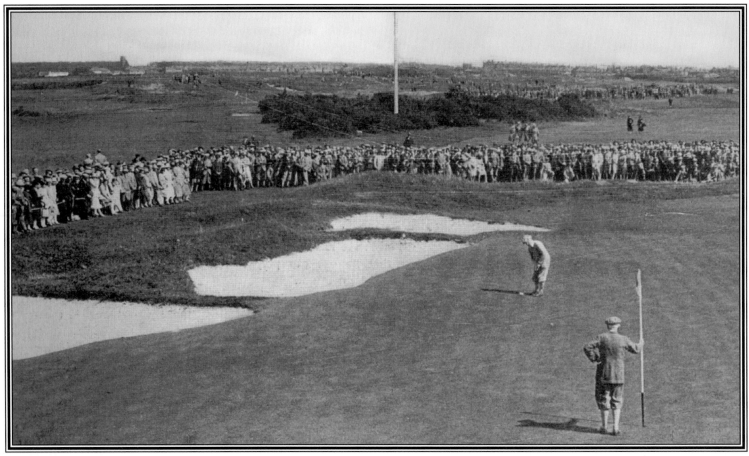

Bob Jones putts on the 18th hole at Royal Lytham and St. Annes during his successful campaign for his first British Open Championship.
The next shot was the one that slammed the door on the field.

ever had before. Whenever I play a bad shot I am conscious the instant I hit the ball that I have done something wrong, and almost always I know what it was. But I find it impossible to think about everything every time I swing a club.

I do not mean that I am in the habit of thinking through the stroke from start to finish as I make it, but over a certain period there are always two or three things that I must consciously look after in order to hit a satisfactory shot. These two or three things are not always the same but they seldom increase in number. If there are more than two or three, I play very bad golf.

Golfing Confidence

One of the queerest angles on the mental side of the game is seen when we begin to consider confidence–what is its effect? how much of it ought we to have? and, in what should we have confidence–in our ability to beat a given opponent or in our ability to play the shots? Many of us have found that we can't play well without confidence of one kind; and that we will be beaten if we have too much of another variety.

Every golfer has a favorite club–a battered old spoon or a mashie with a crooked shaft–which he would not exchange for double its weight in gold. He has confidence in his club and in his ability to use it. And in actuality he does play it better than any other. It isn't all imagination–he doesn't merely think he can play it better–he can really do so because he has confidence in it and swings it easily, freely, and rhythmically.

The better player has this same feeling of confidence, but instead of trusting one of his clubs, he trusts them all, except perhaps one. He has confidence in his swing. He is content to trust himself to take his time and hit the ball. Such an attitude is indispensable to first-class golf.

It doesn't help a great deal to have the soundest swing in the world if that swing is not trusted. There are lots of men who play golf exceptionally well when the issues are small but who collapse when anything of importance is at stake. The fact that they can play well at all shows that fundamentally their swings are good. But what causes the detonation is fear, lack of confidence in the swing which makes them unwilling to trust it with anything that really matters. In the face of such an obstacle, tension takes the place of relaxation, and strain upsets rhythm. The smoothest machine in the world cannot run in a bearing full of the gravel of uncertainty.

That is one kind of confidence, and it is the kind that everyone should have in abundance. When you stand up to the ball ready to make a decisive stroke you must know that you can make it. You must not be afraid to swing, afraid to pivot, afraid to hit. There must be a good swing with plenty of confidence to let it loose.

The other kind of confidence is a different thing, and a dangerous one. In a way it has something to do with the player's opinion of his ability to play the shots, but it works in an entirely different way. Of this kind of confidence we must have only enough to make us feel as we step upon the tee with John Doe–"Well, John, you're pretty good, but I think if I play hard and well I can just about beat you." It must be enough to overcome actual fear or to rout an inferiority complex, but it must not be sufficient to produce a careless overconfident attitude.

Every successful competitive golfer has learned to adopt a certain humility towards an opponent or an open championship field. He knows that no matter how well he plays there may be someone who may play even better. Therefore, although he may be supremely confident of his ability to drive well, play his irons accurately, and putt well, he still is a fool if he is confident of winning–that is, to any greater extent than I have indicated.

Confidence in the club, or the swing, or the shot, aids concentration because it banishes tension and strain; confidence in the result of a match or tournament makes impossible the concentration and hard work required to win.

Careless Shot Destroys Morale

Somewhere at the beginning of this article I made the statement that many fine golfers failed to win competition because they habitually spoiled fine scores by permitting occasional lapses of concentration. Yet, recently, at Augusta, I myself was at least twice guilty of what I had warned others to avoid.

Competitive golf, especially stroke play, demands that the player be continually on the lookout against himself. I do not mean that he is expected to avoid all errors for that would not be human. A number of shots must be mis-hit no matter how capable the player nor how attentive to the game he may be. But unbroken concentration never once distracted from the playing of the shots will save the loss of many additional strokes.

The best competitive golfers are, I think, the distrustful and timorous kind, who are always expecting something terrible to happen–pessimistic fellows who are always quite certain when they come upon the green that the ball farthest from the hole is theirs. This kind of player never takes anything for granted and he cannot be lulled into complacency by a successful run over a few holes. The most dangerous spot where the cords of concentration are most apt to snap is when everything is going smoothly. When the hold upon concentration is a bit weak anyway there is nothing in the world like prosperity to sever the connection.

Over the Hill Course of the Augusta Country Club in the second round of the tournament I got off to a shaky start. After collecting two fives on the first two holes, the ball started rolling for me. The two strokes lost to par on the first two came back at the seventh and eighth, and an additional one was gained at the eleventh and at the thirteenth, so that on the sixteenth tee I had par left for a seventy. I had not made a costly mistake since the second hole and had left the difficult part of the course behind. Each of the last three holes was of drive-and-pitch length, probably the easiest stretch on the entire course.

Yet, although I did not realize it at the time I allowed my attitude toward the rest of the round to become just what it should never be. Seventy was good enough, I thought, and there was absolutely no danger of slipping a stroke on these last three holes. For me the round was over. I had merely to go through the simple formality of holing out on the last three holes.

If I had been intent on picking up further strokes against par as I should have been, I should have been far better off. If the finishing holes were such easy fours, why did I not attack them on the basis of threes? But I did not. I teed my ball on the sixteenth tee, addressed it carelessly, without even one look at the fairway, and hit a perfectly straight shot over the roadway, out of bounds–and this, too, when confronted by one of the widest fairways of the course. The penalty being stroke and distance, I had thrown away two precious shots. That shocked me into consciousness again, and I called myself every kind of a fool I could think of–but that helped little toward getting the strokes back.

GOLF CONCENTRATION

The 9th hole at Interlachen CC during the 1930 U.S. Open where Bob Jones played his famous "Lily Pad" shot.

One shot carelessly played can lead to a lot of greed. I think a careless shot invariably costs more than a bad shot painstakingly played, for it leaves the morale in a state of disorder. It is easy to accept mistakes when we know that they could not be avoided. We realize that a good many shots must be less than perfect no matter how hard we try. But when we actually throw away strokes without rhyme or reason, it is pretty hard to accept the penalty philosophically and to attack the next shot in the proper frame of mind.

"Courageous Timidity"

I think it was J.H. Taylor who made the statement that all of the great golfers he had known had been possessed of a quality which he chose to call "courageous timidity," a most happy phrase, for it expresses exactly the quality which a golfer, expert or not, must have in order to get the most from whatever mechanical ability he may have. Courageous to keep trying in the face of ill-luck or disappointment, and timidity to appreciate and appraise the dangers of each stroke and to curb the desire to take chances beyond a reasonable hope of success. There can be no doubt that such a combination in itself embraces and makes possible all the other qualities which we acclaim as part of the ideal golfing temperament for the championship contender as well as the average golfer. When we have pronounced Taylor's phrase we have said it all.

Golf is not a game of exact mechanical precision. Even the most accurate player in his most effective form must allow himself a certain latitude in playing any kind of stroke. How much this margin ought to be depends, of course, upon the skill of the player and upon how likely he is to make an error. What would be a risky shot for one might be conservative for another. This means that each should know his own limitations and not rush in in foolish confidence to attempt things beyond the reach of his actual ability. Golf is said to be an humbling game, but it is surprising how many people are either not aware of their weaknesses or else reckless of consequences.

Patient Waiting Necessary

What I particularly commend in a golfer is the patient waiting for opportunities. One of the difficult things in the game is to maintain this waiting attitude when the start is bad. A few strokes or a few holes lost at the very beginning often causes a man to blow up completely. Feeling the loss he is impelled to try to retrieve the strokes or the holes immediately. He tries things he can't do, takes foolish chances trying to beat par. A few of these fail, he finds himself going from bad to worse, soon becomes desperate, and finally goes all to pieces.

Any of us has seen it happen in just this way time and time again. We have probably realized then the mistake the poor victim was making, but we failed utterly to read the lesson to ourselves. Just because three holes in a row have been lost it does not follow that the next three must be won. Rather stop the tide and hang on by consistent sane play, picking back a hole here and a hole there as your opponent slips, or when a favorable break turns your ball up within holing distance. A good steady, concentrated pressure kept on an opponent will win back holes quickly enough when they start to come.

Thus is shown the importance of not only patience, but of the elimination of over-confidence. The important thing to be remembered throughout is the necessity for concentration. If a man would play golf well there is no room in his thoughts for anything outside.

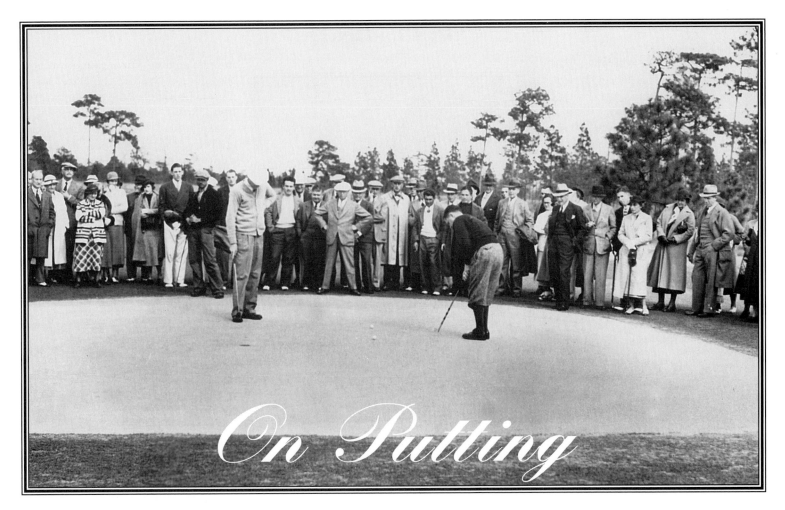

On Putting

The most difficult part of the game of golf is played on the putting green. Whatever may be the relative importance in the long run of the drive, the approach, and the putt, it is certain that it is the putt which mars or finishes the job which the others have begun.

No man has yet been able to win a championship without putting well, taking advantage of his scoring opportunities by holing the putt after a fine iron shot, or saving precious strokes by sinking a good putt for a par after slack play in the other departments had caused him trouble.

One of the questions most frequently put to me is "What are the essential fundamentals of good putting?" And it is a question over which I have pondered quite a lot. I have given more thought and attention to chipping (covered in another part of this book), and putting than to all other departments of the game combined, and I suppose it took me longer to acquire any proficiency there than in any of the others.

Form in golf varies greatly from day to day in every respect, from driving on down, but I think it is harder to putt consistently well than it is to do anything else in the game. It is impossible to prescribe any particular method which will assure good results. The matters of stance, grip, and the position of address should always be left to the player to work out for himself. The main thing is to be comfortable, thoroughly relaxed, with no hint of strain. This is highly important. By attempting to duplicate another method, some players find themselves so cramped and strained that a smooth rhythmic stroke is impossible.

To hole a putt of any considerable length it is necessary to coordinate a number of factors. To find the exact line to the hole and to adjust the speed of the ball so that it will take every curve and roll with precision and curl into the cup, are things which human beings cannot accomplish with mathematical accuracy.

The very uncertainty attendant upon the success of even the well-hit putts should make us doubly anxious to learn to strike every one truly, for if we cannot be sure of the good ones how can we hope to sink the putts which we actually mis-hit with the clubhead?

There is much said about keeping the head and the body still, and taking the putter back with the left hand, and stroking with the right, all of which is very sound advice and helpful to the inexpert putter. But the majority of persons do well enough in these respects. Those who have played at all, quickly realize that they cannot permit the body to sway or move to any great extent, and most of them appreciate the difference between a smooth, flowing stroke and a stab or jab. That much, I think, is accepted and practiced with fair understanding.

Wrist Putting Unnatural

I have noted, however, a very general tendency among certain putters, to confine the execution of the putting stroke exclusively to the wrists. Intent upon preserving a perfectly stationary head and body, the player swings the putter back and forth without taking up any of the motion with the arms, a strained, unnatural performance throughout.

In the first instance, if the arms are held firmly in position, and the arc of the stroke is gained entirely by the action of the wrists, it is impossible to provide a backswing of sufficient proportions for a putt of more than moderate length. If the distance to be traversed is great, it is then necessary to hit hard, with considerable effort and with consequent loss of rhythm. The putting stroke should always have the virtue of smoothness if it has no other.

A putt should always be hit along the ground, never lofted in the air. There again, the all-wrist stroke causes trouble, for, to complete the stroke without moving the arms, the clubhead must come up very sharply from the low point of the arc, and if this low point is reached before, or at impact, the ball must be lifted from the ground.

I believe every teacher will advise that the putter-head should finish low. Obviously, unless it stops at impact, it cannot finish low unless something is done to flatten the arc of the follow-through. And that can be accomplished only by allowing the left wrist and arm to move in a forward line as the ball is struck.

That I regard as the most necessary movement in the whole business of putting. And you see it omitted so many times. The omission results in what I call

little difference. The important thing is the conception which the player has in mind as he addresses the ball, and it is the instructor's task to provide his pupil with a definite condition which he should create before playing the shot. The player cannot see his own mistakes but he can be made to sense his motions just as the instructor senses his own.

From this angle it is easy to understand why it is a mistake to advise a person to keep his body still when putting. In making sure that the body will not

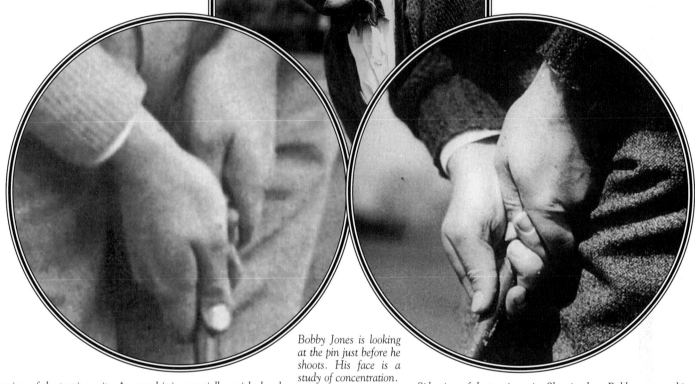

Bobby Jones is looking at the pin just before he shoots. His face is a study of concentration.

Front view of the putting grip. As stated it is essentially a right-hand affair. The late Walter Travis, who suggested this method to Bobby when the latter was a very poor putter, insisted that one hand or the other, but not the two, should control the putting stroke. Bobby opposed his wrists, as Mr. Travis further suggested; employed the right hand; and became one of the best putters the game has ever known. The hands, it will be seen, are precisely opposed, gaining the hinge or pendulum action in the wrists.

Side view of the putting grip. Showing how Bobby reverses his grip for all other shots, to place all of his right hand on the shaft and remove the index finger of the left hand, the overlapping thus being an exact reversal of his regular grip. The putt with Bobby is essentially a right-hand stroke; he takes the club back with the left hand and strokes with the right. The hands start the stroke absolutely in touch with the knickers.

a "locked left wrist" and it may cause almost any sort of error. The remedy is a little more firmness in the left hand grip as the ball is struck, and don't be afraid to let the arm move with the stroke and so remove itself from the way of the stroke.

Body Motion in Putting

The matter of body motion in putting has always interested me. I remember that when I first began to think about how to play golf I was told that putting should be done solely with the wrists; that the arms and body should never move. Obviously that conception of the stroke could not survive the test of actual trial for although the three-and four-footers might be handled by a flick of the wrist, the longer putts require some assistance from the forearms in order to provide enough force without interrupting the smooth rhythmic motion.

Whatever motion may take place in making a putt, if not extraordinary, is so very slight that it is difficult for the eye to detect. It is not important because of any force which it exerts as a factor in the stroke, and whether or not the motion actually takes place at all makes very

move or turn there is a certain amount of rigidity set up which defeats the prime necessity–relaxation.

It is impossible to be quite still and at the same time relaxed, but it is not possible to *hold* one's self quite still and at the same time relax. The very thought of preventing motion causes stiffness. Whatever motion there is should be *permitted* rather than *forced*. This is my conception of perfect relaxation.

The first essential motion is that of the club. The easiest way to accomplish that without strain is by using the arms and hands. If the motion of the arms is sufficient to cause a movement of the body, then the body should move, and will move unless it sets up a resistance of its own.

I will agree that no body motion should be consciously and willfully produced, but if the putt requires a stroke long enough to suggest a movement of the hips or shoulders, it should not be resisted. The attitude of the player towards body motion should be entirely negative, and he may be conscious of it only after it has taken place. But he should never set himself against it. In the interests of timing and rhythm I believe it should be encouraged by a perfect willingness to move upon the slightest impulse.

The one great reason why most players find the long approach putts so difficult is that they refuse to employ the power of arms or body, and so either fail to produce enough force to reach the objective, or they force the stroke, just as they force a drive or an iron, and destroy the accuracy of it.

When the putt becomes merely another golf shot this trouble is removed. If the length is short only the wrists are needed. As the putt becomes longer the wrists must flex more and more, until a point is reached where it becomes more comfortable to move the arms as well.

I think the most important thing to be done on the putting green is to place the body in a comfortable position where it is perfectly balanced, yet free to move at the least suggestion of necessity. There should be perfect relaxation and no strain in any muscle. That done the putt is merely a matter of stroking the ball smoothly and easily toward the hole.

I do not like even to hear anything said about keeping the head or body still. It may be good practice but it is not a good thing to think about because the very effort invariably produces a rigidity which is not healthy. The more naturally one can fall into position the better off he will be.

Watch Result Instead of Method

One of Alex Smith's many dictums on golf has to do with putting-"The most important part of putting is getting the ball into the hole." At first glance this doesn't appear very enlightening but it isn't exactly as inane as it sounds. There are certainly many golfers who actually appear to lose sight of the first object of the game, and devote most of their attention to details of the stroke which, if left alone, would take care of themselves all right. Too much worrying about details of how the hitting is done is fatal to good putting. The stroke is of less importance in putting than in any other department of golf. At least, I am sure there is less cause for concern over the precise form in which it is made. Hence, a comfortable, easy position in hitting the ball is one fundamental requisite. It tends to steadiness in hitting, because a minimum of effort is needed, and it further eliminates any consideration of any special method or pose. Every time a thought is given to stance or stroke it is so much taken away from the accomplishment of the one purpose.

Probably because the objective is so very close, in putting, there is an almost overwhelming temptation to lift the head in an effort to learn where the putt will stop before the ball has fairly started upon its way. Although after the ball is struck the damage, if any, is done past repair, anxiety over the result often will not permit us to stroke the ball calmly in the proper manner.

The most common manifestation of looking up is a continual half-topping of approach putts. Struck with a swing ample for the distance if the ball is fairly hit, the half-top invariably leaves the ball short of the hole, often with a bothersome second putt to make.

A fine remedy, although it may seem a bit drastic, is to keep the head down until the ball has stopped rolling. I know some very fine putters who do that when their putting goes off. It is hard, though, to forego the pleasure of seeing the ball actually disappear into the hole. It is equally effective to be sure that the ball has been actually struck before looking up. That is by no means as hard to do in the case of a putt, as with a full shot from the fairway.

However, the range of the putt is so very important that to gaze fixedly at the ball for an appreciable length of time may be as bad as looking up. In no case must the player concentrate his attention upon the ball long enough for his visual measurement of distance to be disturbed.

Training the Eye

All of which indicates that the first thing in putting to be considered is the slope and speed of the green. It is evident that no matter how accurately the ball may be struck, it is first necessary to select the line upon which it should be started.

As an indication that the line is the important thing, I can truthfully say that I have holed very few putts when I could not see definitely the path which the ball should follow into the hole. In any round there are always numbers of times when the proper line to the hole is obscure. If it were always visible we should miss few putts. But it is always a good practice when the correct line cannot be determined, to borrow generously from any slope and attempt to make the ball pass a tiny bit above the hole. If the ball remains above the hole, there is always a chance that it will at any rate stop not far away. But once a putt begins to roll below the hole, every inch which it travels carries it farther from the objective.

Working on this idea, it must appear that we should concern ourselves mainly with the more general contours of a slope rather than try to account for every little hop or roll which the ball is likely to take. This does not mean that we should be taking a haphazard shot at the

An early view of Bobby Jones' putting stance. Note how the right forearm rests lightly upon the leg. Jones later changed his stance after a lesson by Walter J. Travis.

hole, but only that we should determine upon a line which we want the ball to start, and hit firmly upon that line. Worrying about rough spots in the green has no effect except to make the stroke indecisive, and I believe that bad putting is due more to the effect which the green has upon the player than to that which it has upon the action of the ball.

There is one conception upon which I have always worked with fair success and which might furnish a useful hint to the reader. When putting across a side slope I try to make sure of keeping the ball above the hole so that it will always be falling towards the cup, the object being to make it tumble slowly into the upper side of the hole. If the speed is anywhere near right, the putt cannot finish very far away.

The art of judging slope and speed is not entirely god-given. It is possible to a great degree to develop the faculty. But the major part of any putting practice should be directed to that end rather than to the development of a perfectly accurate stroke.

If day in and day out a man will concentrate upon hitting the ball on the line he thinks is the right one, and with a speed which he thinks is proper, and if he will let the luck and breaks take care of themselves, he will soon find that he is a much-improved putter.

Many times long putts find the bottom of the hole but the man who thinks he can hole them consistently is much mistaken. It is the putt of three yards and less which really counts. Let a player acquire sufficient precision to hole the short putts with regularity and he can afford to take the long ones as they come.

The real test of a good putter is reliability. Not unfailing consistency, for everyone must have his lapses, and not absolute precision with the two and three yarders, but a consistency within human limits which rolls the long ones up close to the hole and rarely slips one of a yard or less.

In the final analysis there is little room for entertaining the hope that putting may be reduced to a science. Good putting is at best a fleeting blessing. Here today, gone tomorrow. It is not likely that anyone will ever attain so close to perfection that he will be able to hole out from fifteen to twenty feet with reasonable certainty. So I think we waste time and energy in trying to perfect a putting stroke which will be as accurate and as certain as that of a steam engine piston. There are too many other things which have to be right and every one is susceptible to human error.

Hints on Holing Short Putts

To miss a putt of two, three, or even four feet seems about the most useless thing in the world. The texture of most of our greens upon which competitions are played is such that no valid excuse is offered the player. In almost every case, one may have the assurance that if struck properly the ball will find the cup.

The greatest difficulty in the short putt arises out of the fact that if we allow for the roll of the green, the stroke must be so delicate and the blow so gentle because of the meager space to be traversed. To strike a crisp and firm, and at the same time gentle blow, requires the very ultimate degree of what we call touch, and firm hitting is the essence of good putting.

For the putter of less extreme delicacy there is always open the method of spanking the ball into the back of the cup. Indeed, where there is a bit of roll to the green, I think that is the best method. If we endeavor to borrow on a short putt, there is always the danger of an error in gauging the speed which will be sufficient to allow the ball to fall off below the hole, or if we have hit it too hard, to keep it from taking the fall until it has passed the cup.

While I favor a free, sweeping swing for putting at middle and long distances, I do not believe that this method is reliable for the shorter ranges. The sweeping stroke is primarily one of delicacy, and delicacy is not so much desired on the holing out putts as direction. I think the best method is to take a short grip on the club and get the head down a good deal closer to the ball. I should also grip the club a bit tighter and strike the ball with a firm left wrist. The first necessity in holing short putts is to keep the putter blade from turning away from the line.

There is no possibility of exaggerating the value of being able to hole all the short or missable putts. It isn't even necessary to hole the long ones if the little ones are certain. I can recall match after match and tournament after tournament which might have been saved by holing a few short putts. And I know that I am not the only one who must repent errors of this kind, for almost every runner-up has missed enough putts under six feet to make him the winner with strokes to spare if he had holed them all.

The putting stance. The ball is opposite the left toe. The heels have a mere half-inch between. The hands are touching the knickers; palms and wrist joints exactly opposed; left eye aligned on the ball; thumbs on top of the shaft.

with the fact that A holds him lightly, and, if B makes no headway even with the aid of his opponent's apparent generosity, he is bound to think that the more experienced man is merely toying with him and will eat him up when he wants to. Suddenly B is left with a two-foot putt which he expects A will to give him, but A is admiring distant scenery and lets him putt. B walks up hurriedly and nervously and misses the simple putt. That ends the match, because B will not hit another good shot.

Obviously, tactics of that kind are not in keeping with the conception of sportsmanship which we all cherish. It is attempting to browbeat or to upset an opponent by something more than superior skill.

To hole every putt, no matter how short, would consume a great deal of time in the course of an eighteen hole round, and where con-

Backswing for the 5-yard putt. The club faces out, or opens normally, but very slightly, owing to the opposed palms and wrists. The stroke is a "stroke," not a sharp hit, but it has a beautiful firmness.

Should Players Concede Putts?

One of our leading sectional golf associations recently put itself upon record as being opposed to the practice of conceding putts, of whatever length, in match play. The matter was discussed in general fashion at the meeting last year of the United States Golf Association.

Of course, the objective in golf is the bottom of the hole, and a golf match should be a test of a player's ability to reach that objective. But I cannot see how it is possible to keep a man from conceding a putt, or even, as Grantland Rice has suggested, a short pitch over a bunker, if he feels like doing so.

The resolution condemning the conceding of putts may have been intended to make impossible certain unfair tactics which could be and have been employed under the present practice. For instance, at the start of a match between A, who is a seasoned competitor, and B, who is an inexperienced youngster, A continues to concede putts to B in varying lengths from a yard up to six feet. B is promptly impressed

Finish of a 5-yard putt; it sank, incidentally. The club obviously comes through with little or no turnover; an effect of the opposed palms. The head seems to turn with the stroke; the body is not held rigidly; there is evidently a tiny easement about the knees and hips, more noticeable the longer the putt. The weight seems perfectly distributed on both feet; rather at variance with the accepted custom of planting it solidly on one foot or the other.

gestion is bad enough anyway there ought to be nothing to make progress slower. Of course, missable putts should not be conceded for they are as much tests of skill as any other shots in the game, but when there is no reasonable possibility that the putt will be missed, I think the ball should be knocked away and the next hole played.

A Cure for Poor Putting

Here is a lesson which I learned many years ago, and which has made my putting infinitely better than before.

In 1921 I was beaten badly in the Amateur Championships by Francis Ouimet, and although I was thoroughly out-played through-out, I could have made a much better fight of it if my putter had not refused to work. I was absolutely helpless on the greens during the whole tournament.

The day after Francis beat me I went over to Nassau, on Long Island, to see Jimmy Maiden, Stewart's brother. We were setting out to play as Jimmy emerged from his shop bearing a rusty old putter which he had christened "Calamity Jane."

"Now, Bobby," Jimmy said, "take this putter and hit the ball for the hole. Never mind about your stroke or your follow-through." And Jimmy showed me a method which he wanted me to adopt. He made me place the ball about opposite my right foot and strike sharply down upon it with the old goose-neck putter, the blade of the putter sticking into the ground and traveling not an inch past the ball. In other words, I was permitted no follow-through at all.

We started out to play, I following Jimmy's instructions to the letter. To make a long story short, I holed so many long putts on the first nine that it became a huge joke to everyone in the game. It became simply a matter of getting on the green and then down the ball would go. I was out in 31 and should have been better if I had played even decently up to the greens.

Of course, I didn't putt that way for very long, and the method suggested by Jimmy did not suit me exactly, but from it I gained one idea which was invaluable, namely, that following through upon the line of the putt has nothing to do with the result. Many putts are mis-hit or swung off line because the player attempts to guide the ball. We must make up our minds that nothing which happens to the club after the ball is struck makes the least bit of difference. When we pick out a line and hit the ball, we do it all. If we make a mistake that mistake remains. It is too late to correct it afterwards.

And while I am still on the subject of putting, I should like to call attention to what I think is a mistaken idea. We have all heard the expressions—"Never up, never in"—and—"Well, I gave that one a chance, anyway"—used as excuses for over-running the hole, and many golfers feel that their duty is well done if, when confronted with an important putt, they hit the ball wildly past the cup. They don't stop to think that for a ball going fast the hole is really only an inch wide–that is, the very center of the hole must be hit— while, if the speed is right, the ball may go in the front, back or sides. Suffer the ignominy of being short if you must, but try to roll the ball just up to the cup. Many of them that are not precisely on line will drop, and in any event, the next one won't be so hard.

The Best of Them Make Mistakes

Just to show that even the best putters miss the little ones occasion-ally, I can give two illustrations by Walter Hagen, whom I regard as the most deadly and effective putter in competition that the game has seen. Hagen at Skokie in the second round, after gaining a big lead with a brilliant sixty-seven in the morning, lost no less than six strokes to par on the first ten holes, mainly through putting lapses. The last one he missed on the tenth could not have been over eighteen inch-es. Again at Worcester I saw him take four putts on the fourteenth from a distance of less than twenty feet.

I am not writing this to cast reflections upon Hagen's artistry with the putter. I think that nothing any one could say would by one whit lessen his well-deserved reputation. But I desire to emphasize the point that if these things can happen to the best, it behooves us of less-er ability to exercise care and caution.

Bob Jones tees off from the 16th hole of the Old Course at St. Andrews during the 1927 British Open at St. Andrews.
(Hulton-Deutsch)

Putting Psychology

It has always been interesting to me to try to determine exactly what it is that makes it possible for a really good putter to experience days when he is as helpless on the putting greens as a babe in arms. I can understand how it can be that a first-class player will occasionally play lamentably poor golf from tee to green, for the long shots require a more complicated swing which demands nicer timing than the putting stroke. It is not surprising that even the best are sometimes off with the woods or irons. But the putting stroke is the simplest of all. I do not believe that there comes a day when the expert putter finds a defect which he cannot discover and correct in a few moments' practice. Yet he may go thirty-six holes putting like an old scrub-woman who had never seen a golf club.

I do not mean by this that I seek an explanation why we do not always hole a good many long putts. I do not appraise good putting by the number of long ones. Luck plays too big a part in these. The telltale putts are those of three, four, six and eight feet, the kind a good putter should hole consistently. It is when putts of these lengths are missed regularly that an explanation ought to be forthcoming.

I have said that I did not believe there was a defect of the putting stroke which a good putter could not discover and correct with a few moments' practice. This is certainly true within my own experience. I frequently have the kind of off days I have described and when I do, it is my habit, if the match behind is not pressing too close, to try a few practice putts on each green. Usually these practice shots come off well enough, particularly so far as an accurate striking of the ball is concerned. But usually too, even after the practice, the next four-footer curls away from the hole.

It's Nearly All in the Mind

I truly believe that a great proportion of putting difficulties is in the player's mind. There are days when one lines up a putt more accurately, particularly the long fellows, and days when the touch is nicer than usual. But when a putt of four feet is missed it is rarely because of a mistake in choosing the line. The mishap is almost always caused by mishitting the ball, either by striking it off line, or by failing to strike it cleanly.

Now the simplest stroke in golf ought to be that required for a four-foot putt. The backstroke need be only four or five inches in length, and there should be no temptation to look up, for the objective lies well within the range of vision all the while the stroke is being played. There can be only one explanation for mishitting–that the player becomes uncertain and worried about the shot and his anxiety sets off tension which actually forces him to hit the ball off line. I have missed some short putts through rank carelessness, but these are very few compared to the number I have missed because I was scared stiff of them.

I think the only time that it is of any use to pick out a spot on the green over which to roll the ball, is when one is making short putts. If the player will locate a spot on the line about halfway between the ball and the hole and hit for that, forgetting that his putt may turn off, he will putt infinitely better. I have always found that the surest way to miss is to worry about some little bump or undulation for which I could find no account.

Bob Jones putting on the 8th green at Winged Foot GC in Mamaroneck, NY, during the 1929 U.S. Open Championship which Jones won in a playoff over Al Espinosa. (P & A Photos)

PUTTING PSYCHOLOGY

Jones putting his way to a new record of 285 in the 1927 British Open Championship at St. Andrews.

Eliminate Worry in Putting

I always find myself more than a little annoyed— and I have heard many other competitors express the same feeling— when a missed putt of three, four, or five feet is greeted by "Oh's" "Ah's" and loud guffaws from the gallery. I am sure that many another struggling contestant has, as I have, wished devoutly for an opportunity to watch the author or authors of the loud noise attempt the same job under the same circumstances. I am certain that he or they should find that many short putts, when viewed from a competitive angle, assume a far different aspect than when seen from the outer reaches of the crowd by a person only mildly interested in the result. It is hard to appreciate how many rolls and tiny, yet important, undulations can be contained in a little over a yard of putting surface, and it is surprising from this distance how slight an error in either direction may cause the putt to stay out.

Missed Putt May Undermine Whole Game

But even granted a just appreciation of the physical difficulties of the strike, the mental or psychological burden completely escapes all but the man who has himself been through it all. To everyone else it is just one stroke–a question merely of a four or five, or a win or a half on one hole. If a man has never been there himself how can he know what the competitor knows–that a loss of confidence in his ability to hole the short putts may ultimately, and in logical progression, undermine his entire game. He has had it happen before and I think it is safe to say that he dreads nothing more than this catastrophe, for when it happens there is nothing to be done.

The thing works out about this way: The player first leaves himself three to five feet wide of the hole on his approach putt; possibly on the first occasion he has run that much past the hole, an easy thing

to do on keen, slippery, putting greens. He misses the putt back. On the next green, he softens his stroke a bit too much, leaves the putt short of the hole, and misses that. From that point on anything may happen. The player feels that he cannot hole a short putt, he tries too hard to lay the long ones absolutely dead, and he loses his touch altogether. The next hope is in the second shot, for he feels he must play all iron shots to within fifteen or twenty feet of the hole in order to be certain of holing out in two putts, and he knows that if he misses the green there is no chance for recovery, or a chip and one putt. In this state it is not hard to see how far the ill effect may extend, especially when tense nerves contribute their bit.

A Bit of Putting Advice

Someone told me a story about an experienced professional who regained his putting confidence by rather drastic means in the middle of a round. Playing well otherwise, he suddenly lost all ability to hole a short putt. After missing several, he was at one hole left with a mean one of about four feet. This time he walked quickly up to the ball, closed his eyes, and rapped the sphere straight into the middle of the cup. He holed the next one or two in the normal way and thereafter pursued his way rejoicing.

I should neither dare to attempt, nor recommend for others, the method employed here, but there can be no question that anxiety and too much care cause most short putts to go astray. When you see a man obviously trying to guide the short putt, or hitting quickly with a short, stabbing stroke, even though he holes a few, if you look for trouble you will not be disappointed. A short putt, even as a long one, must be struck with a smooth, unhurried, and confident stroke. The best way to accomplish this is to decide upon a line to the hole and determine to hit the ball on that line and let it go hang if it wants to. I have never had any better advice in golf from tee to green than was contained in a telegram sent me by Stewart Maiden in 1919. It read-

"Hit 'em hard. They'll land somewhere." You must not apply this advice literally to putting, but its application is obvious. Hit the putt as well as you can and do not allow worry over the outcome to spoil the stroke.

In this connection, it is worthy of observation that nearly every one finds it easier to stroke properly a putt of twelve to fifteen feet. There is a very good reason why this should be true. The player fears he will miss a shorter putt and he fears he may fail to lay a longer one dead, but when he is putting from the middle distance, he merely hopes he may hole out without feeling that he must guide the ball into the hole, and he knows that he will not likely take three putts.

We would all profit greatly if we could cultivate this attitude toward putts of all lengths – and it ought to be easy to do, too, for we all know, or should know by this time, that worry does very little good. If we must be wrong we may as well make our mistake gracefully by choosing the wrong line, as by allowing a nervous over-careful stroke to pull the ball off direction.

Some More Pointers on Putting

Joshua Crane, of Boston, is one of the best putters playing the game of golf today, and he putts with one hand and uses a putter less than twelve inches in length. A banker in Birmingham putts with one hand in his pocket, and Chick Ridley in Atlanta putts better with one hand than with two. These and a good many others have resorted to this means of ridding themselves of the left-hand curse, which spoils more putts than any one thing to be named. Joshua Crane is said to have become so desperate he threatened to give up the game if he could not find a way to keep his left-hand from pulling all his putts off line.

We hear everywhere that the putt is a stroke to be accomplished by the wrists alone–that body, shoulders, arms must remain perfectly still.

Attempting to carry out this idea leads to but one of two results–either the right forearm must be held immovable and the left permitted to move, or vice-versa. But both cannot remain still if the ball is to be struck more than the merest flick. The consequence of either is obvious–the immovable right arm causes the left arm and elbow to go through a ridiculous motion, and a stationary left arm induces the right arm push which is so often seen to be characteristic of beginners.

The putt should first of all be considered to be just what it is–a short golf shot which, except for its length, is like any other golf shot. And when you look at it in that way remember that relaxation is just as important here as in hitting a long drive from the tee. The bad putter sets himself, he assumes a strained position, he stiffens in every muscle, and then, when he thinks he looks like Jerry Travers or Walter Hagen he stabs quickly at the ball in the hope of getting it all over before something dreadful happens. He gives the impression that he is trying to keep everything as still as possible and yet hit the ball.

Avoid a Strained Position

I do not believe that putting can be reduced to a science. I do believe that by constant practice one's average of both distance and direction can be vastly improved, when by increasing the number of putts which come close, the number which fall in will be likewise increased. But the important thing is comfort produced by a perfect relaxation which permits any motion of arms or body which is necessary to avoid strained positions or the necessity for quick-hitting. There is no need to try for a too great exactness in striking the ball for if we could bowl every ball along the exact line upon which we intend it to roll we should still miss a lot of putts, and fail to hole the many which we now make because they stray an inch or so one way or another. From fifteen and twenty feet what we want always to do is to come very close. If we do that, many will go in.

I believe that almost every bad putt is caused by the left hand.

Bob Jones (middle of threesome at the left) watches eventual winner Johnny Farrell play his second stroke to the third green in the U.S. Open Championship at Olympia Fields. Farrell won after a thirty-six hole playoff.

Either because of over-anxiousness, nervousness, uncertainty, or what not, this pesky left hand will now and again brace or stiffen or actually tug at the club, setting up a resistance which inevitably will swing the ball off line. The most common manifestation is, I think, a tendency on the part of the left hand to take hold of the club a fraction of a second before impact and to turn it over, an action which pulls the ball off line to the left.

Restrain Left Hand from Turning Over

These considerations have led me to adopt a certain putting style. It is a style which is not fixed in all particulars, for to adopt a too definite method and position destroys all chance of attaining the relaxation which is so important. First I place my left hand on the club in a position where it is not likely to turn over. On all my other clubs my left hand is placed well over the shaft to encourage a turn over, but when I grip a putter, my left hand is in such a position that the thumb extends down the top of the shaft. It is difficult to turn over farther from that position. Sometimes I feel it necessary to add further insurance against the turn. In that case, I extend my left elbow until it points almost directly at the hole.

From that point there is only one more thing to guard against: That is when the left forearm stiffens and refuses to give way to the stroke, forcing the left wrist to break abruptly, and the clubhead to rise quickly at or before impact. This cannot be protected by position, but one must remember to keep relaxed so that an easy flowing motion is encouraged.

MacDonald Smith says that for him the putting stroke is entirely a right-hand affair. In any case this is not true, and I believe that the average player is less likely to go wrong if he uses his left-hand judiciously. To execute the stroke entirely with the right is probably ideal provided one is able to resist a tendency to lift the club on the backswing. The club must go back inside the line, and this can only be assured if it is taken back with the left hand.

In Actual Application, Pendulum Stroke Physical Impossibility

There is one thing which I wish people would stop talking about and writing about because I think it causes more confusion in a beginner's mind than any one thing connected with golf. That thing is nothing more nor less than the theory of the pendulum putting stroke. It has been described and expressed in different ways, but when boiled down each demonstration resolves itself into a thing absolutely impossible of accomplishment so long as human beings are built as we know them.

Unquestionably a pendulum-like golf club with absolutely true face, swung precisely along the line of the putt and suspended from the point exactly over the ball, furnishes the ideal conception of accurate striking. But so long as human toes stick out in front, and until a golf club turns into a croquet mallet and can be swung backward between the legs, there is little hope that this can be attained. For the present, at least, it seems to me far better that we strive to find some way to improve our performance, using a method more or less familiar to all of us.

The important things in putting are that the putter should be faced properly when it strikes the ball and that it should be striking in the direction of the hole. If these two requirements are met, it makes no difference in the world whether or not the club was faced properly or moved along the projected line of the putt throughout the backswing.

The position of address, being a position of rest, is the logical place to secure a proper facing of the club. The player has opportunity then to set the putter and to place his hands upon the shaft in order to

maintain the position. After that his problem is to swing the club backward and forward in such a way that the club will return to the ball aligned just as it was when it was swung away. If the face of the club opens a little going back it must close as much returning; if it opens more, it must close more.

As I mentioned a few paragraphs back; the putting stroke is in miniature just like any other stroke in the game. Slight alterations in grip and stance may be made to lessen the chances of the more delicate mechanism going astray, but the principle remains the same. The most valuable thing any of us can acquire is the ability to reproduce the same stroke time and time again with the same closing motions, so that striking in the proper direction can be consistently relied upon. In accomplishing this the player is free to adopt his own method, but I shall set down my own for what it is worth.

The anchorage or pivot point of my putting stroke is the right forearm. Except on very long putts this arm, at a point about two inches above the wrists, rests lightly on my right thigh throughout the entire stroke until the ball has been struck; on very long putts this position may be disturbed by the increased length of the backswing. The right wrist is free to flex but remains relaxed, exerting little force itself during the backswing.

The club is swung backward almost solely by the left hand, the motion being guided by the right from the fixed point of contact on the right leg. The club swings always inside the projected line of the

Bobby, too, has his off days, and when he has, it is his habit, if the match behind is not pressing too close, to try a few practice putts on each green.
(Underwood & Underwood)

BOBBY JONES ON GOLF

putt and the club-face opens noticeably.

Of course this method is not offered as a specific. It is still possible to lift the club outside the line or to swing it incorrectly in any number of ways. But this position at least gives me a starting point. The point of anchorage and the relaxed right hand and wrist are two constant factors. The left wrist action is the only variable in the system. It must be determined by experiment and made a constant by patient, persistent practice.

Keeping Head Still— Fallacious Golf Maxim

It used to be regarded as absolutely essential in the execution of any shot that the head should remain precisely in the same position throughout. I have read many articles citing the immovability of my own head as an example, one observer stating that he on several occasions had taken a line on my head against a background and that it had not moved a fraction of an inch.

Becoming curious about this very thing, I had several reels of motion pictures made—ultra speed by the way—in order to see just how still my head actually was. Not in a single case, but in every instance when playing a full shot I found that my head always moved and in an astonishing way. It always moved or turned a few inches backward and returned to the original position by the time the top of the swing was reached; and during the downstroke it moved forward first, then backward as the club was actually coming in contact with the ball. The extent of its travel must have, at times, exceeded four inches.

Of course, I intend in no way to confuse the motion of head with those conscious actions which are within our control. It would be folly to even talk about the motion of the head except for one reason—and that is to convince the player that there is no need to worry about keeping it still.

And just as for the long shots, it is equally necessary in putting, for here, too, the average person, afraid of shifting his body or of moving his head, as he has been warned so often not to do, freezes himself in an engaging posture, and futilely slaps at the ball with a stroke entirely lacking in all the essentials of a golf stroke. Free, easy, and relaxed motion is essential to rhythm and no one can strike rhythmically even a two-foot putt if every muscle is as taut as a violin string.

In putting, more than in any other department of the game, it is necessary to encourage a relaxed action. In no department is it so easy to tighten up as when the merest tap will send the ball the required distance.

I think that in putting, as in making every other golf shot, the player ought to forget about his head. Think *with it*, but not *of it*. If it wants to move let it. But by all means think about the legs, particularly the knees. Let them be not active but relaxed, ready to move in either direction the motion of the swing may indicate. In putting particularly, I think it is very helpful to permit a little motion of the knees, the left forward and the right back during the backstroke, and the other way when striking the ball. It even helps sometimes to consciously produce this motion–anything to break up the tension which anxiety may have created.

Driving from the 9th tee of the Merion Cricket Club during the qualifying round of the 1930 U.S. Amateur Championship--fourth leg of the Grand Slam. (Ralph Miller Library)

On Stance and Swing

For a person beginning to study golf and to learn to play the game it is most important that he step off on the right foot. Without confusing him with too many details and refinements, it is best at first that there be put in his head a definite idea of what it is he seeks to accomplish. Once given a correct conception of the swing as a whole, he is far along the road to playing at least a moderately good game.

To give a person this excellent beginning, I should say could be done by convincing him that what he wants is relaxation. Let him take a club in his hands and lash out with it at any target he can find. Emphasize the play of the wrists, a loose grip, a relaxed forearm, flexible hips and waist, mobile shoulders–in short, a feeling of slackness in every member of the body. Instruction started along these lines encourages freedom. The player at first stands as he chooses and swings as he chooses. The one thing he has to think about is flailing the ball.

After a little of this, when he has obtained some use of the club, and his hands have become accustomed to the feel of it, then is the time to begin to give him detailed instruction.

The stance for the drive. The ball is well away, yet the body position is remarkably upright. The position of the right hand indicates a certain pinching or "feel" in the index finger.

The Stance

The first position of the swing is the stance and position at address. The player should address the ball in a perfectly natural position. By that I mean with feet not abnormally far apart, with body only slightly bent forward, with arms hanging naturally down (not extended too far nor caught in too close), and with the balance so perfect that no sense of strain is felt in any muscle.

Second, he should relax completely. Even a bit of laziness in the attitude is far better than too much tension. He should try to stand easily; even to feel as though he were engaged in an ordinary conversation with some friend whom he has met on the street.

The third step is the waggle, and for those who have not cultivated a relaxed swing the waggle should be full and free with a very supple wrist action. Too much attention cannot be given to the waggle, for it loosens the taut muscles and settles the player more comfortably to the ball. The little adjustments in stance and carriage will be made quite naturally if the muscles are relaxed.

No little comment has been made about my stance, because my feet are so close together. In a way this seems a rather dangerous method, because it affords only a very narrow base upon which the swing may function, and may therefore lead to loss of balance. But I think there are various considerations which justify my narrow stance

The ball, as regards the line of flight, really is opposite the left heel in the full drive.

Here is a picture of Bobby assuming a square stance. Note both feet are parallel to line of flight.

in my own case. In the first place I am short and rather fat, and my center of gravity is low by reason of my build. My feet are ample and get a firm hold on the ground. This latter may be of more importance than one would think. I have observed that nearly every one who has had any success at golf, has had large feet and hands; the one to hold the ground, and the other to hold the club.

That much makes the narrow stance possible for me; My manner of hitting the ball makes it necessary. The one thing I must have in playing almost every shot, especially the long ones, is a free turn in my hips, and as I am more than ordinarily broad in the beam, I cannot afford any restriction in that region. With my feet extended well apart I find free hip action practically impossible.

There are advantages peculiar to both the wide and the narrow stance. The turning in the hips which is the complement of the narrow stance, enables the player to impart considerable acceleration to the clubhead by his body action alone. This style is essentially a free-hitting type and productive of greater length with equal or less exertion. At the same time, it would appear logical that the wider stance with the shorter swing should be the more accurate.

In the interest of players who may be inclined to fashion their own games from watching the methods of others, attention should be called to the importance of first trying to work out the reasons why the player whom they choose to copy uses the methods he does. A tall slender player, no matter what length his swing happens to be, cannot expect to get good results with his feet placed as close together as mine are. His feet must be well apart to furnish anchorage. Similarly, a person who employs a short punching swing, mostly arm and shoulder action, can hardly expect to establish his balance firmly and keep it so on a narrow stance.

Bearing in mind the necessity for perfect balance, the earnest but unskilled player probably figures that he must root his feet firmly in the ground and keep them there. In so doing he is confusing two very distinct kinds of balance. He doesn't realize that a graceful dancer is at all times in as perfect balance as the acrobat who stands with one hand upon the skull of his partner. One is a balance of motion, and the other is a static balance. The balance which the golfer must maintain is decidedly the former.

So much for stance. Now we come to the swing.

The Swing

It is impossible, it seems, to evolve a theory of the golf swing which will please every one. One person tells us we must do so and so, and another says we must do something entirely different. In the end there can exist in our minds nothing but confusion as to what course we must pursue.

It is quite human, of course, to consider that the method which has been found through years of experience to be best for us, must be best for those whom we seek to instruct. But how impossible it is to prescribe each and every movement throughout the stroke. If one could start with the waggle and go through the entire swing precisely in the manner of Walter Hagen or of Johnny Farrell, he would, of course, hit the ball like Walter Hagen or Johnny Farrell. But if he should swing his arms like Farrell and shift his weight like Hagen, he probably would not play at all.

The golf swing is entirely a matter of compensation–making up in one part for what is done in another part. That is the reason that we observe so many different ways of doing the same thing.

To swing freely and easily is the important end to which the efforts of every golfer should be directed. Tense muscles, impeding rather than promoting the progress of the clubhead, take away materially from the force of the blow, as well as tend to pull or push the club out of its natural and proper path.

There is nothing occult about hitting a golf ball. In fact, although the application may be a bit more complicated, we use no more than the ordinary principles of motion which we encounter numberless times every day. Once started in the right line the club will tend to hold to its course until outside forces cause a change.

The great fault in the average golfer's conception of his stroke is that he considers the shaft of the club a means of transmitting actual physical force to the ball, whereas it is in reality merely the means of imparting velocity to the clubhead, rather than applied physical effort of the kind that bends crowbars and lifts heavy weights.

I like to think of a golf club as a weight attached to my hands by an imponderable medium, to which a string is a close approximation, and I like to feel that I am throwing it at the ball with much the same

The top of the swing in a full driving shot. We have here a physical demonstration of the true right-angle of the body on golf; the back is fairly presented to the objective; the hips are as nearly as possible squared with the back and shoulders; the right elbow is compactly held in by the ribs; and if this were an absolute action picture the left arm would be perfectly straight.

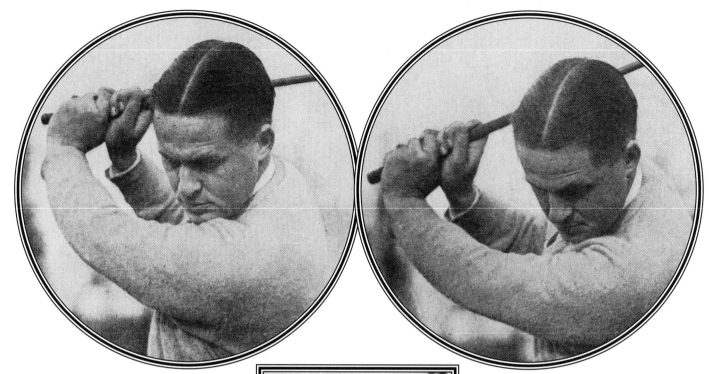

Top of the swing in a full driving stroke. The left arm, being posed, is not as emphatically straight, as in Bobby's actual play, when there is no easement at all of the left elbow. The left eye obviously is in control, the head thus being easily placed and the "sight line" exactly over the left shoulder.

Top of the swing for a full iron shot; say 200 yards with a No. 2 iron. The cast of the head – the left eye being lined on the ball – the dainty grip of the right hand, and the tremendous power coiled in the left hand are all features of this pose.

motion I should use in cracking a whip. By the simile I mean to convey the idea of a supple and lightning-quick action of the wrists, a sort of flailing motion.

Grip First To Be Considered

It is obviously impossible to execute tightly in the hands. I have seen numbers of men take hold of the club as though it were a venomous snake and they were in instant peril of being bitten. The tight grip necessarily tenses all the muscles of the wrists and forearms so that any degree of flexibility is impossible. The proper grip, above all things, is a light one, merely tight enough to hold the club lightly in the fingers, holding the hands close to the body slightly more than waist-high, and to raise and lower the head of the club several times rapidly using only the hands and wrists. That gives a very good sense of how the club should be held.

Another common mistake which has its root in the same misconception is what is called "pressing". The only objection to trying to hit excessively hard is that the effort defeats the easy flexibility of the swing. It does so because again we cannot get away from the conviction that we are moving pianos or shovelling gravel. The tension which ruins the shot is the result of sacrificing speed for force, and even if we meet the ball squarely it does not go so far as an easier and more relaxed swing would send it.

I am not trying to say that we should not try to hit the ball hard, for undoubtedly the harder it is struck the farther it will go. What I am contending for is that we do not mistake what is meant by hitting hard and lose the supple quickness which is the secret of power.

Good Footwork Foundation of Swing

There is a great deal more to be thought of in placing the feet than whether the stance adopted be open or closed. Alec Gerard directs attention to placing the feet in positions which will facilitate and encourage the proper action of the other members of the body. The knee and hip joints ought to be directed and supported in performing the acts required of them.

Take, for example, the man who has difficulty in completing a long sweeping swing or who finds himself forced backward as he hits the ball. Likely he is not supple in his hips and cannot turn his body sufficiently to allow his club to come through. By turning his left foot slightly so that the toe points more nearly along the line of play, he can make it much simpler to complete the swing freely and easily. The scarcely perceptible change eases the strain in the knee joints which hampered him before.

The left side is almost always the one which upsets what we call the "pivot" or "body-turn". It is the left side of the body which should initiate the turn and it is usually there that forces are set up to restrict the motion. The problem, therefore, insofar as it concerns the left foot, involves only the placing of that foot so that hip motion will be facilitated. All golfers have trouble turning either in taking the club back or in swinging it through. By changing the position of the left foot either motion may be made easier.

The right side performs a different function. In the first place, the pivot necessary during the backswing does not involve a flexing or a turn of the right knee as is the case with the left. The right leg simply straightens and has to perform no complicated functions. This can usually be done without regard to the position of the left foot.

But the right foot must be in position to supply a great deal of power, an actual thrust, as the ball is hit. That is shown by the firm hold it must have upon the ground to prevent slipping.

The thing that troubles the average golfer most, seems to be to make use of the weight and power of his body at the same time preserving a perfect balance upon his feet. The most general tendency in this respect is to allow the entire weight of the body to fall backward upon the right foot while the club is approaching the ball in the act of hitting. In this way the player's body, instead of being a source of power, is actually a hostile factor which must be overcome.

Although even the most expert players differ widely in certain matters of form, it is interesting to note that the methods almost all include the same safeguard against any inclination to fall backward. Almost at the same instant that the downward stroke begins, the left heel which has been lifted from the ground during the backswing, plants itself firmly on the sod.

This movement can mean but one thing. It is a conclusive indication that almost the first act of the player as he starts to hit is to shift a certain amount of weight onto the left foot. Very likely the weight so transferred is not a great amount, but the important thing is that all motion of body, arms, and club, is in the direction of the ball, and no part of the swing remains in a position to oppose the power of the whole. That to my mind is the secret of rhythmic swing.

Topping: A Common Fault

It is a fact that topping is the most common of all the misfortunes which beset a beginner, and it is also true that it is the mistake most rare among accomplished players. The reason for this I think is easily found in what I have said before. The less expert player after slumping backward upon his right foot, has moved the center of his swing to a point where, unless he does something extraordinary, his clubhead cannot reach the ball until after it has passed the low point of its arc. Ascending then it is not likely to strike the ball below its center.

A great many people find themselves in trouble at the start because they will not budge the left heel from the ground, and they are consequently so restricted in turning the hips that in order to take the club back shoulder high it becomes necessary to lift it with shoulders and arms.

Many of those who lift the left heel do so in a thoroughly aimless fashion, allowing the foot to turn until the point of the toe only touches the ground and the sole of the foot is presented to the hole. That practice is, of course, just as bad as if no motion at all had taken place, for it wholly destroys the usefulness of the left side of the body. The left leg turns until the knee points toward the ground.

When the thing is properly done, the heel rises considerably from the ground but the foot does not turn from its original position. It is not a difficult movement for it is accomplished simply by permitting the foot to be drawn up by the turn of the hips. The heel should never be raised enough to draw the ball of the foot from the earth. At the top of the swing the weight is borne on the inside of the foot.

At the top of the swing, the weight is borne on the inside of the foot. The left leg turns until the knee points toward the ground.

As I mentioned earlier in this article, the right foot has almost nothing to do on the backswing. There is, however, a slight shift of the burden from the ball of the foot to the heel. The right knee is bent slightly at address and in that position the greater portion of the weight is thrown upon the ball of the foot. When the body turns in taking the club back the right knee straightens, shifting most of the weight from the ball back onto the heel.

From this position two things are possible: either the right foot may remain firmly set, in which case there must be a very restricted finish; or the heel may come up as the stroke goes through to a full finish. Which of the two methods is actually employed depends upon the individual.

There are some who hold that there is actually but little shifting from one foot to another of the weight, and in some cases these have conducted experiments with scales to prove their case. Just how much shifting takes place I am not prepared to say, but there isn't the slightest doubt in my mind that a lateral shift of the hips is necessary to a free rhythmic swing, the shift being backward with the weight as the club goes back, and forward with it as the club comes down.

It is not enough to say that footwork is important. When we reflect that every movement of the stroke is made upon the feet as a foundation, the idea that we should begin at the bottom and work up is not hard to grasp. If your right foot has ever slipped from under you when you were in the act of hitting the ball, I am sure you will certainly see it.

The Straight Left Arm

Sometimes I wonder if our concern over "the straight left arm" is not a useless bother. Many players, I am sure, interpret "straight" to mean rigid, the result being a stiff-armed poke at the ball which has none of the elements of timing or power.

The main advantage of a straight left is that it increases the arc of the backswing and hence the potential power of the stroke. With the left arm extended the club is forced backward and outward to the extreme position without thrusting it with the shoulder –which latter act, I need not add, is disastrous. The wide arc thus achieved, the clubhead may travel through a very long distance, gaining momentum and speed all the while.

The man with supple wrists can well afford to keep the left arm straight, for he can complete a full backswing and ease the tense position at the top by means of his hands and wrists, I think the important thing about the left arm is that it does not remain bent after the downstroke has gotten under way. If it does so, there is a tendency for the left elbow to stray outward and cause the heel of the club to be presented first to the ball, a common cause of "socketing".

But the golfer need give himself little concern about a straight left arm at impact, for if

Bobby Jones driving off in an English tournament. "Golf methods differ," says Bobby, "But basically all consistently good golfers use the same principles in swinging."

ty of preserving a straight left arm at the top of the swing, but what I have not seen satisfactorily demonstrated by anyone is the possibility of playing even moderately decent golf without a straight right arm at impact. In studying many photographs of good players, that is a striking characteristic which they all have in common. Just before the ball is struck, the right arm straightens out and it remains straight for an appreciable space after the ball has been hit.

This straightening process, to my way of thinking, is the source of a large percentage of the power of the stroke. At the instant when every bit of energy which the player possesses is being hurled at the ball, the right arm is the means of transmitting power from the right side and shoulder. One trial is enough to show it is impossible to exert great force if the right arm is allowed to bend. If the elbow softens, the entire burden is saddled squarely upon the forearm and wrists, and a powerful connection straight through to the right leg and to the ground is destroyed.

Apparently, in golf, power depends chiefly on how much winding up can be done without complicating too greatly the unwinding process.

that member is not straight, the player will experience considerable difficulty in the matter of reaching the ball. The point where many left arms are not straight is at the top of the swing, and it does not appear necessary that they should be so.

The important thing is that the left elbow be restrained from moving outward. If its downward motion brings it even closer to the body, and if the forearm avoids a horizontal position, I can see little harm in a slight crook in the arm.

At the top of the swing there is very little motion–only a few inches, which means the difference between good timing and bad. It is largely a matter of a moment of relaxation while getting set to hit. This relaxation must come either in the wrists or in the left elbow, and if the person's wrists are not the flexible kind, he has but one door open to him.

Those who say dogmatically that to keep the left arm straight is correct, and to bend it is wrong, overlook the fact that the golf stroke consists of considerably more than one motion. The result depends not upon the performance of each motion as an isolated act, but upon the way in which all motions are put together to make the whole swing.

Straight Right Arm at Impact

It is easy enough to start an argument anywhere about the necessi-

Power is speed, and speed increases with motion. So the economy of the situation is found in moving the clubhead as fast as possible with movements easily executed by the player himself. The tremendous amount of power in the cocked position of the wrists is apparent if they are held in that position with arms down as at address. From that position by using only the wrists the clubhead can be moved through three or four feet. That can be done very quickly, which means that it is an important factor in developing speed.

The function of the right arm is somewhat similar. Bent almost double at the top of the swing, its potency is measured by the amount of speed it can add to the top of the swing, and its contribution reaches a maximum when it becomes straight. In the machinery of the perfect stroke every force is directed toward increasing the speed of the clubhead from zero at the top position to the tremendous velocity at the moment of impact with the ball.

Controlling the Right Arm

At this point it might be well to discuss what should be done if the right hand is inclined to lead the stroke on the downswing. Many players have this fault, and when trying to diagnose and correct their swings, look upon their right hands as the cause of all the trouble. As often as not, in such a case, a player decides that he must concentrate upon keeping his right hand entirely out of the stroke.

I quite agree that the member in question is the direct cause of a great number of bad shots. But the fault is not that the right hand is applied at all, but in the method of application. Naturally, one cannot hit the ball with the left arm and side alone, and though I have said and am convinced that the right hand should remain subdued throughout the first part of the hitting stroke, there are cases in which I should advise its conscious application under a very definite control.

I believe that this may be an aid to those who suffer from too quick right hand action. Start the club down with the right hand but do it consciously and under control instead of the idea that it can't be helped. The first motion should bring the right elbow close against the ribs on the right side of the body, and the right wrist should come almost vertically downward, at the same time remaining cocked as it was at the top of the swing. After that it will take care of itself and ought not to cause much trouble.

Of course, this is merely a way to keep the right hand from doing mischief, as a means of starting the downward stroke. I think the left is far more reliable, provided the right will suffer itself to be led. The motion is mechanically much simpler, for at the top of the swing the left arm is straight, or nearly so, and a simple downward pull is all that is needed.

Hurried Backswing Ruinous

One essential element of the golf stroke, regardless of what path it may take is a smooth even acceleration from the top of the swing to and through the ball. Anything which disturbs this smoothness and introduces a jerk into the swing is bound to upset the timing or destroy the accuracy of the blow.

This is one of the chief dangers in a hurried backswing, the most persistent fault I have ever had to combat in golf. This tendency to hurry the backswing has been troublesome in the playing of every stroke in the game from the shortest putt to a full drive, and the unfortunate part of the thing is that the more important the shot, and hence

The top of the driving swing. The ball appears a long way from the player; and the position of the club indicates an upright swing; but the compact position of the hands gives the effect of a powerful, semi-flat swing; and Bobby's clubs are well on the flat side in "lie". The stance is so nearly square as, in the pleasant English idiom, "makes no difference."

the greater strain, the more difficult it becomes to swing leisurely.

I suppose there is no more common fault among all kinds and classes of golfers. Especially when trying for length it is hard to resist the impulse to snatch the club down from the top of the swing with all the force which the player can exert. If only always it would be remembered that it is the well-timed stroke, and not the vicious one, which makes the ball travel farthest!

The slow backswing is closely related to the relaxation which we are told is so necessary. Tenseness and anxiety over results produce a hurried swing which is nothing like the leisurely, almost indolent, backswing employed by most of the best players. The fast swing spoils the easy flowing balance of the stroke and throws the player entirely out of his hitting position.

Alex Morrison's idea is that the golf stroke from beginning to end should be as nearly as possible one continuous motion. To be absolutely so is, of course, impossible, for there is a complete change of direction in the midst of the operation. But this change ought to be made with so little effort that the two motions appear to flow one into the other. In other words, the club should go up slowly, and upon reaching the top should begin its descending path just as slowly, rapidly gaining speed until a maximum is reached at the moment of contact with the ball.

It is this picture of gradual acceleration which eludes the average player. Once reaching the top of the swing, he can see but one thing to be done—to hit as hard and as quickly as he can. He does not always realize that the appearance of ease is simply the result of leisurely and well-timed hitting. When the stroke does not go off half-cocked, and when the club has had time to gather speed before the final charge is set off, there is an entire absence of any appearance of intense effort.

Ease, style, form, timing—all these terms applied to golf mean the same thing—economy of effort. They come to mind when we see the force applied where it will do the most good—behind the ball instead

ON STANCE AND SWING

of wasted upon the air. The slow backswing, and a slow leisurely start downward are two very useful things to think about when you are striving to acquire any of these virtues.

The "Forward Press"

While on the subject of the backswing, I should like to say something about what is known as the "forward press."

For many years there has been much said and written about the "forward press," but as much used as is the term, the actual meaning and purpose of the movement is very generally misunderstood.

The "forward press" is apparently a forward motion of the hands just before the club is started back, followed by a perceptible drag which in effect brings the club back with a sling. I say it is apparently that for it is attempted in that manner by a majority of players.

As a matter of fact, the forward motion if properly done has nothing whatever to do with the hands or arms. It is simply and solely a leg motion and its purpose is to set the legs and body into a hitting position . Watch closely any really expert player and pay attention to his knees. You will notice that practically every fine player, just an instant before he starts his backswing, will give a queer little twitch with his knees. In some styles the motion is quite pronounced, while in others it is so quick and slight that it is not easily detected. Johnny Ferrell is very quick with it; Bill Mehlhorn is slower; but they all do it.

The first movement after the waggle is completed should be a quick and very slight turn of the hips in the direction of the hole, the right knee flexing slightly toward the ball and the left leg straightening at the same time. The almost imperceptible motion is transmitted through the arms to the hands, but it does not originate in them. The purpose of the press is to throw the hips and legs into position to start the swing.

The next movement is the real start of the backswing and here again the hips and legs supply the motive force, the hands for a time simply following the lead. This is the "drag" we hear so much about. The hips turn away from the ball and the hands and arms do not move until they are literally pulled away by the left.

The "forward press" and "drag" are, of course, not exaggerated and at times are very difficult to observe. The motion has been regarded as a mannerism and unimportant in the actual stroke. Yet it is the very hallmark of excellence in golf. To watch a man start his club backward (within certain limits) is an infallible indication of his worth as a golfer.

The Upright and Flat Swing

Now we come to a discussion of the upright and flat swing. The difference between these two swings is one which is not generally understood, and the confusion results in many persons misinterpreting advice or instruction received. Many players whose swings are peculiar in some respect appear at first glance to be either upright or flat as the case may be, when as a matter of fact they are the reverse.

The true distinction between the two styles is found in the motion of the body and the path of the clubhead during the lower portions of the stroke. If there is much body turn, and if especially there is an exaggerated turn of the shoulders, the swing must be flat, quickly opening the face of the club upon leaving the ball on the backswing. If the swing is upright there is less twist and more lateral motion of the hips, and the clubhead travels in a path more nearly in the plane of the ball.

Advantages are claimed for each style of play over the other, but it is hard to say which one should be recommended. Almost everything depends, I think, upon the individual; to which method he adapts himself most easily. There are as accomplished exponents of one as of the other, so that the only sound advice is to avoid forcing oneself into an unnatural attitude.

These photos show the amount of turning of the hips that Jones employs for a full swing. It is essential to move the right hip out of the way promptly.

*Bob's maiden pilgrimage to Pebble Beach, California
was in 1929 where he was put out by Johnny Goodman
in the 1st round of the National Amateur.*

The Sound

The average golfer who takes his golf even a little seriously certainly might be pardoned for wondering just what the experts mean when they point out so-and-so as the possessor of "a fine, sound style." Soundness is recognized by all as a most desirable attribute of a golf swing, but I am afraid that merely to point out that such a one possesses that virtue, affords little help to the fellow who would give his right arm to be sound too. Too many times we, who are interested in offering what help we can to those who want it, are too willing to pass over, with such an unenlightening phrase, the very things in which the struggling beginner is most interested. There ought at least to be understood what kind of swing we mean, and what it is that makes a method sound.

Obviously, the sound swing is not a definite reality. We all recognize that no two players swing a club in exactly the same manner, yet certainly more than one deserves to be regarded as a sound swinger. The trained observer and student of the game over a long period of close observance and intimate contact with successful players, in time fixes upon several actions and postures which are common to all. He learns to separate the mannerisms of the individual from the basic elements of his swing, and gradually he builds up a conception of a correct set of motions which he regards as essential in playing the game expertly. When he says that a certain swing is sound, he means that regardless of the variations peculiar to the individual, the method still embraces and accounts for all of the correct actions and postures, or enough of them to assure a high degree of success.

Simplicity Keynote

The first requisite of a truly sound swing is simplicity. In this respect I think that Horton Smith and Miss Joyce Wethered excel all golfers. In the case of each the matter of hitting the ball has been reduced to two motions; taking the club back with one, and bringing it down with the other. I have found many to agree with me that Miss Wethered's swing is the most perfect in the world, but I think it is safe to say that Horton Smith's backswing is the simplest in the world. Either of these two makes an ideal model to be imitated by everyone, for in these two methods it is possible to see all of the fundamentals, without the confusing effect of a great many mannerisms.

It will be found also that the sound swing is a very graceful one. That does not mean that any graceful motion is necessarily sound, but one cannot execute the various motions nor assume successively the correct postures in rhythmic style, without effecting a very pleasing look. The sound swing flows from beginning to end, but it flows powerfully and is graceful because it is correct rather than because it is made so. I know that all of us have seen many swings which were pretty enough but were so only because the player sacrificed power for appearance.

There is at least one thing more that the sound swinger must possess, and that is the ability to reproduce time and again the same old performance. In the end this virtue includes at least the first I have named, for in order to be capable of endless reproduction the swing must be simple.

The one point where it is of the utmost importance that the player be in the correct position occurs at the time when he strikes the ball. A good many players by an extraordinary action of one kind or another manage to right themselves at impact a great part of the time. These are the fellows who play excellent golf almost all of the time yet not quite consistently enough under a big strain to win important championships. It takes a sound swing, fundamentally correct, to stand the gaff of competition.

Keeping on the Line After Impact

Like any other rapid and complicated motion or series of motions, the golf swing is difficult to analyze. It is almost impossible for the player himself to describe with certainty what he does at any particular moment during the stroke. Just as the pianist would have trouble explaining how his fingers find the proper keys without direction from his eyes, so the golfer cannot fix at any instant the relative positions of hands, arms, hips, and clubhead. He can tell what he feels that he does but cannot declare that he actually does it. The hardest question to answer, therefore, is always the one which refers to the fundamentals of the stroke.

It seems to be impossible to separate from the rest of the swing that small segment which is referred to sometimes as the "hitting area." What happens there is too closely related to what has gone before to permit separate consideration. Tommy Armour has always said that Harry Vardon's amazing accuracy was accomplished because the face of Vardon's club remained so long on the line during the backswing—"looking at the ball," as Tommy expressed it—and so soon returned to the line after the hitting stroke had started. There may be a great deal in this, for Tommy's observation is a strict characteristic of an upright swing, which Vardon's certainly was.

But the fact remains that the clubhead actually need be on the line only during the very short space through which it is in contact with the ball. The flat swinger may have more difficulty returning his

Bobby Jones in front of the graph with which he and S.L. Hurt of Atlanta plan to work out some experiments in plotting the path of the club, hands, and shoulders by movies at the rate of 128 pictures per second. The graph is twelve feet square with circles and squares on a twelve inch basis.

Golf Swing

club to position, but, if he does so, there is no reason why his shot should not be straight.

For these reasons I do not like to say that staying on the line is a prime necessity in good iron play. Rather let it be that the possession of a well-grooved swing is what is needed, so that the player may have the ability to reproduce time after time the same motion. If he would accomplish this there must be a compactness of his form and a firm decisive quality in his stroke that will permit no deviation, however small. With a firm grip and a compact swing he need balance only the relaxed muscles necessary for good timing.

One of the greatest difficulties I have had in playing my irons has been to obtain this balance in one particular—to hold firmly to the club with my left hand without tightening the muscles of the forearm and wrist. I like to feel that my left side, especially the arm and shoulder, are guiding the club— holding it in the groove— until it comes time for the big punch, and the only occasions when the machine jumps the track occur when the left wrist becomes wooden and unable to contribute to, and often even impedes, the whip-like crack which strikes the ball.

reach a proper position in any number of ways, and corrections are more easily made when the action is leisurely. Once started downward, the player launches himself upon his venture and right or wrong he must go through with it.

Now there are a number of important things to be watched in the position at the top of the swing. It is possible to write many pages on this phase of the stroke alone. But the one feature which I have in mind now is one which the duffer ignores entirely and which has everything to do with the success of the stroke.

At the top of the swing the shaft of the club, which for the long shots is in a position approximately in a horizontal plane, should at the same time be pointing to a spot slightly to the right of the object at which the player is aiming. This will be found to be a uniform practice among the best professional golfers. It is the natural result of swinging the club back to the top rather than lifting it up as so very many beginners are so prone to do.

Now from this position it is important in what manner the club is started downward. The ne-cessary elevation of the hands at the top of the swing draws the right elbow away from the

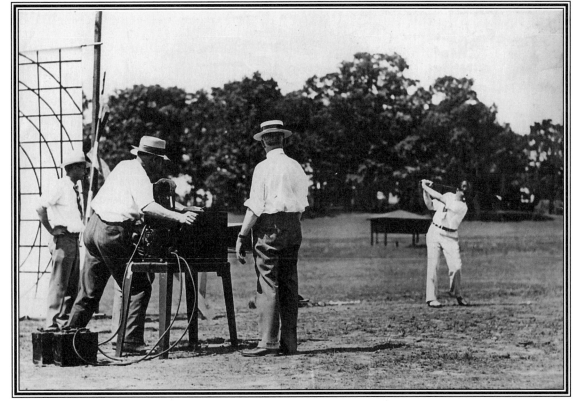

At the top of the swing, Bobby's movements are captured by a "speed movie camera"
on the East Lake G.C. in Atlanta--Bobby's home course since he was a kid. (Wide-World)

Golf Swing
One Uninterrupted Motion

It is always best for the player to consider the golf stroke as the flowing and uninterrupted motion backward and forward from the position of address through the ball to the finish. This view is far more valuable than that which regards the swing as a series of distinct motions. Nevertheless, there are a number of crucial points where proper or improper action may determine the ultimate success of the effort. An error here may be corrected and the effect of the mistake avoided, but a proper start places one far along the road to a happy ending.

This is particularly true of the start of the downward or hitting stroke. The backswing is, of course, important because it is the means of placing the player in position to hit. But it is possible to

ribs where it should have remained until the last possible moment. The elbow is not, however, lifted into the air like the wing of a wounded bird. The right forearm should point obliquely, almost vertically, toward the ground, and be drawn away from the side only by what is necessary to accommodate a full swing of the club.

Watch the Right Hand

A good many players advance thus far with fair success. But the next step usually trips them. The almost irresistible impulse now, when all is in readiness to wallop the ball, is to allow the right hand too much freedom. Immediately that ubiquitous member, which has to be watched continually, whips the club over the right shoulder towards the front of the player whence it must approach the ball from outside the line of flight. Whether a smothered hook or a bad slice results depends only upon whether the club face is shut or open when it reaches the ball. If anything like a decent shot results it may be ascribed to pure accident.

The proper beginning from the position I have described is in the direction in which the grip-end of the shaft is pointing. As the head-end of the club is pointing slightly to the right of the objective aimed at, the grip-end will be directed away from the vertical plane in which the ball rests. In other words, instead of immediately beginning to approach the line of flight as the downward stroke commences, the clubhead should be made to first drop away from that line.

The importance of this movement cannot be overestimated. The right elbow quickly drops back into place close to the side of the body, and the player is in a compact position ready to deliver a blow squarely at the back of the ball. There is no possibility of cutting across the shot.

I regard Chick Evans' swing as a remarkable example of the importance of this movement which I have described. Chick violates one of the most commonly appreciated principles of a good golf swing in the way he takes his club back, lifting it almost vertically upward from the position of address. But he reaches a proper position and when his club starts downward it drops away from the plane of the ball and sweeps through in a fine arc. Reaching the proper position at the top and starting away correctly it makes no difference in what way he progresses upward.

Gradual Acceleration Secret of Golf Swing

There is nothing like an ultra-speed movie camera for revealing truly the various consecutive movements which make up the golf stroke. One may speculate to his heart's content and observe himself blue in the face with the naked eye, but he cannot actually see and analyze the motion without the aid of a recording device more rapid than the human eye. It is of help to learn from the expert what sensations or what "feel" he has as he swings the club, but it is far more enlightening to be able to see what actually happens. The same motion does not necessarily produce the same sensation but it must result in a similar photograph.

Recently I made some high-speed motion pictures of two men with whom I was playing. Both are far better than the average of business-men golfers, playing fairly consistently in the low eighties, and occasionally slipping below the eighty mark at East Lake in Atlanta, where it must be admitted difficulties are not too severe. Both sets of pictures revealed things which I had not noticed before although I have played regularly with both men for years.

One set of photographs showed clearly that the subject, at the very beginning of the downward stroke, bent both knees and permitted his entire body to slump down upon his heels. From this position, extend-

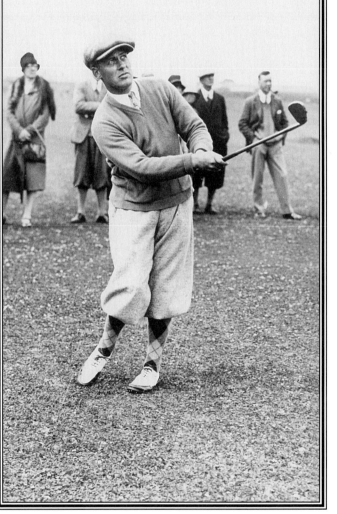

The poetic balance of a mashie pitch. (Hulton-Deutsch)

ing himself in hitting, or "going to work" as Alex Morrison expresses it, the legs straightened again and head and shoulders came up as the punch was delivered.

The other man was equally off but in a slightly different way. His first motion from the top of the swing was made with the left side of the body, by bending the left knee and literally falling forward and downward until his clubhead had almost reached the ball. Then, in order to meet the ball, he had to pull himself up again to about the original level by the time contract occurred. Each swing presented a sort of heaving motion, first downward then upward.

Now, because the golf swing cannot follow the arc of a circle it cannot possess a fixed center. But it is not good practice to permit the head to bob up and down nor to allow the hips and upper parts of the body to move far from the plane in which they commenced operations. To heave the body or to alternately crouch and straighten up only increases the difficulty of bringing the clubhead around to a fair contact.

The most important point to watch and the one at which the trouble usually starts is the left knee. The left knee must bend in order to accommodate the turn of the hips and body made in reaching the top of the swing. But from the moment the motion changes direction and starts downward the left knee begins to straighten. The left leg really must act as a brace against which the player hits. Under no circumstances must the bend of the left leg be permitted to increase after the downstroke has been started.

That is wherein my friends experienced their difficulty. Unquestionably in each case the error was caused by an effort to develop power by beginning to hit from the top of the swing. A more leisurely beginning and a reliance upon a gradual acceleration during the first part of the stroke are the things to which each must school himself.

Freedom vs. Compactness

I believe that everyone will agree that the source of the greatest trouble in golf, not only for good golfers but poor golfers, is tension. This idea has been advanced many times before, of course. The next step is to find some method or methods that will help to relieve tension as much as possible. I think one mistake the average golfer makes along this line comes from trying to keep his swing too compact. He has the idea that this will help him control the head of the club, but about all it does is to make him tighten up and to bring about much more tension than would exist otherwise.

I have seen many fine golfers, in attempting to illustrate what they thought their swings were for pictures or otherwise, stop well before their backswings were completed, when it so happened that in actually hitting the ball they let the clubhead dip a foot or so below the horizontal. What the golf swing needs is all the freedom it can get with as few restrictions as it is possible to make. Don't be afraid to let the swing take its natural course.

I remember reading shortly after the championship at Pebble Beach the comment of some observer who wrote that, after watching a considerable number of the players there, notably Cyril Tolley, he was convinced that much of the talk of the dangers from over-swinging was ill-founded. He pointed out that the majority of players, when they let out for a big shot, as a rule allowed the club to drop below the horizontal at the top of the backswing in spite of the fact that we are usually cautioned that to do this invites troubles and frequently results in disaster. It is something of a satisfaction to me that at least one observer has been so impressed.

It seems to me that there has been a tendency to overemphasize this matter of compactness, or at any rate, that a great many golfers are inclined to go too far in striving for what they believe to be compactness. This is especially true in detail of curbing the swing stroke. Many people have come to believe that a short backswing, by eliminating some of the body turn, simplifies the stroke to such an extent that grave errors will be easily avoided. I have always held the contrary view, and am convinced that a great many more shots are spoiled by a swing that is too short than by one that is too long, and this applies in the use of every club from the driver down to the putter.

Swing Must Have Smoothness

The one quality which a golf swing must have is smoothness. The acceleration from the top must be gradual and the motion must be unhurried and free from any sudden or jerky movements.And in order to accomplish it in this manner, the clubhead must have plenty of time to gather its speed before it reaches the ball.

It is apparent that the longer the arc through which the club travels the less need there is for an abnormal expenditure of energy at any one particular moment. The long path affords plenty of space for building up velocity from the zero point at the top to a maximum at the moment the ball is met.

Horton Smith is a short-swinger who is marvelously accurate as well as very long. But Horton is a tall, powerful chap and he is young. His height and strength make it possible for him to handle the club with ease and precision not in the reach of all of us. But Findlay Douglas says that, as a man grows older and his muscles become less supple, his swing becomes shorter and relaxation becomes more difficult. If this is the case, it would seem that the youngsters would do well to start with a little length to spare.

In any event it is worthwhile remembering that the golf stroke is a swing with the force working from the centre outward, that is, centrifugal, and shortening the arc through which the force is applied does not figure to increase precision. The player who, like Horton Smith, has developed a rather short swing, possibly subconsciously, which carries the element of good timing will no doubt get better results from it than from a swing in which he was consciously striving to extend the limit. But if the natural disposition is toward a long free sweep, I am convinced that any actual effort to cut it down, merely for the sake of compactness, is more than likely to lead to disappointing results.

At the start of the backswing be certain not to lift the club with the right hand.

Start on its backward course by a push from the left side.

A Few Faults and How to Correct Them

Whether one's golfing ambitions are directed at championships or whether they go no further than the low eighty class, one has just about the same problems to solve and the same difficulties to overcome. Hooks and slices and backspin concern the tournament player as much as the dub. And at the bottom of it all, there are certain basic principles which each must observe.

For that reason I thought that it might be of help to enable the struggling beginner to understand the difficulties which a man finds over a period of fifteen or twenty years' experience and study of the game.

Obviously, I can speak with certain knowledge of no one's experiences save my own, so it is my intention to write briefly of the various troubles I have had and how I had sought to eliminate them. Naturally, it is impossible to render oneself proof against any golfing fault. Old and almost forgotten mistakes often creep back into one's swing and cause trouble until they are discovered and put down. We cannot be on the watch for too many things all the time. We can only study the evil and be ready with a remedy once it is recognized.

Like all youngsters I played golf intuitively for a very long while. I didn't know much about what I was trying to do, and when I hit one shot off line the cause of my having done so was the last thing I thought about. Sometimes now I wish I could still play that way.

The first thing about golf which I remember recognizing as a problem to be solved, had to do with the trajectory of my tee shots. Throughout my earlier years in the game my habit was to tee the ball only a small fraction of an inch off the ground—sometimes merely dropping it on the stiff Bermuda grass of the East Lake tees—and to smack a decidedly descending blow. In addition, I always used a club with a very shallow or thin face. The result of such a combination of circumstances was a shot which started low and rose abruptly to the crest of its flight, whence, entirely spent, it dropped lightly upon the ground and stopped very quickly.

This kind of shot was subject to two objections—its distance was curtailed by the entire absence of roll and it was at the mercy of any wind, particularly of a head wind which forced it higher and higher and always backward. The shot was not a boring one and when it hit the ground it was dead.

One quality that a golf swing must have is smoothness. A straight left arm increases the potential power of the stroke.

I tried a lot of things to obtain the trajectory which I wanted—a shot which had sufficient altitude to assure a fairly long flight, and at the same time a shot which would bore into a head wind and strike the ground still going. I have been able to solve the problem fairly well, though even now I occasionally allow the presence of a head wind to bait me into knocking the shot down in my old manner.

The specifics for the remedy are: (1) To place the ball forward about opposite the instep of the left foot; (2) To tee it at least an inch off the ground; (3) To employ a deep-faced driver; and (4) To hit the ball as squarely in the back as possible. The position of address and the height of the tee are merely to make it easier to hit the ball in the back. The depth of the driver face provides a margin of safety needed because of the high tee and inspires a certain amount of confidence in the player.

The chief point in this for the average player is that a sharply descending hit with a straight-faced club is less effective and decidedly more dangerous than the flattened sweeping blow. Where length is desired the rising, quick-stopping shot is not the thing.

Remedies for Golfers Off Form

The most valuable thing an instructor can give his pupil is a simple hint or "tip" which, without undue mental gymnastics, can be made to work on any occasion. When a man is engaged in actual play and something goes wrong, he has not the time to take his swing apart mentally, and by careful analysis get to the root of the trouble. He must have some simple cure, usually a subjective one, which will automatically correct the evil.

As a general rule, I find that to direct my attention to the part of my swing immediately connected with hitting the ball is the most helpful. I am able to correct almost any fault, particularly in driving, by concentrating upon the direction which my hands and clubhead take during the act of hitting the ball and immediately afterward.

Faults developed during the round usually tend in one direction. If you go out without warming up, you usually find that, although you feel that you are swinging properly, the ball continues to drift off to the right, or curl into the rough on the left. You should hit a few shots before going out and make the adjustments then, but it is too late to do any extensive experimenting after the round is started. Whatever change is made, if it is not to upset the rest of your game, must be above all things simple and direct.

I t is surprising how much can be done to overcome baleful tendencies by directing the hands at the moment of contact with the ball. If the shots are going off the line in a certain direction, the source of the trouble may be almost anywhere and you can't stop to locate it, but you may be able to get good results by applying a little counterirritant.

Although, elsewhere in this book in the chapter "On Wooden Play," I have mentioned cures for slicing and hooking, it will do no harm to repeat a few of these to illustrate my point.

We will say then that the trouble is slicing. Now, a slice may be caused by failing to pivot; it may be caused by a too right-handed backstroke; it may be caused in a number of ways. But the absolute direct and immediate cause is nearly always cutting across the ball at impact. What has gone before is merely conducive to that act and only the remote cause of cutting across the ball.

Now, what you do at the moment you hit the ball will not correct fundamental errors in the backswing, but it may set at naught the effect of those errors. So the quickest and surest way to work at least a temporary cure for slicing is to watch the hands and clubhead at

There can be no doubt that the left arm must be straight at the moment of striking the ball.

impact. Stick the right hand straight out toward the hole, and try to send the clubhead through the ball, out to the right of the line. Don't try to keep the ball away from the right side of the fairway for that is the surest way to make it go there. Try actually to shove it out along the right-hand boundary.

In the same way, hooking may be corrected simply enough. It is in this direction that I am most apt to wander, so I have had plenty of experience. I have played whole days, and even one whole week at Minikahda, when I could not relax my vigil for one shot without hooking it into the next county.

On those days I would pick out a spot, not especially, but in my mind's eye, about thirty degrees to the left of the line I wanted to play on. Then disregarding all else, I would hit for all I was worth, watching only that my left hand should go through the ball traveling on a line for that spot. Sometimes I get the same results by trying to brush my left trouser leg with my left hand.

T he point is not so much that you actually do what you think you do, so long as you try to do it. As I said, the hint is purely a subjective one and tends to correct the trouble by trying to exaggerate a departure in the opposite direction. It is only meant for a rough and ready solution to difficulties that cannot wait and it will be of no value to those of us who are idealists in the pursuit of perfect form. But it will get results, which after all, is the ultimate aim.

Try Placing Ball Differently

Very often the position of the ball at address has a lot to do with the way a player hits the ball. Apparently of little importance, this is one of the most vital considerations in hitting a golf ball, not that one position is correct for every player, but because for each player there is one position which, with the peculiarities of his method, enables him to hit the ball most easily and most effectively.

In my particular case this position happens to be a point about opposite the middle of my left foot, and this is true when using any club for almost any kind of shot. Of course, the exigencies of a peculiar situation may alter this position to some extent, but normally it remains the same. With the ball in this forward position, all the power

A FEW FAULTS AND HOW TO CORRECT THEM

of the stroke can be applied behind it—there is no additional tension and loss of power because of a position which requires the player to hold back in order to meet the ball squarely.

It is not difficult to see that if the swing is adjusted to strike the ball in a certain position, even a slight variation in the position of the ball, the swing remaining the same, will cause an error in hitting. And no golfer needs to be told what ruinous results may follow from even the very slightest of mistakes.

Taking the ball an inch too soon or an inch too late may throw it many yards off line at the end of its flight.

Placing the ball at address should always receive minute attention. Too many times we step up confidently and carelessly to play a shot, and fall readily into a position which feels comfortable, and which we think is the accustomed attitude. Without giving the thing a thought, we hit the shot and are at a loss to explain the pull or slice which results. A tiny error is enough and it is very easy to overlook.

For instance, the following: At Winged Foot during the recent championship, I played my irons better than at any other time in my life—that is, in important competition—and I don't think I should have done so had I been left entirely to my own devices.

On the morning of the first day, I went out on the East Course to warm up a bit before starting. After hitting a few drives which went off all right, I dropped back to a number four iron, a club which I use in practice as a sort of indicator to the prospective behavior of all its companions. With it I hit shot after shot, trying everything I could think of, but all of them went to the right of the objective except a few that I tried to keep straight by a vigorous roll of the right hand. These were just as far off line in the other direction. That was not exactly a pleasant situation to confront immediately before starting a tournament.

Finally, T.N. Bradshaw, of Atlanta, who made the trip with me and who was watching my practice, spoke up. Brad has played with me at least as much as anyone and he knows my game. A suggestion from him could not be considered out of place.

"I think you are playing the ball too far back, Bob," he said.

I myself did not think so, but I was in a humor to try anything. So I played the next few a bit farther forward and from that time had no more trouble. This gave me one more thing to think about, but it was worth more than all the others. A slight change of position is hard for the player himself to detect, especially if he plays for any appreciable time in that way. But to move the ball interferes not at all with the swing. To try a different position endangers none of the elements of touch, timing, or rhythm. And very often it will be found to be the exact adjustment required. It is impossible to contend that the same relative positions of ball and feet are proper for every player. But if anyone is off his game, it will do no harm to experiment—to shift the ball nearer the left foot to correct a slice, and nearer the right foot to correct a hook. If it works, it is the simplest specific to be given.

Starting out in the spring after several months of inactivity so far as golf is concerned, the player finds that his clubs have an unfamiliar feeling. As he stands over the ball preparing to hit it, he can't help wondering what is going to happen. There is no such thing then as subjective control, for his muscles have lost the habit of correct hitting to whatever extent the habit had been developed during the past summer.

This feeling of uncertainty in my case means just one thing –hurry– a quick backswing and hasty rap at the ball, always glad to have it over. The mere fact that I feel uncomfortable keeps me from swinging in a long leisurely arc.

To overcome this timidity there are two points which I bear in mind in playing every shot. First, to provide an ample body-turn or pivot on the backstroke; and, second, to make the backstroke slowly. To these might be added an admonition to myself to wait on the blow, for quick-hitting is likewise a temptation. With these things in mind, after a few rounds and a little practice it never is very long before confidence begins to return and the muscles begin to fall back into the old accustomed groove.

The rear view of the finish of a drive. Bobby advises players to hit through in a straight line. (Wide-World)

BOBBY JONES ON GOLF

Bobby Jones teeing off on his first qualifying round in the National Amateur Championship at the Merion Cricket Club in 1930.
Jones scored a brilliant 69, one under par.

Bobby Jones teeing off of the 8th tee at the 1929 National Open
at Winged Foot Golf Club.

Timing the

It is unfortunate that the most important feature of the golf stroke is so difficult to explain or to understand. We all talk about good timing, and faulty timing, and the importance of timing, and yet no one has been able to fix upon a means of saying what timing is. The duffer is told that he spoils his shot because his stroke is not properly timed, but no one can tell him how he can time it properly.

One very common error which results in bad timing can, I believe, be pointed out with sufficient exactness at least to give the enterprising average golfer something to work on. I mean the error of beginning to hit too early in the downward stroke. I have said that it is a common error. It is an error common to all golfers, a chronic lapse in the case of the expert, but an unfailing habit in the case of the dub. I believe it will be found that of the players who turn in scores of ninety and over, ninety-nine out of every hundred hit too soon on ninety-nine out of every hundred strokes. Many who play even better golf and have really decent-looking form, fail to play better than they do for this reason.

Hitting Too Soon

Hitting too soon is a fault of timing in itself. It results in the player reaching the ball with a large part of the power of the stroke already spent. Instead of being able to apply it all behind the ball, he has expended a vast amount upon the air where it could do no good. Apparently everyone fears that he will not be able to strike out in time, when, as a matter of fact, there has not come under my observation one single player who has been habitually guilty of late hitting. Sometimes they fail to close the face of the club by the time the club reaches the ball, but this is always due to something entirely apart from tardy delivery.

The primary cause of this trouble is to be found in the action of the right hand and wrist. If the left hand has a firm grip upon the club, so long as it remains in control, there can be no premature hitting. The left side is striking backhanded and it will prefer to pull from the left shoulder, with the left elbow straight, rather than to deliver a blow involving an uncocking of the wrist.

But the right hand throughout the stroke is in the more powerful position. Its part in the stroke is on what in tennis would be called the forehand. It is moving forward in the direction easiest for it to follow. Because the player is intent upon effort and upon hitting hard, the right hand tends to get into the fight long before it has any right to enter. The right hand must be restrained if it is not to hit before its time arrives.

Increase Speed of Stroke Gradually

I wish everyone could study carefully a few sets of motion pictures showing the proper action of the right side, noting particularly the successive positions of the wrists. In the case of an expert player the wrists remain fully cocked, just as they were at the top of the swing, until at least half of the downstroke has been completed by the arms.

The dub, on the other hand, starts immediately when coming down, to whip the club with his wrists. He forthwith takes all the coil out of his spring and when his hands reach the position corresponding to the numeral eight on the dial of a watch, his wrists are perfectly straight, and all the power left is in his arms and shoulders, to be utilized by any twist or contortion the player can execute.

It is hard to wait, so long as the player is expending anything like the maximum effort. It is therefore wise to work into this sense of delayed hitting, by swinging at first gently toward the ball. I have seen numbers of mediocre players who were able to obtain fine results by exercising a bit of restraint. When once the sense is felt and the drives begin to crack sharply, the speed and force can be increased gradually up to the player's limit.

What Motion Picture Stills Tell

Some time ago I saw in some magazine a two page set of motion picture enlargements of myself hitting a full drive. Underneath the pages the editor, as commentator, called attention to the fact that in starting my downward stroke my body and hips had turned quite perceptibly back toward the position of address before the club had appreciably altered its position at the top. The observation was entirely borne out by the photographs, which illustrated clearly one of the most important details of the stroke.

To a greater or less degree this same thing will be noted in the swing of every good golfer. It is hard for the naked eye to observe the motion precisely. To the human observer, it always appears that the player in starting the down stroke gives a little forward hitch to his hips just as he

Bob Jones poses for high speed photographs (1/50,000 second) at moment of impact for A.G. Spalding & Bros., Inc., in 1935. They clearly show that as the clubhead strikes the ball, it drives in the side of the ball, compressing it considerably has been driven in almost three tenths of an inch, when the ball begins to regain its shape.

Golf Stroke

begins to hit. It is a very quick little motion which is very hard to analyze but it is an essential part of the expert stroke.

What happens is this: The player reaches the normal top of his swing with his wrists not flexed or cocked at the absolute maximum. This is plainly indicated in all posed photographs, for in these only natural and comfortable positions are shown at rest. Because they are posed the position is always one that the player is able to maintain. It is rarely even similar to the posture in which he would find himself if the action could be instantly arrested and the golfer turned to stone.

Cocked Wrist Increases Power

The remarks of the commentator whose words I have paraphrased above, might indicate to some that the club remained stationary because only the hips and not the arms and shoulders moved. Actually this is not the case. The hips, shoulders, and arms all begin the motion before the clubhead moves perceptibly, but this is so because a further flexing of the wrists absorbs all this motion before it is felt at the head of the club. In other words, as the swing starts downward, the wrists bend more, and until they reach their limit in this respect the clubhead does not begin to gather speed. This added cock of the wrists increases the amount of power deliverable at impact.

This is not so much a conscious motion as it is the result of perfect relaxation. It is further a characteristic of the leisurely, **well-timed** stroke which is not in too big a hurry to hit the ball. It is impossible of accomplishment if the wrists are tense, or if the player is too anxious to hit and have it over, for in the latter case, he uses up all of his wrist-cock at the top of the swing.

Photographs Reveal Time Requirements

Golf Illustrated of London published a set of spark photographs and an explanatory article by Captain Phillip Quayle. These photographs are exceedingly clear and reveal to the layman a good deal of what happens when a driver in the hands of a good player comes in contact with a golf ball. Captain Quayle, by means of his spark photography, has been able to record things which the fastest movie camera made cannot approach.

I have heard much speculation concerning the length of time and throughout what space the club and ball remained in contact, and the distance traversed during contact estimated at everything from the most infinitesimal measurement to several inches. Captain Quayle from his photographs calculates that the club and ball are in contact about six ten-thousandths of a second, and that the two together travel in that time about seventy-one one-hundredths of an inch, about as instantaneous a process as one could imagine.

Clubhead Compresses Ball

The photographs clearly show that as the clubhead strikes the ball, it drives in the side of the ball and compresses it considerably before it even leaves the tee upon which it rests. This compression continues until the contact side of the ball has been driven in almost three tenths of an inch, when the ball begins to regain its shape. It is this compression which adds yards to the drive. Captain Quayle figures that the speed of the club during impact is about one hundred feet per second, whereas the initial velocity of the ball is about one hundred and fifty feet per second.

All of which brings to mind that the sole purpose of swinging a golf club is to hit the ball, and that so many of us are prone to overlook that aim. An attractive style, a graceful flourish, and a fine-looking finish are all very nice but Captain Quayle's photographs show that it is only about six ten-thousands of a second that really counts.

Well-Timed Stroke Essential

And again the old problem of timing. More speed on the clubhead means more compression on the ball, and more compression in turn means more yards on the drive. To produce the ultimate the clubhead must reach its maximum speed at the very instant of contact. If we have timed the stroke to reach maximum speed before contact with the ball or after the point where the ball begins to regain its shape, we have thrown away so many yards.

There are just two mechanical requirements of a good golf shot: one is timing, the other is a solid contact with the face of the club faced to the line of flight. Given these the only other elements are the judgment of the player and the favor of fortune.

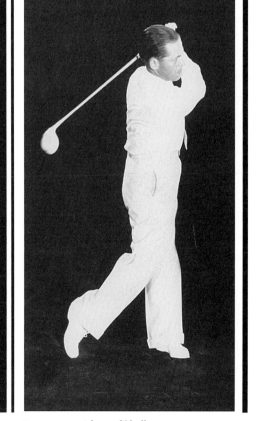

These reveal to the layman a good deal of what happens when a driver in the hands of a good player comes in contact with a golf ball.
before it even leaves the tee upon which it rests. This compression continues until the contact side of the ball
It is this compression which adds yards to the drive.

On Wooden Play

Many instructors incline to the belief that a pupil should begin with short shots and progress to the longer ones. Since I am writing chiefly for those who have played at least a little, in the hope that they will recognize their own difficulties to be the same as mine, it will be easier to proceed as we would play a hole at golf.

In driving, then, and brassie play I have always exhibited two strangely opposite tendencies, especially since I adopted the driving method which I have described as hitting the ball squarely in the back. This method, with the deep-faced club which I favor, demands a high tee and encourages a slightly flatter swing. It is thus most apt to produce a hook if it is not properly timed. Yet in playing a brassie or spoon shot from the fairway, if I mis-hit the shot at all, it will almost always slice, the reason being in this case that the ball must be hit downward in order to get it up from a close lie, and the swing is either too upright or the right hand does not close the face of the club quickly enough.

Considering the drive first the cure is easy to find even if it is sometimes hard to apply. The trouble grows out of my efforts to avoid the rising shot which I described before. I attempt to strike the ball with the clubhead moving as nearly as possible in a horizontal plane, and sometimes my left side is slow to move out of the way of the swing. The little resistance set up there keeps the weight of my body too long upon the right foot, so that the low point of the swing is set backward a few inches. This causes the clubhead to reach the ball moving slightly upward swinging the shot to the left of the intended line.

In order to stop the hook, the most important thing is to make certain that the left side will move easily around as the stroke gets under way. I find that I never get into trouble in this way (it may be, of course, and usually is in some other way) if my left shoulder begins to move at the instant the club starts downward from the top of the swing. That motion starts the weight flowing into the stroke and it continues right on through the ball. When everything is going smoothly, of course no tension is set up in the left side. The ideal situation is complete relaxation. But lacking that, it becomes necessary to move by force that which should itself move naturally in harmony with everything else.

The Smothered Shot

A smothered shot is caused by addressing the ball too far back off the right foot. Very often the player may do this without being at all conscious that his stance is in any way different from his accustomed position. But instinctively as he hits the ball he makes an effort to swing it back upon the proper line. This he can do only by whipping the clubhead through, at the same time retarding the turn of his body. Almost inevitably the abrupt turn of the wrists will turn the toe of the club inward and the face downward. There is nowhere a more complete mess than a smothered drive.

This may not be the only way in which it is possible to smother or hook, but at least it furnishes a reasonable basis for working out a means of prevention. It would seem that if the ball were played forward at address, off the left toe, and care were taken to avoid hitting the ball outward,

neither of these things would be likely. I have found that to be a fairly successful method, at least as applied to myself. It may therefore be successful with others.

The matter of moving the ball to a position opposite the left foot requires no elaboration; the other suggestion may require some. And yet in the end, it amounts to only one thing. In the ordinary golf swing, not freakish in any respect, the left arm must go outward away from the body in order to permit the clubhead to pass outward through the ball. To prevent such a passage, it is only necessary to restrain the left arm and to keep the left elbow in a path close to the ribs of the left side.

Curing the Slice

It is certainly true that the man who hooks most of his tee shots is far closer to being a good golfer than the one who is an habitual slicer. There will not be a great deal of difference perhaps so long as the fault of each remains uncorrected, but the slicer has by far the harder job on his hands.

There are, of course, any number of ways in which a ball may be made to curve to the right, and hence it is somewhat difficult to speak in general terms about a thing which may be accomplished in so many different ways. But if one will watch carefully the efforts of a number of those players who are habitual slicers it will be found that nearly all of them do at least two things alike. First, the right shoulder passes considerably under the left when the

(Above) The slow backswing for the drive

(Left) Stance for the drive. (This was Bobby's former stance. Now he extends his arms to a greater degree for he found this procedure helps his swing)

ball is being hit, and second, the left elbow gets away from the side of the body and projects itself upward as the swing is completed.

These two things are so closely connected that it is hard to know just how to set about correcting the trouble. To one it would be best to say "Keep the left arm close in"; to another, "Keep your right shoulder up." I tried this on my father the other day after watching him hit a few drives from a practice tee. He was hitting every shot with a wide slice although he was apparently meeting the ball with plenty of power. It was quite evident that his trouble was exactly what I have described. He was unable, however, to keep his left elbow down, because his right shoulder had started the swing by moving downward too much, and so it forced his left arm outward. But working from the other end, he found it quite possible to move his shoulders more nearly in a horizontal plane, hitting the ball with the right shoulder relatively high. This position had the desired effect for it forced the left arm to stay close, thus eliminating the tendency to slice.

Hooding the Club

As slicing is the most difficult fault which the players shooting ninety and over have to overcome, it is the common practice among them to hood the club as they address a golf ball. This solution,

The top of the backswing

though a most natural one, is seldom effective. By "hooding" the club, I mean the act of turning the toe of the club forward against the ball so that the face looks toward the ground. Apparently, to the beginner at any rate, that little movement will help him to eliminate the slice by which he loses distance and control. I am afraid, however, that it does little besides encourage the deviation sought to be avoided.

The spin imparted to the ball depends upon the angle at which the club comes in contact with the ball, and not upon the direction in which it is faced. If the club cuts across the line of flight, it is a safe bet that a slice will result no matter how the club may be faced. It is conceivable that if the face were hooded to a degree that would bring it up at exact right angles to the path of the swing, then the ball might be driven straight along a continuation of that path. But the continuation very likely would not be in the direction of the hole.

The tendency when the club is hooded at address, is to draw it across the ball even more than normally, or at least to attempt to straighten it up as the ball is hit. Either impulse obeyed ruins the shot and sets at naught all good intentions.

Although it may sound illogical to suggest such a thing, a far better practice in order to correct slicing, or to produce a slight draw, is to lay the club face off at address. The end to be reached involves meeting

An unusual photo of golfing form. Note how Jones' eyes are still transfixed on the spot where the ball lies until the club passes through the ball.

the ball in such a way that the club is not drawn across the ball, and if the face be open every impulse directs the player to bring it around with his swing. He knows he cannot chop at the ball, and as a consequence his swing becomes flatter and more sweeping. I

The finish of the drive

should advise every habitual slicer to grip the club with the right hand a bit more underneath the shaft and to open the face of the club at address. Then let him swing well around his body and try to roll his wrists into the shot so that the club face will be straight when it meets the ball.

The terms used by many of the pros to explain a hook or a slice convey a good idea of what is regarded as the cause of both. A slice is spoken of as "getting away" from the player, and when a hook results, it is said that he "hung onto the ball too long." Those terms to my mind almost exactly describe the feeling. To produce a hook or, for the habitual slicer to drive straight, the player must have the feeling that he is "hanging on to the ball" and he cannot have that feeling unless he swings through the ball and allows his wrists to turn into the shot.

This brings us now to a discussion of the "intentional slice" and the "intentional hook".

The Intentional Slice

I will attempt to describe here my conception of the manner of producing an intentional fade or slice. After all, the controlled fading shot differs only in degree from the unintended slice which usually ends in trouble.

I find that it is seldom necessary to alter the stance materially or to shift the position of the ball with respect to the feet, unless I want a virtual rainbow curve. I usually address the ball in ordinary fashion except that my left shoulder possibly is drawn back a little from the line of play, and I may stand a very little closer to the ball than I should do for a straight shot. The position at address should be designed to restrict the turn of the body on the backward swing so that the plane of the stroke will be on the upright side.

This much can be said with fair certainty, but I do not care to be understood as doing much more than merely guessing in what I am now going to say:

It has always seemed to me that the most necessary part of the golf stroke is the forward motion of the left shoulder and knee at the beginning of the downward stroke, and I think that it is the exaggeration of this movement which is the primary cause of the left to right drift of the ball. This motion tends to throw the weight forward and to cause the body to forge ahead of the hands and club. It is made up mostly of a lateral shift with little in the nature of turning. All this makes for late hitting, that is, the right hand lags and the clubhead does not come around squarely to the ball, the face remaining open at impact.

After the ball is struck, the hands and arms do not go out toward the hole but slip inside the line of flight and to the left of the objective.

Up to what is properly the finish of the actual stroke, and until the muscles relax again and the club goes up over the shoulder of its own momentum, the back of the left hand and the palm of the right are upward. But this is merely the result of what has gone before and not an end in itself. The finish simply indicates that the wrists have not turned over and that the right hand has been subdued in hitting.

The chief use which I have found for an intentional fade in driving is in combating a right to left wind. British players, having grown accustomed to bothersome breezes are audacious enough to ride a wind of this kind with a pull or hook and thereby gain considerable length. My attitude, however, when confronted by a side wind, has been purely one of defense. I am quite happy to sacrifice a few yards in order to keep the ball in the fairway. A little fading spin to counteract the force of the wind gives very good control.

Often, too, a fade is useful to hold the ball on a dry sloping fairway, or to avoid a dangerous place on the left. When attempting to drive a straight ball, it is impossible to foresee on which side the error will lie, but if intending to slice, there is little chance of driving to the left.

Now, reverting to what I said at the beginning about doing the wrong thing to prevent a slice or hook, I think I can now add something. The player stands upon the tee and he determines that in all events he must not go to the right. So, after taking his stance, he endeavors "with his swing" to place the ball to the left. The likely result is that in bringing the club in toward the left, he will slice into the very hazard he was so intent upon avoiding. In trying to prevent the slice, he will probably do what cannot but produce it.

An exceptional picture of Jones at the finish of a long drive. One can almost feel the amount of power he has put into the stroke (P&A Photos)

The Intentional Hook

I have just tried to explain what I consider to be the best method of playing an intentional slice. I am now going to attempt to describe how I should go about playing an intentional hook, or draw, as the shot is sometimes called.

For me there is little use for the draw or pull except as a means of guarding against a slice where the latter would prove disastrous; and it would be only for such employment that I should recommend learning to bring it off. The hooking spin somehow is not amenable to control to any degree approaching that to which a fade may be subjected. For most golfers the pull is produced by a quite unnatural swing. The tendency of most players, except those who employ the so-called "shutface" method, is to cut across the ball, and they have considerable difficulty in bringing the club around in a flat arc designed to produce a pull.

Whenever, because of a left to right wind or other circumstance which could render a slice undesirable, I attempt to apply a little hooking spin, there are two main points that I look to: first, I stand at a greater distance from the ball; and, second, I turn my body slightly more away from the ball on the backward swing. This is done to flatten the plane of the stroke, and to enable me to swing around upon the ball, rather than to descend upon it from above. In the latter case the tendency is toward a cut.

The most important feature of the drawing stroke is that the clubhead should come upon the ball from inside the line of play, and it should travel outward through the ball. Douglas Edgar, who scarcely ever played a shot without fade or draw, used to say that a slice was produced "by compressing the outside of the ball," and a hook "by compressing the inside of it." Whether or not the statement will bear scientific investigation, the conception is helpful in showing what must be done. Obviously what Edgar meant was simply that a hooking blow must be delivered outward, and that is about all that is needed.

The difficulty comes in delivering the blow in this manner without losing a deal of power and control, hence the advice about standing farther from the ball and turning the body more freely. In this manner it becomes practically impossible to hit in any way except outward and in a sweeping arc.

In discussing the manner of bringing off an intentional pull it is not wise to say too much about the accidental variety lest the impression be made that the two are in any respect the same. Hooking shots caused by stopping the left side are hooks and pulls to be sure, but the swing or stroke which produced them cannot be reduced to control, so that the shot is worthless as a means of getting close to the objective.

One thing more: in playing a pull be sure that the right shoulder comes through a bit higher than it would for an ordinary shot. This enables the right hand and arm to turn the club face up to the ball and over, closing it with a sort of rolling motion which aids materially in producing the desired result.

Pressing Leads to Difficulties

The more one sees of golf, the harder it becomes to make anything out of the various theories about how hard or how gently a ball should be struck. We hear that "pressing" is a thing to be avoided. But when we determine to avoid it, the first thing we know some kind friend will inform us that we are steering the ball and that we should hit it harder.

Truly it is a difficult thing to know just what to do. There are unquestionably worlds of grief ahead for the man who continually goes " all out" after every shot. Extremely hard hitting necessarily involves a considerable sacrifice of control, often with no increase in length, because the ball is not squarely struck. But also there is equal danger when the player "pulls his punch," easing up the stroke in an effort to guide the ball down the middle of the fairway.

In driving it has always been my idea that one should hit as hard as can be done without upsetting the balance of the body, and the timing of the stroke. Pressing causes trouble mainly by speeding up the backstroke. If that can be made slowly and the downward stroke started leisurely, there may be any amount of effort thereafter without cause for worry.

Just after impact. Note from the position of the left arm how it has resisted any turning over by the right.

High Tee Permits Sweeping Stroke

For my manner of hitting, I have better luck with the ball teed a full inch off the ground and in line with the arch of my left foot. Bob MacDonald, in his excellent book says "six inches back of the left heel." But we will not quarrel about that. Bob probably likes to deliver more of a descending blow, while I like better to hit the ball in the back. What I want to discuss now is the importance of properly teeing the ball.

Teeing the ball preparatory to driving off seems a relatively unimportant matter so long as it is done so the club may come at the ball. As a matter of fact, however, most first class players take considerable pains to place the ball properly and often vary the method according to the type of shot desired.

I myself for a normal drive prefer an unusually high tee, leaving the ball as mentioned above, a full inch off the ground, if the surface of the tee is firm. I use a driver with a fairly deep face, and I find if the tee is high I have a much better chance to hit the ball squarely in the center of the club. Also, I do not have a feeling that I must go down after the ball, as I would if it lay close to the ground. The high tee gives me complete confidence to hit with the sweeping stroke which I believe to be an essential of long driving.

The adjustment of the tee is very important in combating a cross wind. I find that by reducing the height of the tee and consequently lowering the ball, I create a tendency to fade the shot perceptibly. If, because of the slope of the fairway, or a right-hand wind, I should like a bit of a cut, I have only to press the tee slightly lower and to stand a very little closer to the ball. It is natural then to hit downward upon the ball and at the same time close in against the left side of the body.

The player must exhibit freedom from tension and stiffness as he takes up his position for starting the swing. (Bettman Archive)

Similarly, if the wind comes from the left, the high tee helps admirably. In that case stand a bit farther from the ball and permit a slightly greater turn of the hips and shoulders during the stroke. The result is a shot bending slightly to the left which will hold dead straight or curl up into a left-hand wind.

Where tee markers are placed generously apart it is possible by taking note of the requirements of the shot, to gain a considerable advantage by teeing on one side or the other of the teeing ground. For instance, if there is a boundary or hazard close upon the right of the fairway, it will make the drive far easier if the player will tee as close to the right side of the tee as possible. He can thus improve the angle of his shot and place himself where he is playing away from the boundary or hazard, instead of alongside or toward it. The difference is small but it is worth using.

The Use of the Spoon

Thus far in our discussion of woods, we have mentioned only the driver and the brassie; let us now direct our attention to the spoon.

For some reason, present day golfers seem to overlook to a great extent the possibilities of the once popular spoon. Possibly that tendency may be due partly to the fact that the increased range of the ball has brought most of the second shots within range of the middle-distance irons, but I do not think that is all of the reason. I know many players who will always extend themselves with the iron rather than resort to the wood. It seems to be a matter of pride with them that they will not allow others to think that they must use a wood club on such and such a hole.

Those who insist upon employing an iron to do the work of the spoon lose sight of the real object of the game. They forget that what counts is the successful execution of the shot, and not with what club it is done. It does not matter if A reaches number fifteen once with a drive and mid-iron and messes up the hole five times, if B is always close with a drive and spoon or brassie.

The spoon for use today should be designed to cover the range between the number two iron and the brassie. By that I mean the club should be of such loft that it can be spared to approximate the range obtainable with a number two and forced to reach nearly that of the brassie. In that way it will cover completely the field assigned to the number one iron with which it ought to be interchanged.

Take my own case as an example. I do not like to play a long iron shot from a tight lie. I never seem to be able to get the control I like to have. So invariably in that case I employ a spoon, playing the shot with a slight cut to get it up quickly. Again I do not like to play a full iron shot with the wind off my right, because I know that I am apt to hook if I do. That is the place for a spared spoon shot fading a bit into the wind for control.

Similarly, as a substitute for the brassie, the spoon works equally well.

Suppose we need a full shot to the green and the wind is blowing across from left to right and the lie is close. In getting the ball up with the straight-faced brassie, the almost necessary result is a slicing spin which, exaggerated by the wind, may carry the ball many yards off the line. But the loft of the spoon will elevate the ball without need of the spin and we can hit hard and confidently straight for the objective.

And to put the spoon to these uses is within the capabilities of even the ordinary player. The modifications in either direction are so slight, that to make them it is only necessary to know what they are. No man who will get a spoon and use it within reasonable limits will ever allow himself to be again without one.

Woods Easiest to Play

I cannot but consider that the wood clubs are by far the easiest to play. We find a great many more people who are weak with the irons or in putting than those who are lacking in driving and brassie play. That certainly ought to make it easier to employ the spoon to do the work of the long range irons, which are the very hardest clubs to master.

The object of the game, however, is not to reach the green with a wood when the shot calls for an iron. In the last analysis, the only excuse for using one club in preference to another is to accomplish better results than could be obtained with the other—to get closer to the hole and into the cup in fewer strokes.

An excellent example of Jones' technique allowing the right side of the body to turn easily around toward the left and the arms swing the clubhead down to the ball.

The Backswing

A Most Important Part of the Game

In learning to do anything, whether it be to solve a problem in mathematics or to swing a golf club, there must be selected a logical point at which to begin. In every study the first step must be to supply the basic knowledge upon which the later development can be made. Yet, although, one would never think of attempting to instruct a pupil in the principles of calculus until he had had a fair understanding of algebra, it is not thought unreasonable that a man can learn to play golf by first studying the middle section of the swing—from the top of the backstroke to impact.

It is true that the entire swing should be as nearly as possible one rhythmic motion. It is likewise true that the ball is not struck on the backswing. It is further a fact that several very good players, by absorbing and counteracting during the hitting stroke the effect of errors committed going back, have managed to attain outstanding skill. Still there can be little argument against the proposition that a method to be reliable must be sound throughout, from beginning to end, and not dependent upon high-speed correction after it has been set in motion. To build to meet this requirement one must start from the first motion, laying each succeeding one upon that which goes before.

That the average golfers do not view their problem in this light is indicated by the fact that nine-tenths of them are wrong from the very beginning, and even those who achieve a moderate measure of success do so by setting one contortion against another to bring themselves to do something like good form at the time they strike the ball. We are all impatient with a new game, particularly so when it happens to be so exasperating as golf, where everything looks so simple and is yet so difficult. It is not surprising that the beginner overlooks the importance of the backswing. To him it must seem to be merely something which has to be done before he can begin to hit. He takes his start from the top of the swing rather than from the ball.

Types of Backswing

If you will stand out on the first tee some Saturday afternoon you will find that you will be able to divide almost all your friends into two groups, merely by the manner in which they start their backswings. You will find that nearly all of them originate the motion solely with the wrists but in two ways. One group will be the "lifters" and the other will be the "rollers". Occasionally you will find a "swinger" but he will be a better player. I think it would be a safe bet that of the two larger groups the "lifters" will predominate. They are the fellows who pick up the club with the right hand, taking it immediately outside the line, and elevating it to the shoulder-position with very little motion save of arms and wrists. The tendency will be to come down in the same way, and to cut across the ball sharply.

The first motion of the backswing should be made by the legs and hips.

The "rollers" are those who initiate the motion by a quick roll of the wrists, which sends the club circling abruptly around the knees. Both of these groups get off on the wrong foot, and their only hope is to get back in step by some equally startling action before they hit the ball.

Mechanics of Swing

The proper way to start the club back is to "swing" it—I think that this conception conveys the idea as well as a thousand words could do. During the first few feet, the motion is sustained by everything but the hands and wrists. Shoulders and hips turn; the left knee bends and moves to the right; and the arms begin to swing backward. Through the first foot or so of travel the wrists are so relaxed that the small inertia of the clubhead causes it to lag behind the hands, the wrists flexing slightly to permit it. All this while the back of the right hand has been moving squarely toward the rear. All these forces of shoulders, hips, and arms continue, and finally with supple, responsive, but not particularly active, wrists the club is swung to the top position where the weight of the clubhead assists the "break" of the wrists which means so much in striking the ball.

This first step, starting the motion, is one of great importance. Begun correctly it is the simplest thing in the world to follow on and on until a proper hitting position is reached. Each step, if it is accomplished correctly at the start makes the next one so much easier.

One thing revealed by fast motion picture photography is that nearly all expert players permit the clubhead to lag behind the arm motion during the first few inches of the backstroke. Pictures showing the player's position when the clubhead has travelled only a few inches show that the hands have travelled farther and that the shaft of the club no longer occupies the same position with respect to the arms as at the time of address, but that the wrists were flexed slightly backward toward the ball.

This is an indication of two important things; first, that the motion of the swing originates back of the hands and wrists; and second, that there is perfect relaxation, permitting the weight and inertia of the clubhead to make itself felt before it is flung back to the top of the swing. In describing this feeling, the pro will tell his pupil that the clubhead should be "dragged" away from the ball or that it should be "flung" to the top of the stroke.

Hip Motion Comes First

That the first motion of the backswing should be made by the legs or hips there can be little doubt. To start it with the hands results inevitably in the lifting upright motion characteristic of the beginner who swings the club as though it were an axe, elevating it to the shoul-

THE BACKSWING A MOST IMPORTANT PART OF THE GAME

der position without a semblance of the weight-shift and shoulder-turn effected by the professional. But there are various opinions concerning the best way consciously to begin the motion.

George Duncan believes that the swing is begun by the knees— that the player "takes off from the left foot by employing a quick knee action and swings the weight over to the right foot." This is all right and may, in certain cases, be true enough. But the trouble is that when the player actually puts his mind upon knee motion and upon shifting the hips first, he is more apt to pull his entire body backward and settle his weight upon the heel of his right foot before his club gets anywhere.

I like Alex Morrison's idea considerably better because it enables the player to accomplish the proper hip shift without altering too much the pivotal point of the swing, that is, without disturbing the position of the head and shoulders. Morrison's advice assumes a position of the left foot such that the toe points slightly outward, away from the ball. The procedure then, as the initial movement of the backswing, is to roll the weight across the ball of the foot; in other words, to slowly turn the foot over upon its inside without, at first, removing the heel from the ground.

This method has, first of all, the advantage of definiteness and clarity. The pupil is not left to experiment with vague conceptions of knee action and the shifting of weight. He has something concrete upon which to fix his attention, and while it may work to accomplish what others advocate, it does do without the necessity of the player's knowing what it is.

Proper Position at Top of Swing Essential

It is important that a correct start be made so that the player will be in a position at the top of the swing to deliver the blow in the most efficient manner possible. To be able to do this his weight must be back of the ball and his club must be in position to be swung around against the ball and not to be chopped down upon it. To accomplish the first of these the shift of weight to the right foot is imperative and, obviously, it is a more easily controlled action if the order is "shift, turn," rather than "turn, shift," for in the latter case all sense of balance would be destroyed. The correct position of the club, the second factor of importance, is more easily accomplished in the manner described, because the shift of weight pulling the club away from the ball at the same time causes the clubhead to come away inside the line of flight, the very opposite of the chopping stroke referred to.

Correcting a Too Right-Handed Backswing

One of the worst faults a duffer falls into involves a too energetic use of the right hand during the backstroke. There are a number of reasons why the left hand and arm should be the guiding force in tak-

ing the club back from the ball, yet in spite of all, and in spite, too, of the player's knowledge and appreciation of all these reasons, there is always a strong tendency to use the right too much. The usual result is a backswing stroke, because when the right hand is used at all it usually elevates the club abruptly, well outside the line of play.

It seems to me that the proper place to effect a cure for a too-right-handed back-swing is in the initial movement of the stroke, or even before that, when the preliminary waggle is being made. A good start means a lot in anything, and this is particularly true of the golf swing, for if the thing is started correctly it is the most natural thing in the world that the motion should continue in the right line.

The right-hand tendency causes the player to pick his club away from the ball at the very start, the clubhead moving quickly away from the ground before the hands have moved perceptibly from their original position. Compare this with the method of the expert

During an efficient backswing, the weight must be back of the ball.

player who literally drags the club away, keeping it along or very close to the ground for several feet of travel. A close study of this part of the stroke will reveal that for a considerable space of time the right wrist is almost completely relaxed, the pushing of the left-hand causing the right hand in its relaxed state to flex back toward the ball so that the clubhead actually lags behind the hands. It will be noted, in studying the styles of all the experts, that the right wrist does not begin to break away from the ball until the club has travelled several feet.

Waggle Loosens Muscles

Although the waggle itself is not a part of the swing nevertheless it is an important preliminary designed to loosen the muscles and to induce a sense of rhythm necessary in order to hit the ball effectively. In the correct grip the right hand is placed in such a position that the palm of the hand is pressed against the back of the shaft. In other words, if the club were removed and the hand opened, the palm would be presented squarely toward the hold. From this position the waggle should be made so that the right hand and wrist flex only directly forward and backward as a fish wags its tail. There should be no roll or turn, and no motion in a vertical plane. This encourages motion in a proper direction once the swing gets under way.

The whole thing is to get away as far as possible from any relation to a chopping stroke. No matter what the shot, the ball must be swept along, and this is impossible once the clubhead is permitted to stray outside the line. The left hand naturally presses inward and it will guide the swing correctly unless the right sets up a disturbance.

Hazards of Abbreviated Backswing

The importance of a full free backswing is a thing I have harped upon considerably without, I believe, ever definitely pointing out to what position the club should be carried. I feel that this phase of the golf stroke is worthy of further elaboration, particularly because it is one in which nearly all golfers err when for any reason the responsibility of making an important shot begins to weigh upon them. The length of the backswing is one of the things which I have to watch continuously, even when I am playing golf almost every day.

Many authorities have urged upon us that to take the club back so far that it passes the horizontal position is to be guilty of a fault which they call "over-swinging." While I admit that it is physically possible to swing back too far—that is, so far that the balance of the player will be disturbed, or his head pulled away from its proper position—still I am certain the temptation or inclination to do so is not present to an extent which constitutes a menace to the player. The average person's tendencies are all in the other direction. His desire, nine times out of ten, is to shorten his swing rather than lengthen it.

In playing a full wood shot my club passes noticeably beyond the horizontal so that, although my hands are high, well above my head, the clubhead dips to about the level of the point of the chin. Posed photographs indicate that at the top my club is approximately horizontal, but motion pictures of a swing when actually hitting a ball show the true position. This is not true of Horton Smith who permits very little cocking of the wrists at the top, but the majority of professionals swing back just about as far as I do.

Length of Backswing Does Not Govern Control

It is a popular notion that an iron club requires an abbreviated backswing just because it is an iron. This is not so. In this respect there is no reason for an iron to be handled differently. The length of the backswing has practically nothing to do with control, and if the iron needs to be swung as fast as the wood, the backstroke employed with it should be just as long. The misconception likely arose because the wise pros rarely play a really full iron. The iron shot is the medium of approaching the hole, a shot the success of which is measured in feet and inches from the hole. For this reason what is spoken of as a full iron shot is not a full shot in the same sense as a drive. The player almost always plays with an iron a shot of less force than the ultimate limit of the club he uses. When driving, the player intends to place his ball in as favorable a position as possible but his direction does not need to be precisely accurate, and it is rarely necessary to limit the distance. With an iron, the ball must be struck only to a certain point and not past it, and the direction should be accurate to a few inches.

The full backswing accomplishes one thing above all others—it gives the player time and room in which to start a gradual acceleration of his swing. It enables him to build up velocity from zero at the top to a maximum at impact without having to hurry. No swing can be smooth if the backswing is stopped at a point from which the club must be yanked downward with no chance to flow easily into the rapid motion.

More short pitches are missed because of an abbreviated backswing than for any other reason. The player has been told to limit the length of the shot by limiting the length of the stroke and in no event to soften the force of the blow. In attempting to play a short shot firmly he invariably chops off his backswing and ruins his timing. He need not, indeed should not, employ a full swing for a short pitch, but neither must he get the idea that the length of the swing should be half, when the length of the shot is half. In any case the club must be taken back far enough to comfortably accommodate the blow to be delivered. The club must be given time to gather whatever speed it is intended to have.

Left Hand Holds Swing in Proper Groove

One of the most glaring of the many mistakes a player can make is to allow the left elbow to bend during the hitting stroke and to let the left arm stray too far from the side of the body. It is noticed immediately by the observer, but the player himself is rarely conscious of just what he is doing. Shanking, heeling, and slicing are the usual results of this mistake.

If one will do a little watching he will find that the left elbow has a more pronounced tendency to fly out when the shot to be played is a short one. This is the reason why most of the real shanks occur on short pitches or spared mashie or iron shots; and it is also a fine reason why the less skillful golfer prefers to hit hard with a less powerful club rather than to play a half shot with another. The ability to keep the left hand moving even on the shortest stroke is one of the really valuable essentials of the expert, a thing which helps to take him out of the class of the ordinary player.

A Right-Hand Complex

Sometimes it is hard to be certain whether this fault, which becomes evident to the observer in the bend of the left elbow, really originates there or whether the right hand, by excessive activity itself forces the error. For a right-handed person the natural inclination is to play the short shots mainly with the right hand. In every other game or activity the right is the hand of touch and of control. Whenever a deft flick of the wrist is required, the right hand is the one used to accomplish it. So when the golfer has to play a wee pitch over a bunker he is likely to make of it a right-hand stroke if he is not careful to do otherwise.

Letting the left elbow fly out is a sure sign that the left arm is not active, that the left hand grip is not firm, and that the left side is not leading as it should be. Such a thing rarely occurs when a player is hitting hard. The obvious result, when such a thing happens, is to present the heel or shank of the club first to the ball. When this happens the shot is about as complete a mess as could be imagined.

There may be some question about the rigid necessity of a straight left arm in the backswing. But there can be no doubt that it must be straight at the moment of striking the ball. Furthermore it must operate all the way down close to the body and never be permitted to break or wander outward.

Movies Clear Up Vardon's Play

In this connection the case of Harry Vardon is interesting. For years the old master has been more or less generally regarded as an exception to the straight left-arm rule. Vardon has always permitted a perceptible bend to show in his left arm at the top of the swing, and critics have thought, and Vardon himself declared, that this bend was not removed until immediately before striking the ball; in other words, that the arm remained bent during almost all of the downstroke. Very recent motion pictures reveal that this is not the case, that Vardon straightens his left arm almost as soon as he starts his club downward, completing the action before his clubhead passes the level of his head. This is comforting news for it has long worried a lot of people to explain how Vardon could have played such masterful and consistent golf with a such a factor of uncertainty as was believed to exist in his swing.

To sum up: If I had a beginner to teach I think I should school him thoroughly in making a proper start and a correct back-swing, before I should permit him to strike a ball. It is always easier to follow a motion correctly started than it is to initiate it into the proper direction. There is a confusing something about taking off from a position of rest which leaves the average beginner in a state of helpless perplexity.

On Iron Play

Nearly all of the driving troubles which I have discussed, such as fast swinging, stiff wrists, steering, are found in playing the irons. But iron play differs in one very important respect from wood play.

In playing any iron, the degree of accuracy required is much higher. The problem is not to get as much range as possible, but to hit the ball as far as the hole and no farther. This feature makes it desirable, except in certain special instances, to hit a shot with backspin which will cause it to stop very quickly after striking the ground.

Where one of my earliest troubles with the driver was a tendency to hit the ball too much downward, one of the most persistent of my errors with the irons is a desire to hit the ball too much upward. It is strange of course that this should be the case, for it would seem that whether my tendency were in one direction or the other, it would remain the same no matter which club was being used. To understand why it does not, it is only necessary to take account of the different objects in view in playing the two clubs—the driver and the iron— one requiring roll and the other a high quick-stopping shot.

Apparently when one takes a mashie in hand to play a neat pitch to the green over a yawning bunker, his first impulse is to lob the ball high into the air. I have seen numbers upon numbers of duffers who attempt to obtain backspin in this way. They never stop to think that the lofted club was given them to enable them to secure altitude without this necessity.

The backspin is not merely a means of stopping the ball after it strikes the ground. It is also the agency which steadies the ball in its flight through the air and holds it true upon the line to the flag. Anyone who has tried to pitch out of heavy rough,

Starting the backswing

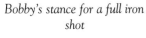

Bobby's stance for a full iron shot

where it was impossible to impart spin to the ball, will be able to appreciate how much the spin adds to control. Played from a heavy lie the ball often darts from side to side and may finish yards away from the line on which it started and there is no way to foresee in which direction the shot will go wrong.

In playing an iron, and by this term I mean to include the pitching clubs as well, it is imperative that the player "stay down to the shot." That means that the left side of his body must not strain upward as he hits the ball. Left shoulder, left hand, and the clubhead must all stay down, and the weight of the body must have shifted with the stroke until most of it is borne by the left foot.

In the perfect iron stroke the clubhead descends upon the ball and sends it on its way, passing afterward, still downward until it strips the grass from the ground and rips a divot from the sod. In order to accomplish this kind of a stroke, it is important that the left hand grip be firm and the left arm straight at impact.

Acquiring Underspin

I am sure that we have all heard—I certainly had it drummed into me in my younger days—that to strike a ball with

Midway of the backswing

The top of a swing for a full iron shot

underspin, the hands must go through the ball without turning over; that is , with the back of the left hand and the palm of the right hand upward. To accomplish this without an unconscionable break of the wrists, the right shoulder must go considerably underneath the left. And I have always maintained, mistakenly I now believe, that the shoulders should not operate even nearly in the same horizontal plane, but that, in the hitting stroke, the left shoulder should be uppermost and the right shoulder below.

Working on this theory I have had great difficulty in bringing the clubhead up to the ball in a true position, the tendency always being to open the face of the club at impact because the right hand wanted to lag or lay off. Possibly that may account for a life-long habit of turning the toe of the club slightly toward the ball at the address. However that is not so very important.

What I now believe to be proper in hitting an iron shot consists largely in keeping the right shoulder up and in hitting a crisp blow against the left hand. The effect is this: if the right shoulder is allowed to go under, the little finger of the left hand is presented to the ball, and there is an appalling tendency on the part of the left elbow to jump out of its proper position close to the side (a very efficient cause of the dreaded "shank" which I will explain later). In keeping the right shoulder up, the left elbow is forced in against the side and the back of the left hand is presented to the ball. The abbreviated finish, after a crisp spanking blow is easy now, whereas, from the old position, it was impossible without seriously straining the left arm.

Of course, this one may go the way of my other pet theories, but at least it helped me win a championship and has given me an assurance and accuracy with an iron club wholly unknown to me before.

Use Lofted Iron
Playing from Heavy Lie

The average golfer, when he finds himself with a close lie, or with his ball lying deep in heavy grass and a shot of 150 yards or so to a closely guarded green, is at a loss concerning the shot to play. The first thing that crosses his mind is that he must lose some length because of the lie of the ball, since it is not sitting high where he can hit it squarely. With this thought, and with the idea of compensating for this loss, he will select for the shot a stronger club than he would use if the ball were lying well.

Ordinarily, it is dangerous for a player of whatever ability to force an iron to its ultimate limit, but the situation which I have described is one where such a thing is necessary. There are a number of reasons for this, all of which should be understood by the player who expects to intelligently work out problems where the shots he learns on the practice tee have to be varied a little, or supplemented with a small amount of ingenuity on his part.

*A spared shot can be more effective than
one which forces a club to its limit. (Hulton-Deutsch)*

*The finish of an iron shot to the green.
Notice the perfect follow through. (Hulton-Deutsch)*

When the ball is lying in heavy grass or in a small hole or depression, it becomes necessary to swing the club in a sharply descending arc—literally to dig the ball out of the haven which it has found. This necessity takes loft off the club—hooding or closing the face until a mashie becomes effectively a number four iron, and a number four as strong as a number three for a normal lie.

Now, when it comes to hitting the ball let us see what happens. The ball is lying so that it is apparent to the player that force will be required to dig it out, and whether consciously or not, he is going to hit it a good bit harder than he would ordinarily.

There is no possibility, theoretical or practical, that any sort of a half or spared shot can be played to offset the decrease in the loft of the club which I have mentioned.

This much takes care of the range of the shot, but there is one other argument in favor of using the more lofted club.

Everyone knows how impossible it is to play a backspin shot from a heavy lie, the grass cushion between the club and the ball preventing the clean contact needed to impart spin. So in order to stop the shot within reasonable or calculable limits, the player must depend entirely upon elevation, and no club straighter than a number four iron will do the trick.

If he can't make the distance with the number four, in nine cases out of ten he would do best to play safe rather than attempt the use of a more powerful club.

Spared Shots or Half-Shots More Effective Than Forced Ones

Considering that iron play is the real offensive part of the game, it may be interesting to see just what sort of iron play places the ball close to the hole. There is ever in every golfer's mind this problem: Is it better to use this club and hit hard, or that one and spare the shot? Throughout a full round of golf do the forced shots or the spared shots finish closer to the hole on the average?

The control of a spared shot is considered to be beyond the reach of the average player. He is thought to be on much safer ground when he is blazing away at each shot with every ounce of power in his body. But it is not necessary that a person should be able to play a mashie shot with a mid-iron. All that he needs to do is to bridge the now small gap between each of his many clubs so that he may have control throughout every foot of the difference between his wooden clubs and his putter. Every stroke which utilizes less than the full power of the club may be called a spared shot, and I think the spared shot within certain limits is more effective in the long run than that which forces a club to the utmost.

Of course, I am speaking about getting close to the hole, and it is well to remember that to do that it is not enough to hit the ball on line. I have heard many players tell of hitting a shot directly at the flagstick but add that it finished at the back or front of the green, as though that were not their fault.

A half shot serves the player well in the wind and abnormal conditions.
(Ralph Miller Library)

They would likely consider the shot a bad one if its length were exact, and its direction forty feet off. But range and direction are equally necessary. The subsequent putt is not made a bit easier by the fact that the second shot was on line.

I have found that when I play an absolutely full shot with any iron club, I usually find myself many feet past the hole. There must be some places where the distance is exactly right for a full shot, but I am never able to find them. I think though the explanation may not be hard after all.

When the player has once determined that a full shot is required, he hits the ball hard concerning himself only with the direction. Very likely in sizing up the shot he has unconsciously allowed himself a little leeway. But in playing less than a full shot with

both distance and direction in mind, his aim is to drop the ball at a certain point. His long practice and training enables him to do it.

Years ago, it could be truthfully said that in the half-iron shot lay the difference between the great and the near-great golfers. That was when the only iron clubs in the bag were the cleek, mid-iron, and mashie, and when the player was forced to moderate his stroke for the intermediate ranges. The man who could not play a half-shot in those days was helpless if his requirements called for something less than a full bang with an iron and more than he could get with his mashie.

The old order has changed somewhat. Today a man may call upon his mashie-iron, or spade, or number two. He generally has seven or eight irons, so nicely graduated in loft that to secure the proper range becomes largely a matter of selecting the club.

But even the improvement in implements and the advent of new ones has not entirely effaced the value of the half-shot. It is still the weapon of the fine player and serves him well in the wind or under more or less abnormal conditions.

Tommy Armour has a great liking for half and three-quarter shots. Rarely does Tommy force his irons. Reared upon the wind-swept Scottish courses, long continued necessity has made him favor the shorter, more compact stroke. Walter Hagen, on the other hand, learning his game upon inland American courses, will play a full shot wherever possible.

Bobby Jones at the finish of a short pitch shot to the green. Notice how the club shaft is choked

Walter feels, very much as I do, that the greatest danger lies in constraint.

I remember how Hagen played the fourteenth hole at Whitfield in our match in which he gave me such an artistic lacing. We played the hole twice and each time I used a spoon, and I didn't spare it either. But Walter pasted his ball each time with his murderous long-handled driving iron and each time he was nearer the hole than I was. The second time he holed his in two. I had played the same hole almost daily with Armour. He preferred a spoon or brassie with which he did not need to extend himself.

Of course, Hagen can play a half-shot. He simply does not like it.

Do Not Restrict Backswing Too Much

I think that most people have trouble with the less-than-full shots because they restrict the backswing too much. "Half-shots" implies "half-swing." It seems difficult to avoid that idea. But a half-shot is really neither half a swing nor half a shot. The stroke is a gooddeal more than half normal and the ball travels a good deal farther than half the maximum range. The half-shot can more properly be thought of as something less than a full-shot, though of the same type.

As I said the great trouble with most of us is that we employ a half-swing for the half-shot. We remember the advice that we should regulate the length of the shot by the length of the stroke, but we forget that the backswing is not the stroke that is meant. Neither is the first part of the downward swing. The length of stroke which determines the range is fixed by the point where the wrists begin to unwind and to put the last ounce of power behind the club.

In playing a half-shot, I think the swing should be of nearly normal fullness. That makes for rhythm and good timing and prevents hurried and jerky hitting. The blow must be firm and decisive. Slack hitting to cut down range is fatal because it destroys control. Accuracy cannot be sacrificed upon any consideration.

In order to preserve this crispness and still restrict the range, I like to feel that I am delaying, just a trifle, the delivery of the blow. In other words, I do not begin the unwinding of my wrists quite so soon as for a full shot, and when I do begin to hit, the effort is not so vicious.

As a general rule the average player has much difficulty with the spared or half-shot. When he begins to shorten his swing or to ease off a bit in the delivery he gets into trouble. The half-shot requires a little more skill than has been granted to the ordinary golfer.

So I think that players, other than experts, will do well to choose the less powerful club and hit a harder blow and this for two reasons: First, the obvious one, that the ball is thus more apt to be fairly struck; second, because most of our greens are built up in the rear and the situation is consequently less embarrassing if the ball is left short of the green. The shot too strongly played, if it goes over the green, leaves the player where he must play a very delicate approach back over a bank to a green which slopes away from him.

The above is based upon the limitations of skill imposed upon the average player. Now suppose we are dealing with one who is happy and confident with the shot of less than full strength. What must he do?

The first thing to consider is the construction of the green to be approached. Does it require a high pitching shot designed to fly all the way and stop quickly, or is the front left unguarded so that a measure

Good rhythm and timing in playing a spared stroke comes from nearly normal fullness which prevents jerky hitting.

of run can be used? If the green is closely guarded then the forcing shot is the one to play. A full shot with almost any iron will carry the ball high into the air, and if it is struck even nearly correctly it will come down with very little run. The spared shot is invariably lower in flight and is not a quick-stopping shot.

The direction of the wind may also influence the decision. For best control against a breeze, the half-shot with the stronger club is always easiest for me. The ball must be kept moderately low to prevent the wind from blowing it off its path, and the low shot into the wind will stop quickly enough. Playing downwind it is best to use the shorterclub because then is the hardest time to use backspin. The stopping must be done by altitude alone.

All this is, of course, more or less instinctive. It can be acquired only by experience. One must play a lot of golf before he can know just how hard to hit for a given range. The thing to learn is to hit the ball fairly and firmly with the moderated stroke. The rest will come quite naturally.

A Cure for Shanking

Of all the terrible things a man may do to a golf ball, the most demoralizing and the most mystifying is to "shank" it— which is hitting the ball with the socket of the clubface instead of the face itself.

I should describe the cause of shanking as a failure to keep the left elbow close in to the body when the ball is being struck. That, in turn, is caused either by bending the arm too much at the top of the swing, or by making the hitting stroke too much of a right-handed affair from start to finish. If the left arm is relaxed too much at the top, the elbow is left in the ideal position to be thrown away from the side, and the only way to prevent its going out is to pull down hard with the left arm.

By assuming the position of address with left arm crooked and left elbow held out from the body, one can see immediately that the socket of the club is the very first thing to be presented to the ball. It is then difficult to see how a shank could possibly be avoided.

But knowing causes does not help much unless the knowledge leads us to a remedy, and there we are always confronted with the difficulty of finding a method of presentation which can be readily understood and applied. My own suggestion would be this: try to brush the left trouser-leg with the left hand when you hit the ball. I realize that while that might work very well for me, because I play always with my hands and arms abnormally close in, the person with more orthodox style and with the ball farther away might have to imagine a golf ball in the left side-pocket.

Prevention Often the Cause

I have a friend here in Atlanta who probably knows more about shanking than any other person in the whole world. For several years, the mere mention of the word was enough to start him going, for it seems that in this peculiar malady, to try to prevent it is the surest way to bring it on. My friend, after playing excellently, once reached the final round of the city championship, and I went out to watch the match. In the eighteen holes which I saw, he hit ten iron shots, of varying length, in the socket. I didn't have the heart to ask him how many he hit there in the rest of the match.

But now he has cured it, and can talk about his experiences with equanimity. It is from what he told me, more than from my own observation, that I have learned, I think, how socketing or shanking is caused and may be prevented. I know that my friend consulted several well-known professionals, among them George Duncan, without success and finally got the solution from Stewart Maiden.

The conception which Stewart Maiden made Chick Ridley use, and which ended Chick's troubles with shanking, is probably easier to understand than any I could suggest. It was to drive his left elbow straight at the ground from the top of the swing.

However it is done, it is one of the essentials of good sound golf that the left arm must operate close to the body. When it begins to roam around in the outer spaces, it always causes trouble of one kind or another. Just remember that and work out the easiest way for you to remember to keep it there.

There is a story that we, in Atlanta, like to tell of one of my friends who was afflicted with the terrible habit of shanking mashie shots. One afternoon my friend, playing extremely well, reached the fourteenth hole as the sun was declining. Just as he approached his ball to play a mashie shot to the green, he was accosted by the East Lake greenkeeper, who innocently made the observation that it was certainly beautiful out there in the shank of the evening. So, you see, it doesn't take very much!

The best judgment in the world and the most careful consideration of hazards and other dangers are of little avail if the shot is not well struck. (Ralph Miller Library)

Aerial view of the deciding match of the 1930 U.S. Amateur Championship over the links of the Merion Cricket Club as Jones captures the fourth leg of the Grand Slam. (Wide World Photos)

Judging Distance Difficult

The two prime requisites of every golf shot are distance and direction, and although reams and reams have been written about hitting the ball on line for the flag, I don't remember ever to have seen any advice on the other equally important feature. Possibly the faculty cannot be developed in one who was not born with it, and perhaps I shall be wasting my time and that of my readers, by attempting a dissertation on the art of judging distance.

A short while ago I read in the "British Golf Illustrated" an article on the subject by Hilton, and that so eminent a critic should hesitate to offer advice has made me fearful that I am treading on dangerous ground. Mr. Hilton confines himself to wondering if the gift depends upon good long-range vision, and to observing that the professional player is ordinarily a better judge of distance than the amateur. I am not sure that Mr. Hilton has not done about all one can do in this field, and yet I feel that I have had some experience which may be helpful to the average player.

To the average player who plays almost all of his golf on one course, rarely playing away from home, or at least not enough for him to give serious attention to his problem, it is mystifying to be dropped upon a strange terrain with no familiar landmarks to give him his bearings. Usually he can be depended on to add at least five or six strokes to what would otherwise be his normal score. He seldom knows what club to use, or how hard to hit the ball, and if he requests information he doesn't quite trust it.

Now, if the average club member had opportunities for playing more on courses strange to him, there is no question that he would play a better game at home. The one difficulty which troubles him abroad and which he recognizes, is his inability to correctly estimate distances. And that is exactly his biggest handicap at home, although there he doesn't appreciate it as much.

Countless times due to an unusually heavy breeze, or some other change in conditions, I have seen the men with whom I play misjudge a shot by many yards. The expression of honest amazement when a well-hit shot falls short is sometimes amusing, but the fact that the error was not one of hitting does not help the score very much.

Don't Rely on Card Distances

The great trouble with the one-course golfer is that he habitually gets his bearings by calculating his position with respect to landmarks—so far beyond a certain tree, or so far from the crest of a hill. And when he plays a strange course he looks too much at the distances on the card. He arrives at his conclusion respecting the next shot by subtracting the supposed length of his drive—an estimate which is never accurate—from the figure set down on the score card as the length of the hole—which is usually wrong.

Suppose someone told you to step out on a polo field and hit a golf ball exactly 150 yards. How would you do it? You would probably select a mashie because it is popularly supposed that an ordinary mashie shot will travel about 150 yards. But when playing to a green 150 yards away you must not go 135 or 165 yards. If you do you get into trouble. And if you always play the same shot for the 150 yard distance, an error of 15 yards either way for any sort of breeze is a small allowance.

JUDGING DISTANCE DIFFICULT

Walter Hagen watches Bob tee off from the (then) first tee during the 1935 Masters Tournament. (Wide World Photos/NYT)

Let the Eye Judge

When playing a strange course I never look at a score card to get the length of a hole. I sometimes consult it as a matter of curiosity to see what the par is, or how many three shot holes there are. But, even if the length is correct, it doesn't mean anything, for if you don't know how far you have driven, it won't matter much whether the hole is four-twenty or four-eighty, you still must figure on the next shot independently of the first.

It is far better to approach each shot with an open mind, ready to play a distance commensurate with what the length of the shot appears to be. On a blind hole, of course, there is nothing to see and one is apt to be wrong. But on the ordinary layout where everything is in plain view, the eye is the most accurate aid we have.

I once told a friend that the easiest way to determine the distance to the hole was by considering the size of people around the green. His reply was that there never were any people around the green when he was playing. I had to admit that in that case he would have to give up that method, but insisted nevertheless that it was effective. The principle is, of course, quite sound and works really better when there is not a crowd but only one or two men. The apparent height of the flag will also serve when the full length of it is visible.

I played one round at St. Andrews in practice when a trick of this kind was absolutely our only guide. We were playing a late round and towards mid-afternoon a heavy fog had blown in off the North Sea. It was so thick that we were unable to distinguish the flag from distances of more than a hundred and twenty-five or fifty yards, and our only means of determining either distance or direction was by keeping a sharp watch on the match ahead while its members where holing out. I do not remember what scores we made so I cannot offer them as

proof that the system worked well. You must accept my statement that it did.

Player Should Be Observant

Most errors of judgment in the matter of range are occasioned, I think, by failure to observe and take account of all the ground between the ball and the green. There is nothing more deceptive than a shot to a green slightly elevated and with a hidden swale in front. Invariably the hole appears to be closer than it is by the length of the swale, and no reliable conception of the shot can be obtained without walking forward for an inspection. It is always safest to make sure that you have seen everything.

The average person who has little opportunity to play various courses cannot hope to play with the assurance of a man who spends his entire time on courses he has never seen. Our most popular exhibitionists have acquired the knack of getting the range at the first glance, and they have learned to rely on something besides local knowledge. I suppose they have all developed systems of their own. But I am sure that none of them counts the yards; it's so much easier to think in terms of the proper club to use. After constant play of this kind it is just like throwing a stone; you don't think about how far you are going to throw or with what trajectory, you simply take one look and let it go.

Judgment of distance, as I have said, is most likely a gift, and Mr. Hilton calls it such. Possibly these suggestions which I have made will help no one. I do believe, however, that a little more thought given to this phase of every shot will help everyone. It is just as important as a true swing.

Playing Short!

On Pitch, Run-up, Blast, Chip and Other Short Shots

In an earlier chapter dealing with iron play in general, I merely touched on the subject of backspin. I will attempt to discuss it more fully here because of its great importance in this department of the game.

It is a common belief that in playing a backspin shot with a mashie-niblick the ball must be struck in a way that will permit the face of the clubhead to go through entirely open–that is, looking skyward. Another way of expressing the same thought is that the back of the left hand should be upward. The supposed object of such instruction was to prevent any roll or turn of the wrists, a movement which was thought to produce overspin and a break from right to left in the flight of the ball.

Truly, an open clubface at impact produces a slicing spin, and an accentuated roll of the wrists usually results in a hook. But it has been demonstrated, to my satisfaction at least, that neither the hook nor the slice has a thing whatever to do with backspin.

Backspin is not sidespin, and it is not obtained by drawing the clubface across the ball. The spin which causes the ball to stop is the natural result of contact with a lofted club. If the club had no loft–if the angle of its face were vertical–every bit of the force of the blow would be directed toward the center of the ball and no spin would be imparted.

But a mashie-niblick has about forty-five degrees of loft and when it strikes the ball, even in a perfectly normal way, a goodly portion of its force is exerted along the circumference of the ball and so starts it spinning. The maximum spin would, of course, be imparted by a club of 180 degrees loft, which would, to the fullest extent, "cut the feet from under the ball." The mashie-niblick is a compromise which impels the ball forward as well as gives it backspin.

The difficulty with the open-face idea is that in attempting to carry it out there is danger of taking the ball on the upward arc of the stroke. The face of the club, then, is moving in a path more nearly at right angles to the plane of its face, and begins to approximate the suppositious club with no loft at all. Instead of a crisp, firm punch into the ground–a stroke which will produce spin–the shot becomes merely a lob wholly beyond control.

It has helped me a lot to gain this conception of a mashie-niblick pitch. Placing dependence upon the loft of the club and realizing that I myself was not obliged to do it all, have added much on the side of confidence. The chief considerations are a clean contact between club and ball and a good firm hit.

I am sure every golfer at one time or another has been surprised by a half-topped mashie-niblick shot which is brought up quickly on the green, stopped by powerful backspin. That, of course, is the extreme case where the club met the ball a descending blow just below center. A greater proportion of the force was exerted on the circumference

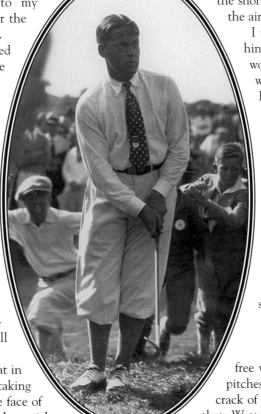

The chip shot is played with the feet close together and the ball off the right foot. The ball is struck with a straightforward blow and is pitched without spin.
(Ralph Miller Library)

and hence a more vicious spin was produced. A lower trajectory accounted for the difference in range.

Flexible Wrists for Short Pitches

Since I first began to play golf I have always had trouble with short pitch shots, and have consequently given that department very careful study.

I have never felt that I could play a pitch of fifty or sixty yards with an ordinary mashie-niblick and have any hope that the ball would stop within a reasonable distance after it struck the ground. The longer shots bothered me not at all, for when I was able to play a full shot the stopping problem was simple. It was for this reason that I continually resorted to the niblick for the short pitches so that I could lob the shot high in the air.

I think that watching Watts Gunn gave me a hint about mashie-niblick play. It was the wonder of all at Oakmont in 1925 how Watts was able to get so much "bite" on his pitches. He was stopping them more quickly and more surely than any man in the whole field. It is probably no compliment to my powers of observation that I have required nearly three years to find out why he was able to do it.

In the first place, I was wrong when I tried to keep the clubface from turning away from the projected line of flight. To attempt that induces a restricted wrist action, and hence lessens the sharp, incisive quality of the blow. I realize now that I have always had the feeling that I was bringing my club against the ball mainly with my arms and shoulders.

Watching Watts and experimenting with my own game has convinced me that free wrist action is necessary in playing the short pitches–and the shorter the shot, the more like the crack of a whip should be the stroke. I have noticed that Watts does not move his hands backward an abnormal distance, yet he appears to do so because of his flexible wrists. The hitting stroke is slow in proportion to the length of the shot, until the flick of the wrists takes the ball sharply and cleanly from its resting place.

It is a mistake to believe that short pitches can be played in the same way as longer ones. When the shot is long enough, there is no need to do anything except hit the ball a clean blow. The loft of the club will take care of the spin. But a shot struck softly in the same way, although it may afford the same pleasing sensations, will nevertheless scamper across the green like a frightened rabbit.

I believe this shot is easier to control than the full niblick shot which I have been using. The niblick is a splendid club for the very short pitches over guarding hazards, but its loft is so great that it becomes very dangerous when used for anything like the full extent of its range.

Bunker Practice

No matter how expert a person may be in the use of his iron clubs, nor how consistently accurate off the tee, still in order to count himself a finished golfer, he must acquire more than a fair amount of skill in recovering from hazards. Strangely enough, although it is recognized that even the best players in the world get into trouble often, recovery work is about the last thing that the ordinary player will practice. I have seen any number of them hammering away for hours from a practice tee or playing pitch shots from a fine green fairway, but I have yet to see one in a bunker unless he had to get there.

To explain the method one should use in extricating a ball from sand is a very difficult proposition. The whole thing is so much a question of touch–striking an exact balance between the force of the blow, the loft of the club, the weight of sand taken, and the distance to be traversed–there is really no way to tell another how to play the shot. In other cases where there are fewer variable conditions, it is possible to lay down rules of some practical value. But this shot which the player refuses to practice is the one which must be learned by practice alone.

As I have said, how hard to hit the ball and how much sand to take behind it are questions which each player must determine for himself. There are, however, two points which can be mentioned and which ought to be observed.

The first one is the one most important and most often ignored. I consider it an essential of good form in playing any kind of a blasting shot from a bunker (I am not considering cases where the ball is lying cleanly enough to be clipped) that the face of the club, no matter which one is selected, be laid off or back at address. This does not mean that good shots cannot be played with the face of the club slightly hooded.

But the reason for the laid-back face is obvious when one thinks of what must happen when the hooded club takes too little sand—a wild shot yards over the green. The laid back face pops the ball more abruptly into the air and will permit, without disastrous results, a quite considerable error either in the amount of sand taken or in the force of the stroke.

The other principle I should recommend is that a full—or nearly full swing be taken in all cases whether it is intended to employ a violent stroke taking plenty of sand behind the ball, or to strike more lightly a mere fraction of an inch under the ball. The reason for this is that I think the more leisurely swing, where there is ample time and room to reach any force desired, enables the player to maintain a more accurate sense of what he is doing than a stroke of the short, choppy variety.

The average player is apt to regard with wonderment the apparent ease with which the best pros flick a ball from the sand close enough to the hole to get down in one putt. They think how they themselves would likely use two or three strokes getting out of the same bunker. If the leading players in an open championship were compelled to lose a stroke to par for each bunker visited, it is safe to say they would not be the leaders long. And it is always well to remember that these men did not learn to play out of bunkers by practicing shots from a practice tee or fairway.

Notwithstanding all this, I do not recall seeing a player, other than an expert, practicing bunker shots. Bunkers are unquestionable things to be avoided. The pity of it is that we cannot avoid them every time, and the man who visits them most spends the least time in learning how to get out.

I fancy that if the player who happened to be bunkered near the green, simply set himself upon recovering to a good position—merely onto the putting surface—with a little practice he would have little difficulty in achieving that result. But when he tries for more, attempting a delicate pitch to get close to the hole, he is undone by his ambition. If he would accept the penalty of one stroke, get out without losing more, and play steadily on, I am sure his game would noticeably improve.

There is another angle which may be of more cumulative effect than the actual loss of strokes. Each disaster usually means three or four uncertain holes before the player's balance and poise returns to normal, and each bunker, more of a problem.

It might be well, if the player can find no convenient bunker not in use, to follow the example of the English amateur who rented one for the season and spent regularly four hours per day blasting balls from its depths.

A bunker shot is not unlike an auto crash. You can recover from either. A water hazard is more like an airplane crash. You can't recover from these.
(Ralph Miller Library)

Three Types of Bunker Shots

There are three separate and distinct types of shot which may be employed from the sand, and every one peculiarly fits a different situation. For the sake of convenience, we may call them the chip, the blast, and the cut-shot, although these names mean very little without some explanation of the manner of execution.

I should like to consider first the ordinary blasting or explosive shot, both because it is the most popular among average players and because, if only one shot is to be learned, it is the most generally useful. The safest course, whatever the lie of the ball or the location of the hole, is almost always a full blast, taking plenty of sand and making certain of getting the ball at least out of the bunker.

For the player who would become adept at bunker play, the blasting shot should be put to no such general use. There are times, of course, when its employment is prescribed by circumstances and its omission would be foolhardy –viz., when the ball is lying in a heel-mark or footprint, or when the bunker is very deep and the hole not too far beyond the edge. When the only safe course appears to be to attempt only to get onto the putting surface is another time this shot will be found useful.

The conventional manner of playing the explosive shot is apparently the best. Our most proficient players exhibit little variation of method in this department. The ball is played from a point opposite the left foot or slightly in front of it. The player

stands fairly erect, with the feet not far apart. The club–always a niblick–is taken near the end, and a full swing is employed. The swing is full, but unless the ball is lying in an extremely bad place, there is no particular necessity for an excessively hard blow, the object being ostensibly to move only the ball, not the bunker!

Up to this point we have encountered little difficulty.

There are two means of regulating the range of a full blasting shot;first, by the loft or angle of the club;and, second, by the mass of sand taken behind the ball, the force of the blow varying little. If full range is desired the club is faced up to the ball with its normal loft and as little sand taken as the lie of the ball will permit. As the range is shortened the club should be laid back and away from the ball (no attempt should be made to cut across the shot) and more sand taken behind it.

From this kind of shot the ball goes up with practically no spin and falls almost lifeless upon the green, taking whatever roll the topography and speed of the green may give to it.

The only difficulty to be encountered is the weight of the sand to be taken, and that the player will have to judge for himself, considering whether the sand is wet and coarse, or dry and powdery.

Chip Shot Most Dangerous

Just as the blasting shot is almost always the safest, the clean chip is uniformly the most dangerous. It has its uses, however, when the bunker is shallow and the ball is lying neatly on

When chipping near the green, the player needs an unhurried stroke, thus allowing the ball to enjoy a normal roll to the hole.

top of the sand. When everything is propitious and the player himself feels a little cocksure, it may work. The only rule I should care to lay down with regard to this stroke is that a more lofted club be selected than would be required for the same shot from the fairway.

That will permit striking the ball a little higher and thereby lessen the danger of spoiling the shot by hitting the sand.

The Cut Shot

And now, turning to that which I have called the "cut-shot," I think immediately of Freddie McLeod. I have seen Freddie do so many remarkable stunts with this shot that I have almost been converted to a believer in its value. But Freddie's use of it and mine are sadly different– that is, sadly for me.

Freddie plays the ball relatively far in front of his left foot, his body facing the hole. Using a full and vicious stroke, he literally tears the bottom off the ball. The club is laid back about as far as possible and passes under and across the ball, imparting to it a terrific spin. I have often seen Freddie's ball pitch as much as two yards past the hole and come running backward until it stopped on the very edge of the cup. I have seen it go in at least twice.

I had waited patiently for a number of years to see what would happen if Freddie ever hit one a little too high. When he finally did half-top one I was not in a position to enjoy it as I should have liked, for I happened to be in line and nearly lost an ear.

But this shot is not for the rank and file of golfers. The nicety of execution which it requires is beyond

In playing a stroke off clean sand, the main thing is to strike a descending blow which will get you out of the bunker even if you take it heavy.

the reach of most of us.

The Modified Blast

I should like now, in a few words, to indicate my own preference in the matter of extricating the ball from sand around the green.

When my ball is lying cleanly, or nearly so, and there are no unusual dangers attendant upon the stroke, I cannot help feeling that from the bunker I ought to get close enough to the hole at least to render not unreasonable the expectation of getting down in one putt. I have found that wherever a chip cannot be employed, I cannot be sufficiently accurate with the blast and I do not dare try one of Freddie McLeod's cut-shots.

The solution for me has been a modification of the blast, which has some of the earmarks of the cut.

First, I must have a reasonably good lie. I take my stance with feet close together and body almost erect, and facing slightly toward the hole. I always use a niblick, and lay it back just a little bit. Then, with a generous half swing and free wrist-action, I try to take sand just under the ball, not over one-half inch behind where the ball is resting on the sand. The length of my swing is almost always the same, the range being controlled by the force of the blow. The merit of this shot, as I see it, is that it is easier to control than the blast and, while more dangerous than a full explosion, is much safer than the cut. Except in extraordinary situations, there is little chance that the error on one side will be great enough

to leave the ball still in the bunker, or on the other, to send it over the green.

When played in this fashion the ball has considerable spin, imparted by the face of the club which is roughened by the thin layer of sand upon it, so that it is possible to pitch boldly up to the hole with assurance that there will be little roll.

It must be borne in mind, however, that this shot cannot be employed from a bad lie. Neither can it be used from furrowed bunkers.

In writing of these three types of bunker shots, I do not mean to imply that there exists no other legitimate way of accomplishing the desired results. Imagination plays a fairly important part, and there certainly is no place on a golf course where the player's flare for originality can have freer rein than in a sand-trap. Once there, he has the selection of any number of means of getting out, granting, of course, that his ball is not lying in a diabolical furrow, nor in an innocent-looking, though equally obnoxious, heel-mark.

Situation Determines Shot

When a man walks into a bunker, he is generally in a very unsettled state of mind. Approaching his ball upon the fairway, he can be reasonably sure that he can use whatever club or shot the distance and terrain may demand. But on the sand, his situation is vastly different, for there he must accommodate his ambitious intentions to the lie he has been lucky enough to draw. And rarely, indeed, is he met with a situation entirely familiar to him,. for the very smallest hump of sand back of the ball may make impossible, or at any rate too dangerous, the shot which he had determined upon as suited to the occasion.

I always remember, with much satisfaction, a shot which I played at Columbus in the last round of the Open Championship.

It was on the thirteenth hole. I had just holed a four at the long twelfth and had been informed that Joe Turnesa, playing two holes ahead, had taken six on that hole, and five to the thirteenth. I began then to have some hope of winning, for I was now only two strokes behind, and if I could get my four at thirteen, I would be only a stroke behind with five holes to play.

But the thirteenth was against the wind that day, and my spoon

In the controlled blast, the backswing is on the long side, but the club is merely floated into the sand behind the ball, producing a shot with some backspin.

second, hit with every intention of bringing it in from left to right into the wind, held straight to the line and finished in the trap to the left of the green. The ball was lying near the left bank, leaving the full width of the bunker to be played over. The hole was a scant ten or fifteen feet beyond the opposite bank, and about six feet beyond the hole was a terrace, which would carry the ball far away down the slope if it should pass over the top of the rise.

In this situation, an explosive shot or blast was of no use, because the ball, with no backspin, could not be stopped short of the terrace. It was likewise impossible to chip because my ball lay too far from the opposite bank of the bunker; and, finally, I did not dare try to cut the ball up with lots of backspin because, if I took too much sand, I should leave it in the bunker.

I do not know what I should have or could have done had not the bank of the bunker been low and not too precipitous. As it was, it was only a little over two feet high and sloping. My only chance lay in a run-up shot, hoping to take the bank with the proper speed. I hit the ball with a mashie-iron, scuttling it across the sand, and watched it climb the bank. Luckily, it curled down the slope and came to rest four feet to the left of the hole!

The general tendency, I think, is to overlook the possibilities in a shot of that nature. I admit that it does appear unworkmanlike and amateurish to run a shot through sand and out of a bunker, but it sometimes becomes necessary to disregard appearances. A few disasters resulting from a desire to display brilliant technique are enough to harden even the most sensitive nature. It is best to keep always in mind the ultimate object in the game–to approach the hole.

It must be appreciated that backspin cannot be imparted to a ball embedded in the sand or lying in a heelprint. A mass of sand must be taken. (FPG Photos)

Which example of the use of imagination in golf, brings us now to a more complete explanation of the run-up shot.

The Run-Up Shot

It is hard to blame golfers in America for failing to appreciate the uses and advantages of a skillfully played run-up shot. The habit, or perhaps the necessity, of keeping putting greens well soaked with water has done away with most of the need of run-up, although there are always times when it can be turned to advantage. But for the most part, the soft greens hold out an irresistible invitation for the more spectacular pitch, and the holding turf has made it possible for designers to place bunkers close enough to the hole to demand a carrying shot.

Although lack of familiarity with the run-up has caused the majority of players to regard it as a very difficult shot, it is actually far simpler and far less risky than the pitch. There is often cause for wonder when we see a player of moderate ability continue to pitch, pitch, pitch–getting some close, and some miles away, when almost any sort of skill could roll the ball up somewhere near the hole. That is the greatest virtue of the run-up–it will never finish very far away.

The player's early experiences with the run-up shot are not happy ones because he is apt to hit the ball in the same way as he would if playing a pitch, trying to obtain the run by hooding the club and shoving the ball along close to the ground. Sometimes that method works passably well, but a ball so struck will be affected by every irregularity of the turf over which it runs. Even the faintest trace of backspin may cause the ball to check its speed at the first rough spot it strikes, and that is usually the result of a knock-down stroke with a lofted club. The amount of run must be an almost certain quantity.

The shot ought rarely to be played with any club of more loft than a number four iron. The straighter face assures that the ball will glide smoothly over the fairway and will not lose its speed before it reaches the putting surface.

I carry in my bag a cleek shafted to a little more than putter length which I use for run-up shots of thirty and forty yards. It is very useful for it makes of the stroke very little more than a long approach putt.

In reality I suppose the stroke to be employed for this shot is more like the putting stroke than any other. It is a sweep from beginning to end, and should by no means include the free wrist action and the sharp biting blow so necessary in playing a pitching shot. I can think of no better idea to fix upon than that of "rolling" the ball, rather than of driving or forcing it along.

I do not think it matters much whether the wrists are turned the right over the left as is so often advised. The stroke is too simple to warrant worry over such matters. If the ball is struck fairly, it will do all the running that is necessary.

Occasions are very rare when there is any appreciable advantage to be gained by attempting a run-up shot of more than thirty or forty yards. Usually from distances greater than that, the pitch or the pitch-and-run are safer shots, for the delicacy required becomes less as we move away from the hole. The shot played from a distance of fifty or sixty yards which is designed to pitch a few yards of the green with enough run to carry it up to the hole, is not a run-up. Run-up shots in the sense I know them are those which cover considerably more than half their travel on the ground. It is obvious that to fulfill that requirement the shot must be comparatively short.

The peculiarity of the stroke in the run-up shot is the taut left forearm and almost rigid left wrist. The club is taken back with almost no aid from the wrists, and swung through the ball largely by means of the arms and shoulders. There is very little opening of the clubface on the backswing, and the ball, played farther back than usual, is simply batted along the ground.

The chief difficulty involved in any run-up shot is to strike the ball in such a way that neither its direction nor the length of its roll will be greatly affected by inconsistencies in the earth or turf. Many a pitch-and-run has been spoiled by striking in a place where the ground is softer or where the grass is heavier than was expected.

Simplicity Always Best

The fact that the use of a straighter club in this stroke eliminates some mechanical complications, would recommend the use of such a club to the vast majority of golfers, for simplicity above all is what they should seek. When you make a choice between the pitch and the run-up, you are not trying to create opportunities for displaying your skill. The only legitimate reason for playing either shot is that it is easier. It is nearly always the simple, straightforward method that wins in golf, because then when the shots go wrong, as they must sometimes do, they do not carry so far afield.

In choosing between the pitch and the run-up, many things have to be considered. First, the lie of the ball. Many players cannot pitch accurately with a heavy-lying ball, or with a ball imbedded in clover. In either case, the run-up is much simpler and should be played rather than take the risk of a bad pitch. If the ball is lying cleanly, then pitch if you like.

Of course the condition of the ground in front of the green is most important. I have seen men try persistently to run-up on courses where the fairways were not smooth, or where the speed of the fairway was greatly different from that of the green. Of course, such attempts were mere folly. It was naturally impossible to foresee what kind of a roll the ball would take.

The point is that both the pitch and the run-up have places in the repertory of every good golfer. Each is immensely useful at times, and much difficulty may be avoided by a judicious mixture of the two.

The great value of a hazard is not that it catches a missed shot, but it forces a miss on a timid player.

Long Approach Putts and Pitch Shots Hardest

It is my opinion that if a vote were taken among the professionals and the leading amateurs to determine the most difficult shot to play, the count would be almost equally divided between the very short pitch over a bunker and the long approach putt. These two strokes require a nicety of judgment and a delicacy in execution which exceed by far those required in any other shot in the game. A few feet more or less may mean the loss of one stroke at least and sometimes more, in either case.

The very long approach putt is difficult mainly because it is so hard to determine just how much force is to be put into the stroke. To be successful it must leave the ball within a yard or less of the hole, and when the distance to be traversed is sixty or seventy feet, that is a very small margin, especially if the green happens to be very keen and hard to judge.

Whenever my long approach putts begin to leave me six, eight, and ten-footers to hole, if I inquire into the cause, I usually find that my backswing is hurried and too short. The approach putt requires a leisurely ample backswing, long enough so that the ball may be swept away with a smooth stroke.

This same broad arc is also helpful in playing the wee pitch. This little shot more than any other, tempts the player to hurry the stroke. The sight usually seen is a club dashing quickly up and down, and a ball dropping gently into the sand almost under the player's nose. The short chopping stroke is induced by a desire to put backspin on the ball, and the player feels that he must hit firmly to produce the spin. He will find a far greater measure of success if he will lighten his grip on the club and permit himself a little longer, and much slower, backswing.

Most failures from bunkers result from topping because tension has upset the stroke.

Gripping the club less firmly permits a freer wrist and forearm action with which to flick the ball across the intervening hazard. The shot is always a dangerous one, but it is certainly one of the prettiest in the game when executed properly.

The Chip Shot and the Putt

Earlier in this chapter we discussed the chip shot in connection with bunkers. Here I should like to discuss it in its relation to the putt.

I have heard it said many times that a chip shot should be regarded merely as an extended putt and should be played with substantially the same stroke as is used in the putting. In general terms, the chip and the putt are parts of what we call the short game, but beyond that there is absolutely no relation between them. Each requires a different technique, and proficiency in one department by no means carries with it success in the other.

The design of the player when chipping from just off the putting surface, is to place his ball in position where the putt which follows will be as simple as possible.

It is beyond all reasonable expectations that a person may hole a chip shot. Therefore little will be gained by playing always for the hole. Naturally, if the ball can be rolled to the edge of the hole, the putt will be simple whatever the condition of the green. But there are times when a four-foot putt uphill is a far less annoying proposition than one of half that length across a keen slope. It is well to keep in mind that the success of the chip depends upon the success of the putt and is not measured by the number of inches separating the ball from the hole.

There is nothing more trying than the playing of a medal round when one is chipping badly. To be continually struggling to get down in one putt after the chip shot, is likely to undermine the staunchest determination. It is rare when a competitor plays even one round in which he has not a lot of chipping to do. If he is not adept at the shot, the question becomes merely how long good putting will stand the strain. Sooner or later the strokes will begin to slip away.

I think it is a bad idea to use one club for all kinds of chip-shots and short run-ups. Familiarity with the implement, of course, has its advantages, but it is practically impossible to secure a club which is effective from all distances and over all conditions of turf and terrain. It is far better to be able to play the shot with any club which may be indicated by the shot at hand, so that the proportion of pitch and run may be accommodated to any position of the ball or hole with respect to the edge of the putting surface.

Methods of Play

Nearly every successful golfer is a skillful player of the chip shot. Nearly all of them play the stroke with any club and with each club in two distinct ways. In one case, where the green is not especially keen and where the cup is set far

enough back from the edge of the putting surface to accommodate the normal run of the ball, the shot is played with feet close together and the ball off the right foot. The ball is struck a straightforward blow and is pitched without spin, taking its normal roll to the vicinity of the hole.

In case the hole should be cut very near to the edge of the green, or if the green should be keen or sloping, the expert places the ball opposite his left foot and plays the stroke with the face of the club lying off slightly. Pinching the ball from the ground in this way, the spin imparted causes the ball to drag during the first part of its journey upon the green and comes to a stop after a gentle roll.

The first method requires considerably less delicacy and finesse and is always the safer shot if a club can be found which is capable of making the shot in that way. Usually, but not always a chip which requires spin with one club can be played normally with a club of more loft.

I think crouching is the worst mistake the average person makes when playing a chip shot. You will observe any number of players who stand to the ball with feet wide apart and bodies bent far down, taking a grip upon the club at the very bottom of the leather. Such an attitude invariably produces a tenseness which destroys all chance of executing a delicate stroke.

I should urge most strongly that a player acquire aptitude with several clubs for the purpose of chipping. I have found for myself that one club cannot be made to meet the exigencies of all kinds and lengths of chip shots. I like, except upon extraordinary occasions, to employ the club which will permit me, using a straightforward stroke, to pitch the ball just to the edge of the putting surface. For example, if my ball lay fifteen feet off the green, with the hole thirty feet from the edge, I should play a mashie, whereas if the ball lay only three feet off the green I should use a mashie-iron.

A great many players employ successfully what is known as "drag" on the chip. This is done by opening the clubface slightly and striking a sharp blow at the bottom of the ball. This is a refinement, however, which adds unnecessarily to the difficulties of the shot. It appears to me much simpler, if spin is needed for the mashie, to play a straightforward shot with either mashie-niblick or niblick.

Of course, no general observation can be made to take care of all the vagaries of chipping.

It is best to keep the trajectory of the ball as flat and allow for as much run under the conditions as is possible in the short chip.

Brains and Imagination in Golf

The ambition of every man who plays golf, whether his average game be seventy-two or ninety-five, is to take strokes off his score. That is the aim of Walter Hagen as much as of the rankest duffer in any club. The great difference is that Hagen, aside from any improvement in his mechanical ability, knows that he can save stroke after stroke by simply using his head.

The business-man golfer takes lessons. He reads books. He imitates good players. He buys new clubs. He does everything he can to improve his swing. his shot-making ability. But he overlooks one important feature. He doesn't ask himself if he is scoring as well as he ought to with his present ability.

In every club there is always at least one man who has the reputation of "making a poor game go a long way," the man who seems always to beat a player a bit better than himself. He doesn't do it by any divine inspiration, nor yet by any trick of fate. He simply uses his head, analyzing each situation as it confronts him, always keeping in view his own limitations and powers. That is what we call judgment, and it is a lot easier to use good judgment than it is to learn to swing a club like Harry Vardon.

Let a person post himself at any particular point on the course during the progress of the open championship, or of any really first-class tournament and watch the entire field of 150 players or more go by. Of that number he will, of course, be impressed by the Farrells, Hagens, Armours, and the others who bear illustrious names. But I am sure he will be surprised at the number of fine shots played by men of whom he has never heard. And if he is an intelligent observer, he will appreciate that these fine shots are not mere accidents. What then is the difference between those who finish always at the top, and those who sometimes finish not at all?

The answer is, I think, in what I have mentioned above—the ability to use one's head. The successful man carries a resourcefulness and a character of judgment, the lack of which dooms the other fellow, despite his mechanical skill, to a permanent place among the "also-rans". Knowing what to do, and when to do it, is the necessary complement to mechanical skill which maintains a few men at the head of the procession with many others clutching closely, but vainly, for their coat-tails.

The faculty, which the first-class player possesses, of quickly sizing up the requirements of a shot on a strange course, choosing the club, and the method of playing it, is what I mean by resourcefulness and judgment. On a course that is well-known such decisions are made automatically, and it is then that skill alone is required. But to conquer an unfamiliar layout, considerable work must be done by that which

lies between the ears.

Fortunately, sound judgment can be acquired in golf in much easier fashion than can mechanical skill. Experience over various courses and under varied conditions will teach a lot to any man. If he can play the shots, the rest can be learned by proper thought and application.

The average golfer may ask what this has to do with him! Really a good deal, for by training himself to visualize and plan each shot before he makes it and by giving careful thought to his method of attack, he can improve his game even more certainly than by spending hours on a practice tee. Some men, for one reason or another, can never learn to swing a golf club correctly, but everyone can improve in the matter of selecting the shot to be played.

The importance of good judgment is undiminished by the fact that the average player has fewer shots at his command than the skillful professional. The problem is nevertheless the same–how best for the particular individual to play the particular shot. Good judgment must take into account the personal equation as well as the slope and condition of the ground, and the locations of bunkers and hazards.

Here is one example showing how a man can waste strokes and lose holes uselessly. I played a while ago in a fourball match with my father, who plays a fairly good game, in the eighties as a rule. He was playing a match against another member of our party with whom he was about evenly matched. On the seventeenth hole, Dad hit under his ball on the drive, dropping in the road just over the lake. His opponent topped into the water and played three from the bank.

I particularly noted how Dad's ball was lying in the road. It actually invited a full shot with a straight faced iron. But there was a five-foot embankment ten yards ahead. The green was so far distant that the longest shot would still leave seventy yards or more to go. The other man was in the rough in three. The best he could be expected to do was to play on in four, leaving two putts for a six.

Dad needed, in this situation, only to play conservatively up the fairway with a mashie, another mashie shot to the green, take two putts for a five, and win the hole. He could not hope to do better even if his long iron came off, for the green was a full three-hundred yards away. But he didn't stop to think it all out! Bent upon hitting the ball as far as possible, he took the long iron, half-topped the shot, and the ball, striking into the bank, barely hopped up into the fairway.

Harry Vardon and Bob Jones at the 1920 U.S. Open Championship at the Inverness Club in Toledo, Ohio.

BOBBY JONES ON GOLF

Having wasted a stroke, he was little better off than before. Now, he could not carry the bunker twenty yards from the green. He played short of it with an iron, pitched on the green in four, and holed out in two putts for a six. His opponent, as it turned out, messed up his iron shot, but chipped to the edge of the hole and secured a half.

Those are the things that not one golfer in a hundred will trouble himself to think about. To take chances is perfectly proper – when there is something to be gained and when there is a reasonable possibilty that the shot can be made. But where is there even an excuse for taking a risk when in no conceivable way can benefit result?

I believe that if a person will approach every shot with a cool head, if he will look carefully to what lies before him and think two or three shots ahead, he can improve his average score by from four strokes upward. If you are in trouble, you know you can get out with one club in a certain way, and you think you might get out with another club in another way. Before you try that other club in the other way, think whether or not you will gain anything if it works—not merely whether you may send your ball a few yards farther down the fairway, but whether you will there- by gain any measurable advantage.

Imagination an Asset

Imagination, it has been said, is something that a golfer should not possess. To a certain extent, that is true. It is certainly a bad thing to have too clearly in mind, when hitting the ball, all the many kinds of disas- ters which may befall the stroke. Then, if ever, is the time to have a single-track mind which can hold only the immediate objective in view.

But the golfer who is devoid of imagination of any kind will certainly never rise far above medioc- rity. In the main, the shots

Bob's friends watch him tee off in an exhibition with Billy Burke, Johnny Revolta, and Horton Smith.

from the tee and through the fairway, have become stereotyped and require no originality. But ever so often there arises a situation which is novel and puzzling. Behind a tree, or on the down-slope of a bunker, the player needs imagination and resourcefulness as well as mechani- cal accuracy.

At St. Andrews, the people are still talking about a shot made by Francis Ouimet on the seventeenth, the famous Road Hole. The road back of this green is one of the terrors of the St. Andrews links, and to be in it is regarded as absolutely fatal, for the green is very small, and a terrible bunker awaits the approach which is too strong.

Ouimet's ball, on this occasion, went not only into the road, but across it and on to within three or four inches of a stone wall seven or eight yards beyond the road itself. His opponent was safely on in three so that Francis appeared to have lost the hole, although he had played only two, for he seemingly must play away from the wall with his third, pitch on –if he could– in four, and take two putts for a six.

Francis approached the ball, looked it over for a moment and drew

a niblick from his bag. Instead of playing the obvious shot to safety, he squared himself to the ball as though intending to drive it through the stone wall. Then, to the amazement of everyone, he banged the ball into the wall with the lofted club, and it came back like a shot, cleared the road, pitched onto the green and stayed there–a shot bril- liantly executed, it is true, but far more brilliantly conceived.

Hagen's Remarkable Recovery

I once saw Hagen play a marvelous shot from a bunker–I am sorry I cannot remember just where it was, although the shot itself stands out prominently in my memory.

His ball was lying in heavy grass on the steep slope of a large bunker. The bank was almost sheer and Hagen's ball lay about half- way down it. The green lay across the bunker, and the ball very close to the edge. It was impossible to raise the ball from the precipitous down-slope sufficiently to clear the opposite side of the bunker, and at the same time drop it quickly enough to hold the green.

I remember thinking what a mess Walter had gotten himself into! But apparently he had not, for with a big mashie or some such imple- ment, he played almost a full shot straight into the opposite bank of the bunker. The ball popped neatly onto the green, up near the hole and Hagen holed the putt.

Of course, without some good fortune, the ball might not have fin- ished so near the hole. But it looked at first as though it would need some luck to get on the green. The average man would not have dreamed of playing the shot in that way. The concep- tion was that of a genius.

Prevent Waste of Strokes

Situations like these break up the monotony which there undoubtedly is in golf. For hole after hole the shots go along smoothly enough, causing very little mental distur- bance. But sooner or later something happens and a brand new situ- ation comes up.

Very likely, it is something like the two I have mentioned, some- thing outside the realm of past experience, calling for a shot never tried before. Then is the time that we need imagination, and a lot of it!

Years of practice and instruction are needed to round out a sound, workable method of hitting a golf ball. For a great many men, it is impossible to give to the game more than enough time to become ordinarily proficient at making the shots. Most of them never will be able to drive like Johnny Farrell, nor to play an iron like Tommy Armour, nor to putt like Walter Hagen. But by using their heads they can learn very quickly to prevent the useless waste of strokes.

"Warming Up"

To think too much of the swing while playing a golf shot is usually disastrous. It is a difficult matter to be conscious at the same time of every detail of the stroke and still retain a modicum of concentration upon driving the ball to a desired spot. It is this difficulty which leads the average golfer to believe that the expert player must have nothing to worry about except hitting the ball.

We hear so much talk of "machine-like play" and the like that it is no wonder that a good player is thought of as an automaton who keeps swinging his clubs in the same groove day after day. Of course, it would be an exceedingly happy circumstance if such were the case, but it is unfortunately not yet so, and not likely to be so as long as those mortals who are unwise enough to struggle with the game remain in their present stage of advancement.

The expert has to make use of his golfing intelligence and experience every time he strikes a ball, and it is his ability to quickly discover and remedy defects in his swing which enables him to widen the space which separates him from the ordinary player.

That is the one great reason that I always try to manage five or ten minutes practice before starting upon a competitive round. The practice is not, as some may think, indulged in for the purpose of learning something new nor yet in the hope of substantially increasing skill already possessed. The sole and only purpose is to make whatever adjustments may be necessary to gain confidence and control.

When a player steps to the first tee without having hit a ball that day, he is taking a step in the dark. In every case he must feel his way for the first few holes until he can become oriented, and discover whether his clubs are going to feel like broom handles, fishing poles, or anything else than the ordinary golf clubs.

I do not think it matters a great deal whether the preliminary practice is satisfying or not, although if time permits, it ought to be continued until the shots begin to go. In five minutes one can hit as many shots in the practice field as in five or six holes of actual play, and that should give ample opportunity to "get the feel" of every club. In this little work-out, or warming-up skirmish, I like to give every club a little attention—that is, a few shots each with driver, spoon, mid-iron, mashie, and mashie-niblick, followed by a half-minute or so on the putting green with three or four balls.

Chick Evans appeared at Minikahda with a full set of clubs equipped with square grips. "I like them," explained Chick, "because I can feel the corners and always know where the clubhead is." That

Here's Bobby making a full turn away from the ball with all his majesty.

is exactly what the few minutes of practice does for other people; it gives them a sense of location; they begin to know how their clubs will behave that day.

Often, of course, no irretrievable damage will be done by starting off cold, but it is almost certain that many uncomfortable moments will be experienced. It is never wise to count upon playing into one's best game after the match has begun. The time to get up steam is while waiting at the station, not after you have started your journey.

While on the subject of practice, I should like to say something about the value of the practice net.

Net for Practice Golf

A few years ago, I was introduced to what was then to me a new form of practice golf—the practice net. It impressed me with the tremendous possibilities of practice at home in the spare moments of busy days, when there is not time to go out to the golf club. Every golfer is anxious to improve his game and should be interested in finding or making opportunities for doing so.

On the lawn by the side of his home in Yarmouth, Maine, Don Abbott, whom I was then visiting, rigged up a splendid driving net. The backstop was of canvas and the sides and top were screened with netting for a distance of twenty or twenty-five feet. Underneath was the turf of the lawn from which iron and brassie shots could be played as from a good fairway. Such a contrivance occupies a negligible amount of space and affords the golfer a place to practice where he needs no caddie and very few balls.

While I whacked away at a few dozen shots with Don's clubs, I found myself wondering just how much was this kind of practice worth and how did it compare with playing in the wide open spaces! I also asked myself how much good did people who winter in the North get out of those indoor golfing schools which have become so popular of recent years.

Quite obviously practice in a net is better than no practice at all, for it keeps the muscles trained to their proper jobs and prevents the softening of the hands which brings blisters in the spring. Even if that were all it would be worthwhile, I think. But there is more!

Driving a full shot into a canvas thirty feet away does not offer the thrill involved in striking a ball down the middle of a beautiful fairway. Much is left to the imagination to say that this one would have sliced or that one would have gone straight. The little niceties of the fade or draw, and of low or high trajectory cannot, of course, be developed when the continuous flight and behavior of the ball cannot be observed.

Only one-half of the golf shot is at command. Hitting the ball is all there is and we are denied the satisfaction of watching the good ones and spared the agony of beholding the bad ones; which, after all may be more than a fifty-fifty break in our favor for all attention can then be given to the swing.

But I believe that nearly every one can know by the feel of the ball upon the club whether or not it has been properly struck, and can at least in this way school himself in true hitting. That is half the battle and if spring golf can be begun with an accurate and correct swing, the little adjustments for range and direction will not be found difficult.

Mental Hazard Removed

Probably the greatest defect in this scheme of winter practice is that one of the fundamental difficulties and beauties of the game is removed from the play, namely, the sense of responsibility –the mental hazard. It would seem to me far easier to produce a perfect swing when standing in front of a net which must stop the ball within thirty feet, than when confronted with an iron shot of 180 yards to a closely guarded green.

In the first case, there is nothing to worry about. Whatever happens, the next shot will not be played from a sand pit and no six or seven will mar a good score. In actual play the mental side of the game–the mental hazard–is one of the principal testing components. Without its threatening uncertainties golf is really no longer golf.

But I am convinced that net practice can bring about an enormous improvement in technique in mechanical ball-hitting as detached from the playing of the game. It will then remain to be seen if this technical improvement can be brought onto the field under the strain of a full round of golf.

I am frankly impressed with the value of a net at home for winter practice. Nearly every business man works his hardest in winter and has little time for play even if weather permits. But any of us can spare a half-hour or so every now and then to hit a few dozen shots.

Practice Avoids Trouble

Here is a good place to speak of bunker practice, even though I mention it again in the chapter on the playing of short shots. Too much stress cannot be laid on this type of practice, as the greatest difference is always noted in the play around the greens.

As the play grows closer to the cup, and the need for touch and delicate control becomes more exacting, the one who has not been in intimate contact with his clubs for a great while will surely suffer. There is a great difference between the accuracy required to place a full iron shot on a fair-sized green and that needed to guide a ten foot putt into the cup.

On every course, the weight and fineness of the sand is likely to be different, and since almost every shot from the sand is played according to the character of the surface upon which the ball rests, the niceties of bunker play vary for almost every course. In other words, while the fundamentals of the stroke remain the same, the ultimate success of the shot depends entirely upon the exactness with which the resistance of the sand is estimated.

It is almost impossible to exaggerate the disturbing effect upon one's entire game produced by a feeling of uncertainty concerning one's ability to recover well from bunkers around the green. The great value of a hazard is not that it catches a shot which has been missed but that it forces a miss upon the timid player. How much greater is this mental effect when the player knows that he has not the ability to recover if he makes a mistake?

Whether a golfer plays in championship tournament or not, a few minutes of practice is an excellent plan to follow.

Bobby, just having finished a practice putt. His heels almost touch and the hands are close to his body.

On the Correct Grip

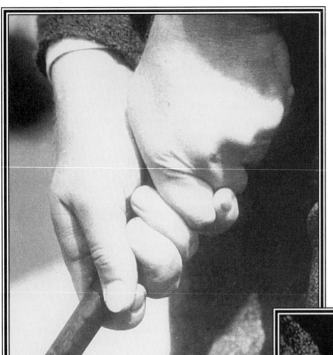

and allowances must be made for these variations.

The exact nature of the grip which will prove best for each individual player can be determined only with reference to the capabilities of the hands and wrists of the individual. Regardless of physical limitations of whatever nature, to assure control and power a golf club must be held in the fingers. It may, of course, lie against the palm in places, but the fingers must wind around and control it.

Occasionally we run across people whose hands are so short that they have difficulty in managing the club entirely in the fingers, because they cannot encircle the shaft. For them it is often necessary to remove the padding under the grip in order to reduce the size. If that operation does not do the work, then wood should be taken off the shaft underneath the grip, until it is comfortable in the hands.

The hands are extremely low; the left holds firmly; the right delicately, with more than a suspicion of "pinch" in the hold of the right thumb and index finger. Bobby holds the driver and all other clubs well up to the end

The person with large, strong hands has a very definite advantage in golf. Sometimes I think large feet help too, but the hands are most important. I like to see hands that nearly cover the leather part of the handle, for you know then that the club will do their bidding.

The average person who has never played golf, when handed a club, wants to take hold of it in one of two ways; either entirely in the fingers or, like a baseball player, entirely in the palms. The former is preferred by women, while the latter has favor with the men, probably because of their universal training in college or high-school baseball. Yet neither will work with a golf club.

Because the hands are the points of contact and of control of the club, it is immensely important that they be set in a proper fashion. In developing the grip, the player should adopt a method which will enable him to handle the club with the least possible effort. Grantland Rice says that the hands and legs tire first in golf—the former wield the club, and the latter support the body. I should go even farther and say that the hands are most likely to tire if there is the least strain in their position on the club. To handle a club weighing fourteen ounces, when more than half the weight is concentrated at a distance of more than a yard from the point of control is no light exercise, you can be sure.

There is in the Garden City Golf Club on Long Island, a cast of Harry Vardon's hands and grip upon a club, and they look as though they belonged to some giant of Brobdingnag. Someone once remarked that Vardon, walking down the fairway, appeared to be carrying a bunch of bananas under each arm! Still, taking all these physical characteristics into consideration there are certain principles which cannot be overlooked in setting the hands of a beginner upon a golf club.

If the player takes the club entirely in his fingers, he quite obviously cannot manipulate the small shaft with certainty, and the same is true if he grasps it like a baseball bat. But there is a still greater objection to both types of grip. With the club held solely in the fingers, it is impossible to bring the clubhead to the ground without arching the wrists and arms upward. In this position the wrists are almost powerless.

It seems to me that there has been in our best instruction a tendency to overlook the importance of a proper position of the hands upon the club. The usual formula is to advise that the club be held in a "manner comfortable to the player," and that feature is very important. Obviously, there may be, and often there is, considerable difficulty to be encountered by one person in adopting the exact grip used by another. Human hands differ almost as much as human faces,

But no argument is necessary to show that both methods are wrong. It would probably be best now to follow with a few suggestions concerning a better way.

admitted asset to the golfer.

It will be found that most of the star performers of today employ a grip which in its essential element differs little from the grip which has been named for Harry Vardon. The Vardon grip is an overlapping one, and while some of the better players interlock and others neither interlock nor overlap, the positions of the hands upon the club vary little among them all. In nearly every case, the hands are opposed, the left against the front of the shaft and the right against the back of it, with the V's formed by the thumb and first finger of each hand pointing directly upward in the line of the shaft. The variation from this in a particular case will be found to be very small.

Leaving out of consideration the fact that the grip determines to a great extent the position of the wrists, it is also important in regard to this question of obtaining leverage upon the club. To this end, the best grip is the combination finger and palm affair. The club is grasped by the fingers but it is pressed almost diagonally across the palm of each hand.

As I grip the club, the shaft rests squarely upon the second joint of the index finger of each hand, and passes across the palm, emerging midway between the base of the little finger and the wrist. In this way I have a contact with the club greatly exceeding the width of my hands, and when in addition the index finger of my right hand is extended and crooked around the shaft, I have increased even my leverage upon the club. I do not think that the thumbs should be placed upon the top of the shaft, for in that position they restrict the free swing. Slightly upon the side, forming a letter V with the index fingers is the best position.

Many players would do well to consider carefully if they have enough strength in their hands to use the interlocking or overlapping grip. Although these grips make for compactness, there is a necessary loss of leverage

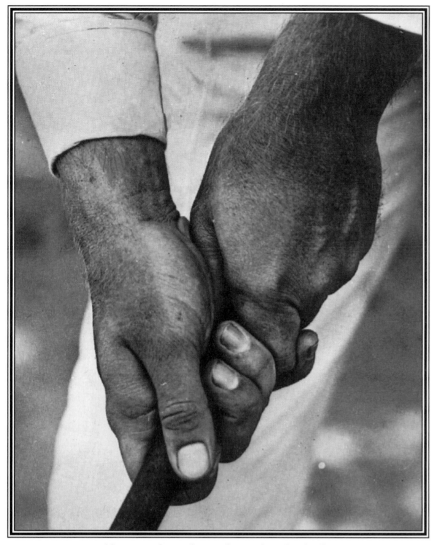

Bobby Jones shows the grip he employs for the drive.

Compactness and Leverage

There are two things to be considered, from a theoretical viewpoint, in determining the proper grip compactness and leverage. Our two hands must fit closely together upon the shaft because our two arms are of the same length and they must work together. That much, of course, is undisputed, so the problem is really a paradox—how to get the hands far apart while keeping them close together.

The question of leverage is the troublesome factor. On the average driver, forty-two inches long, the clubhead would be at least thirty-four inches from the right hand of the player. That means that holding on to eight or ten inches of wood of comparatively negligible weight, a person must control the clubhead, weighing seven to nine ounces, with a lever arm of thirty inches or more. It is easily seen that to do so requires a generous spread of the hands upon the club.

To illustrate the importance of leverage as applied to the golf stroke, take hold of the club with the thumb and forefinger of each hand at points four inches apart and waggle the clubhead back and forth. Now drop the lower point ten inches. In the latter position, a great deal less effort is required to move the club. Of course, for proper control the intermediate fingers must be on the club, but I believe that the two most positive points of the grip are with the thumb and forefinger of the right hand and with the two smallest fingers of the left hand, and that these points should be as far apart as the spread of the hands will permit. That is one reason that large hands are an

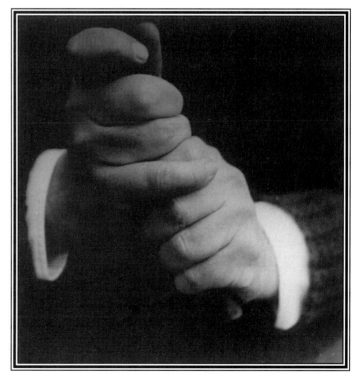

The fingers twine around the shaft providing an ample spread to make manipulation of the clubhead easy.

ON THE CORRECT GRIP

which may be fatal to a player with small or weak hands. When the little finger of the right hand is lapped over the index finger of the left, the spread is decreased so much. For women always, and for men not blessed with large, strong hands, I should recommend the old-fashioned grip with no overlap or interlock. It has recently gone out of style because it has been thought that one simply must use the Vardon or some other kind of grip. The older and plainer style has lost none of its efficacy, and serves as well as popular variations.

Flexible Wrists an Important Feature

Supple wrists are unquestionably to be desired in playing golf. Where speed is the essential quality, rather than strength, tense muscles ought not to be tolerated, for the muscle that is hardened by strain is not capable of rapid movement.

But nearly everyone at some time carries this notion of relaxation too far. In order that what is called a "free wrist action" may be encouraged, the tendency must be to relax the grip upon the club to an extent sufficient to impair seriously, if not destroy, the control which the player has over the club-head. Swinging with considerable force upon the ball, either the rapid motion prior to impact or the actual contact with the ball itself, may cause the club to turn in the hands and spoil an otherwise perfect stroke.

In my opinion, the left hand is the one that should hold the club steady. I think it matters very little indeed how lightly the right hand may rest upon the club up to the very moment of hitting. But a weak left-hand grip of a flabby left wrist may be utterly swept aside by an incorrect action of the right hand.

Bobby's grip for all shots except the putt. This was the regular overlapping or Vardon grip. It was actually first employed by British Amateur Champion Johnny Laidlay (1889, 1891).

A Happy Medium Needed

The great problem, of course, is to keep a firm grip upon the club and at the same time to use the wrists freely throughout the swing. The firm grip tends to tighten the muscles of the forearm and hence to bind the wrist into the set position at address. That would result in a stroke we should expect only from a wooden man. But if a firm hold is retained on the club with the left hand, there need be no fear of using the wrist too much, for the natural exertion of hitting will bring the left wrist up firm to the ball.

There need be no unusual tension in the grip of the thumb and forefinger of the left hand. The important members are the last three fingers of that hand. The firmness there gives excellent control and in addition discourages any desire to open the fingers as the club is stopped at the top of the backswing.

Stiff wrists destroy timing, rhythm, and every hope of control. It is a condition which places the direct control of the club in the shoulders and body of the player rather than in the hands where it should be.

It has been particularly striking to me that nearly all of the young players whom I have observed within the last few years have one common tendency. All of them seem to want length at whatever cost and they have, whether consciously or not, adopted the obvious but most dangerous means of getting it. They turn the left hand more to the upper side of the shaft and drop the right hand underneath it. The first effect of this change is to increase greatly the power of the wrists, because as they lash into the stroke the clubhead can be moved through a greater distance in the act of turning into the ball. This much is fine so long, and only so long, as it is under perfect control. But the most even temperament and the best trained muscles cannot remain in perfect concert all the time, and when a swing of this kind is not clicking, the error will be exaggerated in its effect upon the shot.

The position of the hands which I have described places the entire body in a strained position, where the natural tendency is to pull the left shoulder upward before the ball is hit and so strike the ball an ascending blow. Since it is thus difficult to keep the clubhead travelling close to the ground, it will be noted that the players addicted to the habit of gripping in this manner are more likely to top their drives than others who employ a more orthodox style. Shots mis-hit in any way must reach some sort of difficulty but no foozle can be as complete as a top.

Where Should Club Be Grasped?

Ted Ray points out that although much attention is given to teaching a person in what manner he should hold a golf club, very little is ever said about where he should hold it, a detail which may be equally as important as any. Usually in buying a new club a man takes care to secure one of the proper length, that is, of a length which will permit him to reach the ball comfortably when addressing it in his normal position. That is as it should be. But there are fourteen or more inches of leather on every golf club and these inches were not used solely for the purpose of increasing the manufacturer's cost.

Obviously, the club should be held as near as possible to the end when playing a full shot. So long as the club can be controlled, every inch of additional length in the shaft means additional yards on the end of the drive. But still there is danger if the player is not careful that the left hand may approach so nearly the end of the shaft that a firm grip will be lost while the swing is in progress. The safer course is to leave at least a half-inch of the shaft projecting beyond the left hand. There is then always enough to hold.

When playing into the wind it is generally accepted as good practice to take a shorter hold upon the shaft. The swing is thus shortened and the club is more definitely and easily controllable. The swing becomes not tight but more compact and there is less likelihood that the ball will be driven high in the air. Generally speaking, however, the proper place to hold a wood club is the point at which it balances best in the hands and where the player is most comfortable holding it.

With the irons it is an entirely different story. The shots which confront us during a round are unfortunately not all exactly suited to a full shot with any club. We must play three-quarter shots, half shots, and even wee pitches, and we must have control of the club at all times. It is so difficult for any but an expert player to employ less than a full stroke and at the same time retain the firmness and crispness which is the first requisite of a good iron shot. Not everyone would be able to do it at whatever point they should grip the club, but many by continuing to hold the club at the end make the accomplishment impossible.

The travel of the hands is not greatly reduced when playing a half or three-quarter shot and if the effective length of the shaft is not shortened, a firm crisp blow will likely pass the green by many yards.

With the pitching clubs, the hands should progress down the shaft as the hole is neared. For example, when playing a mashie–niblick pitch of a hundred and twenty yards, the club may be held close to the end; but if a shot of forty yards were attempted with the same club held at the same point,

Finish of a putt. Note the hands carefully opposed, the wrists working exactly against each other. In other shots the left hand is more on top of the shaft. In the putt also the overlapping is done by the forefinger of the left hand instead of the little finger of the right.

it would be necessary to soften the stroke in order to avoid overplaying the green.

There is one more thing in this connection which it is always well to remember. It is the complaint of all golfers that on some days they have the "feel" and on others the magic touch entirely deserts them. Many times I have found that by shifting my grip upon certain clubs, particularly the driver and putter, I have been able to bring back the touch with those clubs. Often the slightly altered balance of the club–making it feel lighter or heavier as the grip was shifted down or up–was the only thing that was needed to restore the accustomed confidence in it.

After playing golf persistently for twenty years, and after I had developed what I conceived to be a fairly sound method and had become rather set in my ways, I had the notion that I should make no more changes, only practice and try to machinize what I had.

However, I hit upon a defect in my iron play which had to be eliminated and I approached Jimmy Maiden, brother of Stewart, who happened to be in Atlanta at that time, explaining to him my theories.

"I think you are quite right in your own case, Bob," said Jimmy, "but don't forget that the position of your hands will very nearly determine what you must do with your shoulders. Your idea works very well so long as your grip remains the same. Look out that you don't unconsciously alter that."

I confess that I had some difficulty at first in seeing just what Jimmy meant. But he went on to explain, and when I understood, I could not fail to agree. The conception is such a good one that I shall attempt to describe it in my own words, for I believe it will be a great aid to correct thinking about the grip and swing.

How Grip Determines Shoulder Action

Obviously, it is desired that the face of the club should be squared to the line of flight when the ball is struck; to drive a straight ball on the proper line it is even necessary that it should be so.

If the club face comes onto the ball at any other angle, the only chance of obtaining decent results is that the spin and curve on the ball may correct in flight the error existing at the start.

Remembering now that the face of the club must be brought squarely up to the ball, this is how the grip determines the shoulder action:

Supposing that the grip is with the right hand well underneath the shaft of the club, to get it into that position the right arm must drop down until, instead of being uppermost at the address, it is below the left. Likewise the right shoulder is drawn down and the left shoulder appears correspondingly high. If that is the position of address, naturally in striking the ball, the right shoulder must go under.

This, then, upsets my theories that for good iron play the right shoulder had to stay up.

To be sure, applied to my own case, my right hand being on top of the shaft, the rule was correct, but it does not hold for everybody. As Jimmy explained, the shoulder action is affected by different grips.

Nerves in Golf

Of all ways in which nerves are manifested in golf, the strongest malady is that which seems to paralyze the player to an extent which makes it virtually impossible for him to start the swing. Whatever the sensation is—fear, uncertainty, or lack of determination—once a man is caught in its grip, he appears to be hypnotized at sight of the ball.

In golf, often on a simple shot, the player waggles his club and looks at the hole and the ball, until all his powers are required to move the club backward. Cyril Walker, back in 1924, after he had won the Open Championship fell a victim to this strange hypnosis. No one ever tried harder than Cyril to speed up his play for he realized that his slowness, in addition to affecting his own game, was a bother to his partners and opponents. "But," he confessed, "even when playing an apparently simple chip, I get to waggling and thinking about the shot, until I become absolutely frozen."

Apart from other considerations, an affliction or habit of that kind ruins the shot, for by the time the waggling is over tense nerves are frayed and every muscle is as taut as a steel band. There is no place left for freedom and rhythm. After one or two such experiences the player begins "fighting" the ball, approaching it in anything but a complacent frame of mind.

Merely to play quickly in order that the agony may be speedily ended will do little good. Indeed such procedure is probably worse than to waggle indefinitely. But a player should form a habit of playing promptly, eliminating all waste energy and unnecessary strain. There is always more ease, grace, and rhythm in the swing that begins with one or two leisurely regulated waggles, and proceeds without hurry and without hesitation. In this respect George Duncan is very pleasing to watch. There is no fussing with the feet, no twisting of the clubface, no uncertainty about the position of the hands. George falls immediately in position over the ball, then with one look and one waggle, he starts it on the way.

Mental Composure Necessary

People who do not play golf have difficulty in understanding why sudden noises or sudden motion in a player's line of vision usually upsets him and causes him to miss the shot. Apparently, baseball and golf require the same sort of concentration, yet a ball player nearly always has to produce his best in the midst of a din of cheering.

The disturbances which annoy a golfer are not those which begin before he addresses his ball and continue throughout the time he is making the stroke. In a measure, it is possible to shut out all consciousness of a continuous noise. But when someone shouts out of dead silence, or a whistle blasts shrilly in the distance, the player cannot be prepared for it.

On two or three occasions I have made golf shots before a baseball audience. I have stood in the batter's box in Atlanta and fired balls at the center field fence. And playing before a baseball crowd, one is bound to get a baseball reception. Few in the stands were golfers, so I was freely admonished to "knock it over the fence" or to "lose it," all the while I was hitting the ball.

Bobby Jones playing before one of the numerous crowds that always follow him in big championships. Sudden motions or noises are often disconcerting, he states. Note the evidence of strain in his features.

Unexpected motion is quite as distracting as noise. If a person standing behind a player so much as moves his foot, it may be enough to cause the eye to wander off the ball.

The golfer's sensitiveness to apparently trivial, outside disturbances, is far from being affected. It is very, very real, and something he cannot cure. Golf is not a game of action. It is a game requiring complete mental and muscular composure and there is not room nor time for other matters.

Tips for Nervous Golfer

Very often, I think, when we are trying to take strokes off our score, we attach too much importance to new theories of the swing, and overlook the fact that we are not getting everything we should out of the mechanical ability which we possess. Good golf, like any other human endeavor, is dependent upon human efficiency, and that is determined exactly as in the case of a steam engine and is fixed by the percentage of latent power or ability which can be turned into real effective work. The elimination of waste power and the turning of every force to advantage is the secret of high efficiency.

Every golfer is of limited ability—some more so, others less. We can't always help that. But I believe that I can make a few common sense suggestions, which have nothing to do with technique, that will help to take strokes off any man's game.

The first real big lesson I learned, and it was medal competition that taught me, was that every stroke in the round was of equal importance, and that each one was worthy of, and demanded the same amount of concentration. Before I had much experience I would invariably allow myself to become careless when confronted by a simple-looking shot. A wide fairway or a big green was always the hardest for me to hit. But no golf shot is easy, unless it is played with a precise and definite purpose, and with perfect and complete concentration upon results. The easiest way to assure minute attention on every shot is to cultivate a frame of mind that will be satisfied by nothing less than perfection. If it looks easy to play onto the green, try to get close to the hole; if it looks easy to get within the ten-foot radius, and then try to lay it dead. Always strive to go as far towards the ultimate end of holing out as it is reasonably possible to go.

The surest way to collect sevens and eights, and to pile up a disgraceful score is to become angry and rattled. It won't cost much in the way of strokes when you slice a drive or pull an iron if you throw your club away or curse your luck because you still have time to get over it before the next shot. But if you look up in the bunker and leave your ball sitting where it was, you had best think twice before you hit it again.

I discovered long ago that I had to control my temper in tournament play as a matter of utility, aside from considerations of decent behavior. My first reaction, when I had indulged my temper before spectators, was one of shame and regret, and when I came to the next shot, I was still thinking more of the temper I had shown than of the shot I was then trying to make.

Sometimes I thought how useless would appear my anger if by any chance I should lay the next one dead, or hole a putt and retrieve my fortunes. But in whatever direction my embarrassment led me, the result was a loss of effectiveness, not only for the remainder of that hole, but for several holes thereafter until I could bring myself back to earth.

No virtue in this world is so oft rewarded as per-

Another view of Bobby playing before a crowd. Here again his face shows signs of physical strain.

severance. Don't give up just because you are bunkered in three, and your opponent is on the green in two. You might hole out, and he might take three putts. It doesn't happen often, but you can never tell. I myself have found the value of playing the fifth shot just as carefully as the second. In former times I used to fly off the handle after I had messed up a couple of shots and would usually throw away two or three more strokes as the result. But I can appreciate now that it is just as important in medal play to hole a good putt for a seven as for a three.

Take Your Time

I used to be a very rapid player. I am still fairly fast—after I have taken my stance. But at Merion in 1925, I discovered that I was missing a lot of shots simply because I was hitting the ball too soon after I had reached it, especially on the putting green. Having walked up to the green at a brisk pace, and elbowed my way through whatever

gallery there might have been, I had been putting quickly while my breath was coming in short gasps and my ears ringing as I leaned over the ball.

Realizing that I was making a mistake, I resolved that no matter how much time I consumed I was going to tranquilize my breathing before I made another putt. So I began to take great pains to study the line. I really did not study the line, for I have never been able to see more rolls and humps in a minute than I could in five seconds, but I was giving my breath a chance. You have no idea what a steadying effect upon the nerves can be had by doing some little thing in a natural manner. Light a cigarette, pick up a twig, or do anything to take up a little time, you will find this will help to calm you nerves.

And that applies equally to shots through the green. Don't hit the ball until you are ready, until every other consideration has been excluded from the mind.

Another thing that often helps: When you have located the line to the hole and addressed the putt, often something gets blurred and you lose the line. Don't go ahead and putt anyway for you must surely miss. Step away and start over again. You didn't have a chance at first; you might make it now.

Worry Detrimental

In playing any golf shot, it always helps if the player can shut out from his mind all worry over the result of the effort, at least while he is in the act of playing the shot. It is well to be apprised of all dangers, and the chances of failure, and the penalty likely to be incurred in the event of such failure ought to be weighed carefully before deciding upon the shot. But after taking the stance, it is too late to worry. The only thing to do then is to hit the ball!

I have touched on this subject before, but I do not believe it is possible to stress it unduly. It is not an easy matter, even with the assistance of a first-class teacher, for a man to develop a sound golfing style. But it is possible and practicable for a person to cultivate an attitude toward the game which will enable him to get everything possible out of his known capabilities.

Medal competition is the most diabolical sort of golf because it puts so many worries into the player's head. Unseen rivals are pictured as never missing a shot. When we ourselves make a slip, we feel that every man in the field is going to take advantage of it. We cannot conceive that the others are likely having difficulties at least equalling our own. Strangely too, every report borne about among the gallery which reaches the player's ears has to do with the marvelous start, or "three birdies in a row," made by someone else. If a man listens to and credits all these reports, he can hardly be blamed for stumbling a bit.

Harry Vardon always said, "No matter what happens, keep on hitting the ball." No man was ever successful at medal or match play without some such philosophy to work upon.

Suppose your opponent plays a beautiful iron shot dead on the flag, and from the place where you stand his ball appears to be within inches of the hole. What will you do? Very likely you will strain every muscle and nerve to lay your ball beside, or closer than, his. You will try so hard to do this that you will probably hook or slice into a bunker and permit your opponent to win the hole without the necessity of holing the putt!

What you should do is about as follows: Tell yourself that your opponent's ball is not likely to be as close to the hole as it appears to be. Probably he is short, and at least may have left a very missable putt. Tell yourself, also, that you are going to try to hit your shot well in order to get close to the hole, but that you will make sure that you get on the green somewhere within reasonable holing distance so that your opponent will at least have to hole his putt to win the hole.

Lots and lots of holes are won by good second shots which look formidable and yet are not really so deadly as they appear. An approach may stop only six or eight feet away from the hole, yet there still remains the putt to be holed, which is not always a simple procedure. The man who keeps one eye on the ball on the green while he is playing his own, is simply looking for trouble, and he usually finds it.

On the putting green, too, it is often hard to keep from thinking about the importance of the putt rather than about hitting the ball

Bobby Jones plays a chip shot in an exhibition to benefit the unemployed over the links of the Essex CC in West Orange, New Jersey in September 1931.

properly. The thought that a miss may mean defeat, or at least an almost hopeless position, is often an absolute bar to concentration. The observer can usually tell what is in the player's mind by the way in which he strokes the ball, even when the putt, by good fortune, tumbles in. A quick, nervous jab betrays the anxiety in the player's mind.

The Strain of Competitive Golf

While I realize that only a very few of my readers have championship ambitions, or desire in any way to acquire great reputations as competitive players, I can't help thinking that even to those casual golfers who play once a week or less, with never a thought of even a club competition, it must be interesting to see how the other fellows feel about things, and to see what difficulties they must encounter

which the average player is never called upon to meet.

Innis Brown, I think, said that there was no strain in sport as great as the pressure of the last nine holes of an open championship when the pace was hot and the field close. I could not be prepared to go that length for I have never engaged seriously in any other sport, but I can say that there is nothing else like it in golf.

In no length of play in vogue today is physical condition—that is, endurance and stamina—of more than passing importance. General good health, without intensive training or conditioning is sufficient. Golf is not exacting upon the physical powers of a man, but it is trying upon his nerves, and the nervous strain usually reacts in some way upon the physical body.

I remember standing beside my ball in the eighteenth fairway at Columbus, gazing toward the green, and wishing devoutly that my knees would stop knocking together long enough for me to hit the ball. Up until that shot I had been nervous, of course, but the tension had been all of the kind that fires the muscles with energy and fills the heart with determination. But when I reached the point when I had only to play an iron shot to a wide-open green and go down in two putts to win the championship, I suppose I got the "buckague." I began to think how miserable would be a failure at that point. My attitude became entirely defensive where before it had been aggressive, and right now, I think it was only the merest accident that I got that shot onto the green.

I suppose everyone has experienced the feeling that I have tried to describe, but I have encountered another difficulty to which I think I may claim sole rights, and which I am unable to overcome. It has its inception, I suppose, in some mistake of diet, but it is nevertheless directly traceable to nervous disturbance.

During the past three or four years, throughout the early morning of every day of competition, I have found myself continually on the verge of active nausea. It cannot be that my breakfast causes it for I am rarely able to eat anything at that meal; and it cannot be, as Ty Cobb has found in his case, that the cream in coffee is to blame, for I give up everything even remotely connected with milk or cream when engaged in competition.

Whatever is the cause, it is most unpleasant and it usually renders me unable to button my shirt collar or to put on a neck-tie at least until late in the morning. When I played Evans at Minikahda I went tieless and with my collar open all morning because of it.

Nervous indigestion, or nausea, whatever you choose to call it, is by no means peculiar to golfers, nor is it a malady to which only one man of a class may lay claim. Competition in sport has come to be a very serious business—at the time—and those who engage in it are going to have to suffer the temporary discomforts which it entails. It is a safe guess that every man in a golf tournament is carrying a burden of one kind or another. Each and every one is always glad when each round is finished, sometimes when each hole is passed. But there is something about it which always makes them come back for more.

At Harvard my roommate was captain of the track team and performed for it in the quarter-mile event. I don't believe he has in his life run the distance, even in practice, without at the end becoming violently ill and on the verge of collapse. But the next afternoon he was at it again and as keen as before.

There is no question that nervousness causes a digestive derangement which may impair efficiency. That is the principal reason that I avoid taking on a quantity of food during the day when engaged in competition. Easily digested food, and as little of that as possible is the best order.

High-Strung Temperament Best

I used to think that if I could suppress a feeling of nervousness when starting out to play a match, I could then play a better and more thoughtful game. I have since come to think that the man who goes placidly on his way is often the easiest fellow to beat, for it is only the high-strung temperament that rises above its own ability to meet a great occasion.

Watts Gunn is the outstanding illustration. Playing in local or minor sectional tournaments Watts is very likely to be beaten by an inferior player, simply because he cannot become anxious about the outcome until it is too late. I have seen him time and again allow himself to become two, three and even four down, before his peril would rouse him to play the kind of golf of which he is capable. But if he starts against Sweetser, or Von Elm, or anyone he fears, he is a worthy opponent from the very start.

Von Elm and Sweetser, two great match-players among the amateurs, are of the nervous type. They are as high-strung as any thoroughbred race horses. It is that which makes certain that they will never descend to plodding mediocrity, that they will always be at the top of the game.

Almost every contestant leaves the first tee with a certain amount of apprehension in his soul. But a lot of them make the mistake of

trying to assume an indifferent attitude which it was not meant they should have. In trying to quiet a pounding heart or still a trembling hand, it is quite possible to fall into a lazy slackness which cannot be shaken. The competitor who can keep himself "on edge" is the hard man to beat.

Concentrate on Game

In playing competitive golf there is nothing so important as concentrating upon the game. And, unfortunately, it isn't simply a matter of concentrating upon the shot while you are standing over the ball. Just as soon as one shot is played the player's mind becomes busy with the next and the only rest comes after the last putt is holed.

To illustrate how serious a lack of concentration can be, here's a little incident which occurred when I attended my first open championship. I was struck particularly with Jock Hutchison. Jock had played magnificent golf in the qualifying rounds at Toledo, and was looked upon by everyone as the most likely candidate for the championship.

I first saw Jock in that round as he approached the twelfth green. The twelfth at Toledo is a long three-shotter and Jock was on nicely in three. He ran his approach putt up about three feet past the hole, and as he walked forward to hole out he caught sight of my head, craning over some conveniently low shoulder. "They won't drop today, Bobby," said he, and continued with some Scotch sallies which started the gallery twittering!

Jock Hutchison and Bob Jones as they started their first round in the 1930 U.S. Open Championship at Interlachen GC. (P&A Photos)

At that time Jock looked a certain winner but he slipped a few strokes in the closing holes and finished one stroke behind Ted Ray, who won. I thought then, and have since, that Jock Hutchison, if his Scotch blood had given him the proverbial dourness instead of a gay wit, would have been champion many times.

To a man with the temperament of Hutchison, distraction may be relief, but to the other ninety-nine of the hundred, golf is an exacting game which requires every bit of one's attention.

Of course, ideal golfing temperaments are not always heaven-sent. The calm thoughtfulness of Johnny Farrell as he steps up to a shot is not secured without effort. But Johnny has learned like many others that that battle must be won before the shot is played, no matter how many minutes are required.

Farrell, however, is not unique in the possession of nerves. Everybody has them, and they always make themselves known on a golf course.

Fear of What Might Happen Leads Golfers Into Trouble

In golf the chief difference between practice and actual play is the sense of responsibility which attaches to every shot played during the round. There are many who can produce a fine swing when it is aimed at a daisy but cannot repeat the performance with a ball before them. There are others who hit perfect shots off a practice tee but lose the knack upon the course; and there are still others who play well enough until they find themselves mixed up in a tournament.

This would certainly indicate that there are varying degrees of responsibility which different golfers can bear. The game of one can stand very little, of another a bit more, and so on. And even the stoutest and most determined somewhere, sometime, encounter strains which snap the cords of concentration.

This disturbing sense of responsibility which ruins so many shots and so many rounds is nothing in the world but fear—dread of what may happen to the shot about to be played. This is the way in which bunkers around the green exert their greatest effect. Few of them are placed so close to the hole that they will catch a well-hit shot. But the player takes one look at the expanse of sand and immediately finds himself on the defensive. His effort is to avoid the bunker rather than to hit the shot. He flinches on the stroke and spoils the shot.

The last look of concentration before Master Bobby Jones begins his backswing. Bobby is 14 years young here.

New Layout Easiest First Time

Most of the pros will say that a course is easier the first time played than for the next several rounds. The reason for this is quite obvious. The player, unfamiliar with the course, sees only where the shot should finish. He has the line pointed out to him but no one takes the trouble to warn him of the hazards. He then hits the ball direct for the objective with no thought of trouble ahead.

In playing various charity matches I myself have gained a little experience along that line. I have found that if the putting greens are good and the distances not too hard to judge, I almost always play a course better the first time than I do for the next four or five rounds. It is one of those phenomena which are hard to explain without resorting to some speculation.

Worries Detract from Game

When the player is familiar with the course and has played it many times, as each hole comes up to be played, it is natural, I think, for him to conjure up in his mind visions of the ways in which he has encountered trouble on that hole. He will remember how he sliced his second shot into a trap and took a six or seven. Then as he hits the ball he will be determined to avoid the trap at all costs. There is then a part of his concentration taken up with something he ought not to do, and that is so much taken away from the ability to play the stroke correctly.

When playing a course for the first time there are no unpleasant recollections coming up to spoil the shot. The player usually sees only the flag and the green, and if his glance does fall upon a guarding bunker it is only for a moment. The hazards are all a part of the background, instead of being in the center of the picture.

The ability to hit the shot for the flag and to let trouble take care of itself is a rare attribute among golfers. I think it is one of the chief fortes of Walter Hagen and Harry Cooper. Neither appears to give a thought to what may happen to the shot. I am sure that they see only the green as a possible destination for the ball.

I suppose it is some complex of this sort that has caused me to find upon every course at least one hole that I simply cannot play. Once I get into trouble on it, I cannot play it.

Play Full Shot

Fear is also the cause of the ruinous habit of steering the shot. Nothing is more certain to swing the ball off line than a too determined effort to guide it straight.

Very much the same results follow when the player is in two minds about what club to use or how hard to hit the ball. The feeling of uncertainty usually causes him to hit the shot halfheartedly or to attempt at the last instant to put in a little extra power which he feels he needs. When there is any doubt about the shot to play it is my idea that the best plan is to select the less-powerful club and play a full shot.

Those Hoodoo Holes!

The ideal golf course must require strategy as well as skill, otherwise it cannot be enduringly interesting.
A really great course must be pleasurable to the greatest possible number.

On nearly every golf course I have played I have found at least one hole which has completely baffled me at every attempt. In every open championship I have had some "jinx" hole which, in the four rounds, has cost me a hat full of strokes. And the hard thing to explain is that these holes very often have no common characteristics, no features of design, upon which I can lay my finger as having penetrated a particular fault in my game. I seem to have as much trouble at short holes as long ones, and throughout a week's play, I will have trouble day after day at the same holes.

Possibly the best explanation of this is that I yield to a sort of weak-minded conviction that a particular hole has the "Indian Sign" on me and am therefore really beaten by it before I get to it. Somehow, when I begin a round, on the very first tee, I start thinking about getting past that cursed hole, and it worries me until I get past it, and usually afterward, if I waste a few strokes there.

After you have played a hole badly and have continued to do so, you often find yourself wondering what has been so hard about it. Sometimes you simply can't think of any reason why you should have taken that six, and you could never believe you had done so if the figures were not on your card.

Both Simple and Severely Trapped Holes Hard

There are just two classes of really difficult holes on a golf course; the first is made up of those that are so exacting, so severely bunkered, that they just escape being unfair; the second class embraces those holes, so familiar in Britain, whose simplicity is disarming and upon which you can take a lot of strokes without getting into much trouble.

Naturally, any hole which demands a superbly accurate shot to avoid trouble is a hard one to play. Almost every hole on the Oakmont course comes within this class, and the fifteenth notably so, because it requires two shots of the kind mentioned. I do not have to seek for a reason for having trouble there. It was simply a matter of too much hole.

But most of the others were easy affairs, with nothing much in the way of a good shot, and plenty of room on the green. But a very large green often makes a hole difficult. The long approach putt is about the hardest shot in the game, at least for me, and any green which is large enough to make possible putts of thirty and forty yards is a terror to me.

Targeted Green Preferred by Good Iron Players

A good iron player will always prefer to shoot at what, in golf parlance, is known as a "targeted" green; that is, one clearly defined by bunkers and elevated in the rear. If the shot is not unfair, a green of this kind is much easier to hit than one which has the appearance of covering half the horizon. The tremendous expanse of putting surface has the effect, I think, of relaxing one's concentration. The shot appears so easy that it actually becomes hard. Somehow, you can't get

THOSE HOODOO HOLES!

away from the feeling that on the green is good enough, when in reality the long putt may be harder than a short pitch.

Of the two kinds of holes which I have named, I think the innocent-looking, disarming ones are the hardest to play. The obviously difficult holes put us on our mettle, and though we may miss the shot, we never do so from want of trying. The only way I see to conquer the others is to play only for the flag and forget how large the green is.

An Uncomfortable Mental Hazard

Harold Hilton, the great English amateur, is reputed to have conquered certain holes by playing them a dozen times after dinner in the long British twilight, until he felt that he had overcome whatever fear had at first seized him. Certainly, Mr. Hilton's plan was a very good one as his record will attest. I must confess that I have often thought of trying it myself, and more often regretted that I had not. It appears to me to be the only reasonable way to convince oneself that the hole is not impossible after all.

The feeling is far from comfortable to start upon every round of a championship with visions of disaster upon a certain hole in one's mind.

Golfer Who Could Ignore Fear Would Be Good

It is, of course, a great tribute to a golf course, that no competitor can feel that his troubles are over after he passes a certain hole. Too many of the courses offered for competitions afford few worries except upon a few holes. Usually if the player gets past a certain point without suffering material damage, he feels that he can go the rest of the way in comparative safety.

I wonder what Mr. Hilton would do if he found troublesome not a hole or two, but nine of them all in succession. I should think that would be too many to play a dozen times in the evening, even in England.

Yet for weeks at home, I will continue to play the first nine badly and the second nine well. Then for no apparent reason the worm will turn and all my good scores begin to come on the first nine. It seems to run in streaks.

One or two psychologists have undertaken to tell us something about the golfer's worries.

I wish they could tell us more, for if ever a man can learn to bring himself into the right frame of mind, and can learn to approach each hole and each shot with a mind in which there will be no fear of future, nor remembrance of past, difficulties, he will be as nearly unbeatable as it is possible to be in a game of uncertainties such as golf unquestionably is.

In 1926 Bobby Jones and the US Walker Cup team played a match against "The Moles" at Woking, England. The Moles prevailed 6-3
(F.R. Furber; The Times).

BOBBY JONES ON GOLF

Bobby Jones negotiates a grass bunker in the 1928
United States Amateur at Brae Burn Golf Club.

Negotiating the stymie required a niblick
chip over the opponents ball.

Last look of a champion before extracting
the ball from a difficult lie.

The Part Luck Plays in Golf

The 1928 National Amateur Championship at Brae Burn GC where Bob's ball on the sixth hole nearly found the brook. (P&A Photos)

We have all heard, and most of us have had occasion to know, that luck plays a great part in all golf matches. Whether long putts are dropping, or whether approach shots are bounding toward the hole or away from it, makes all the difference in the world. The effect of luck of this kind is cumulative and often it is not recognized at the time. It makes its appearance simply as superior skill.

Often in golf we see luck so colossal that it is really shameful. Impossible results are obtained through nothing more than the merest chance.

It is, of course, impossible to participate in or witness a great deal of competitive golf without recognizing the tremendous part played by the breaks of fortune. In any game in which a ball is driven over an uneven terrain the element of luck is bound to be of great importance. Two balls striking the ground only a yard apart may finish, one in a bunker, the other near the hole. That, of course, is expected. But why a lucky bound or a putt that stays out or goes in often changes the whole aspect of a match is not so easy to explain.

Sometimes the winning of one hole which in itself is not important, a long putt that drops or an iron shot finishing close to the hole; or even a careless or indecisive stroke from his adversary, will give to one player a feeling of confidence and determination to win which transforms him from a listless human into a whirling dynamo.

Of an occurrence based on the last contingency, no better illustration can be given than the amazing transformation in Chick Evans' appearance in the match with Reggie Lewis at the Engineers Club in 1920, when Lewis missed his putt to halve the hole and win.

As Chick walked slowly onto that last green, he looked to be hopelessly beaten, and his manner showed plainly that he thought so. All the while Lewis was preparing to play his chip from behind the green, Evans was pacing to and fro across the lower edge. He fidgeted with his putter and with his cap, unable to stand still. But when Lewis missed his putt and the match was even—Evans seemed to be struck with an electric charge. If his tired body was exhausted before, there was no sign of it visible as he came rushing up the slope to the first tee. Chick was all eagerness to win now that he had been given another chance.

Such an incident is enough to bolster a player's morale and he goes romping on to glory.

But more intangible than that is another "something"—call it luck or anything else—which on certain days seems to hover over the golfer and prevents his doing anything wrong. The golfer speaks of it when he says that "the ball was rolling for him."

When the ball is rolling for you no score is impossible and it doesn't seem to matter much whether you hit the shots correctly or not. It is an inexorable sort of thing from which there is apparently no escape. That is, for the opponent. The player himself does not want to escape it. If you are a believer in predestination, I suppose you can figure that you have been allotted a certain score for that day and make it you must!

In this connection, the most astonishing experience I ever had was at Flossmoor this past fall. The occasion was a one-round medal competition to honor the memory of a splendid Chicago boy and fine golfer, Warren Wood. The members of the British and American Walker Cup teams journeyed over from Wheaton, where they were quartered, to take part.

We started off in a four ball match—Bill Tweddell and I, paired against Phil Perkins and Chick Evans. We were getting a very late start and none of us was too serious, all wanting to save something for the Cup match two days off, and a good bit more interested in our match upon which we had a wager of a dollar Nassau than in compiling a score. Winning the competition was something none of us expected to do.

I started badly enough, and a five at the short seventh left me at that point three over an average of fours, and three over par. Then something happened! The ball began to roll for me, and the next eleven holes were done in thirty-six strokes! If I had suddenly started to play that kind of golf; if I had hit the shots any better from that point on, there would be nothing remarkable about the occurrence. The point is that I did not do that. I missed as many shots on the last nine as I had on the first, but my score was lower by a matter of seven strokes!

Threes on the eighth and ninth were made possible by pitches which brought up close to the holes and putts of ten and six feet respectively. That was all right, and I was willing to accept credit for them. I felt it was about time I did something for my side. At that Bill and I only halved both holes, for Chick holed a three at the eighth, and Phil one at the ninth.

On the tenth I pushed my drive to the rough and played out into a bunker short of the green. So that I might join in the search with the others for Phil's ball in the rough back of the green, I played my shot and holed out for another three that might easily have been a five. The next hole, a short one, I got in three because a badly pushed iron shot refused to go off the edge of the green. At the next hole, two fairly good shots and a seven yard putt yielded another three, and the short thirteenth was made in three uneventfully.

At the fourteenth a short pitch stopped a foot from the hole and another three resulted. That made seven three's in a row, at least four of which could be called lucky.

Then came the fifteenth, and I was beginning to be suspicious of all this prosperity. Off the tee I hit a wild drive to the right among some imposing trees. As it disappeared I heard a crack and saw the ball come spinning back into the fairway in easy reach of the green. Four there, and three at the next.

At the seventeenth my second shot–an iron– was badly pulled and a good bit too long. But I had been allotted a four there so a ten-foot putt went in. Four at the last made thirty for the last nine.

I give my word that with the way I had been playing, a thirty-six or thirty-seven would have been a satisfactory score.

There is no way to explain the amazing difference in the scores up to the eighth hole and from that point on in, except by saying that "the ball was rolling for me." Every golfer knows what it means. It is a whole lot more effective than all the skill in the world.

A Blind Niblick Shot

I should like to give here two other instances of this phenomenal luck that stand out in my mind, not because they occurred in championship matches, but because they were instrumental in helping my partner and me win two matches which we were very anxious to win.

The shots which I am going to describe were almost identical in character, and both came from my club. Other than that I can claim no credit for them, and little more for my part in the matches which they helped to win.

My partner in one match was Jock Hutchison, and in the other Jess Sweetser. Both played brilliantly–indeed, I think Jock played the finest golf I have ever seen.

The first one with Jock was at Memphis in 1921 just before the national amateur at St. Louis. Jock and I were playing Mitchell and Duncan at the Colonial Club. The match was all square, or we were one or two down—I can't remember which—when we came to the eighth hole of the second round.

The green at this hole was built up quite high in the back and I had gone over with my second shot. I had played the role of spectator most of the day and was anything but hopeful of having any great share in the match. Mitchell's second shot lay a bare two yards from the hole, but Jock was only ten or twelve feet away. I thought that the best thing I could do would be to get my ball up on the green and out of the way as quickly as possible.

The difference between a winner and near-winner is the ability not to play a shot carelessly or with over-confidence.(USGA)

The back of the green was so high and the flag was so near the front that it could not be seen from where my ball lay. I grabbed a niblick from my bag, ran down the bank, paused only long enough to swipe the ball without looking at the flag, and dashed back up the slope to the green. I reached the top just in time to see my ball disappear into the cup! Mitchell missed and we won the hole, and I am sure that I had no intention of doing so.

Jock came home in 31 against a par of thirty-six, and I had a three on one hole where he took five. At that we won by only two-and-one.

A Great Comeback

The second with Jess Sweetser occurred in a match against Hagen and Sarazen in 1923 at Winged Foot. Walter and Gene had us five down at lunch and we were doing plenty of good-natured kidding. Jess and I got the worst of that, too, for it is difficult to produce any effective repartee when you are five down.

But in the afternoon, Jess and I had our inning. With a very little assistance from me, Jess with two birdies and some beautiful golf, had cut their lead to two holes. And then at the tenth, a spoon shot of about 210 yards, everyone was on the green but me. My ball lay in the rough grass fifteen yards to the right and down a steep slope. The shot was an almost exact duplicate of the one at Memphis, although this time I did look at the flag. But, in some unaccountable way, it went in too!

The most astonished person in the whole crowd, on both occasions when those shots went in, was myself. If I had earnestly and painstakingly tried to play either, they could never have come close to the hole.

When Hagen Turned the Tide

I might give numerous instances where one little bit of luck has turned the tide. Very often, indeed, the effect upon the result is much greater than in either case I have mentioned. For instance, although I did not see the match, I am confident that had not Sarazen knocked Hagen's ball into the cup at the sixth hole of their Florida match, the result would have been very different, might even have been as great a victory for Gene as it was for Walter. Gene had won three of the first five holes and was left with a short putt to win the sixth. But Hagen stymied him with his long putt, and Gene, set upon winning the hole, knocked Walter in for a win instead. Sarazen's psychological advantage was thereby transferred to Hagen, who proceeded promptly to win the next two holes to bring the match back to even terms.

In golf, we can never tell when the tables of fate will turn. The holing of one long putt may set us off on an inspired burst which will sweep us off our feet. So we can never be sure of victory or defeat until the last putt is in the hole. Until then we must play every shot as well as we possibly can. Having done that, we can do no more though the heavens fall.

Fighting the Wind!

Bob Jones putts on perhaps the most treacherous one-shotter in golf--the 12th hole at Augusta National Golf Club. This 1935 practice round included
Dick Metz, Ed Dudley and Ky Laffoon. (Frank Christian Studios)

Although conditions of ground and weather do objectively affect the playing of golf, a great deal of the adverse effect is caused by the state of the player's mind. A hard wind or a heavy rain inspires in the player a feeling of combativeness or of desperation, and prevents him from going about his business in an equable frame of mind. He is tempted to strive to do a little bit more than he can—to hit a little harder, or to exercise a nicer control. Only after a lot of experience, does one learn that best results are reached by refusing to regard the elements, except as a circumstance to be considered in deciding upon the character and direction of the shot. If we regard them as definite contrary forces which must be overcome, they in reality become very powerful enemies.

It has always been my opinion that a gale of wind was more trying on the nerves of the player than upon his mechanical ability to control a golf ball. No degree of perfection has yet appeared which will not be affected to some extent by a high wind. Every player in the field will miss more shots because of it, and encounter hazards which otherwise might have been beyond the reach of an ordinary mistake. Under these circumstances, it is appallingly easy for one to lose one's head, to become unduly depressed, and to throw away additional strokes quite needlessly.

When one remembers that a thirty-mile cross-wind will cause a drift of approximately ten feet in one thousand yards' travel of a high velocity Springfield bullet, it is not surprising that a cross-wind will deflect the flight of a golf ball. The wind effect, of course, is less upon a well-hit shot than upon one which has been hit with a spin, carrying it in the direction of the wind. It is possible to hook or slice into the face of the breeze just enough to make the ball travel in a straight line. But in any event, the current of air is as much a part of the golf course as the fairways, hazards, and greens where the ball comes to rest.

The wind directly behind or directly against the player bestows in each case compensating advantages and disadvantages. The following wind adds yards to the drive but it makes the approach shots far more difficult. Often a steep pitch played downwind is blown completely out of control. The opposite wind materially lessens the range of all the shots but it makes much easier the shots to the green. There is a great deal of comfort in the knowledge that a pitch can be played boldly for the hole, with the certainty that the wind will stop it no matter how hard the green may be.

In playing across the wind, the player has two courses open to him, either one promising as much disaster as can be found on a golf course. These are the times when he needs most a finished control of his stroke, a keen ability to estimate the force of the currents, and plenty of nerve to back up his judgment and execution. The two shots between which he must choose are, first, a straight shot off line into the wind, allowing just enough so that the ball will drift back to the objective; or, second, a shot directly on the line with just enough draw or fade to counteract the force of the breeze and straighten the flight of the ball.

I say that a good deal of nerve is required in either case because when one sets oneself for a shot under these conditions it is apparent what a mistake will mean. Errors are never slight when a wind is blowing, and the ball, once out of control and at the mercy of a gale, is likely to be carried far afield.

To me it has always seemed the safer practice to hit a normally straight shot designed to ride in on the wind. If it comes off right the ball travels almost on a ruled line until its force is nearly spent, when the effect of the current is more easily felt. This method is simpler because the normal shot is a straight one and the only complication is the allowance for drift. If one elects to draw or fade into the wind, there is added to the wind factor the difficulty of executing a controlled hook or slice.

Separates Good and Bad Golf

In any open championship, it is interesting to note the havoc wrought among the leading competitors by even one windy day. Nothing has yet been devised which provides such an infallible method of separating the sheep from the goats. The separation is not always accomplished on the basis of inherent ability, but a gusty day always annihilates the competitor who has been eking good scores out of poor golf.

I can think of no more apt illustration of this process of separation than what happened to me in the Western Open in 1920. On the first two days the air was calm and the course very fast. At no time was I playing what the English call "convincing" golf, but my inaccuracies were never sufficient to cause me a great deal of trouble so that by good putting and a fair share of luck I scored a 69 the first day and a 70 on the second. But the concluding day dawned with a fairly formidable wind blowing and I was a goat–for that day, at least. I don't believe that I played worse golf than on the previous two days, but iron shots which had found the outer reaches of the green were now falling into sand pits, and drives which had barely missed the rough were now missing nothing. To my 69-70 was added a disgraceful eighty-three. The men who had been making 72's and 73's by playing good golf continued to make them, and went on their ways rejoicing.

No especial degree of skill is required to overcome a wind of less than gale velocity. It is surprising how little directional effect is had upon the flight of a ball which has been truly struck. Of course, a head wind greatly curtails range, and often makes it impossible to reach some of the longer holes in two shots. But a well-hit shot will

Bob Jones successfully defends the British Open Championship in 1927 at St. Andrews.

cling tenaciously to its projected line until its force is almost entirely spent. At the end of its flight, the ball may slide this way or that, according to the wind, but that small amount of drift is easily allowed for.

But a strong wind will completely ruin a mis-hit shot. If a cross-wind once gets hold of a hook or slice veering in the same direction, there is no limit of the course to which the ball may not go. Errors are magnified ten times and shots which ordinarily would escape penalty often cause the loss of several strokes.

Many players—particularly the fellows who score close to ninety—allow themselves to be stampeded by the wind. They feel the necessity for doing something which they have not the skill to accomplish and, in attempting it, it is likely that they will commit a greater error than if they would simply hit the ball and let it go at that. Seldom is the ordinary club member called upon to play on days when the weather ought to give him a great amount of trouble. If he would refuse to be annoyed because he could not reach a few holes in the accustomed number of stokes, and would make a small allowance each time he confronted a cross-wind, in the end his score would be little affected.

A good number of golfers who have a right to be rated above the average are quite happy with the game so long as conditions remain pleasant and normal. But a little wind or a drop or two of rain immediately throws them into such a panic that they can by no means do themselves justice. Sometimes their dejection reaches the extent of complaint and protest against a situation which they can in no wise alter. It is, of course, reasonable to expect that unfavorable weather will add a few strokes to the score in the end, but there is no reason to allow a toll of a dozen or more.

Walter Hagen last year furnished an outstanding example of what can be done by keeping and using one's head. It was in the second round of the open championship at Olympia Fields. Walter had gone out in 40 and had played the tenth hole only of the incoming nine when he was overtaken by a veritable torrent of rain accompanied by some amount of wind. I had finished only a short while before the storm broke and had reached the shelter of the clubhouse in time. Looking out from my window I could scarcely see through the rain to the tenth tee, not over 100 yards away. I naturally thought of Hagen's situation. Out in 40, it seemed unlikely that he could better that figure coming home. An eighty for the round would mean, substantially, elimination.

But Hagen did on that nine what no golfer in the world could do as well as he. He shut his eyes and his mind to the rain and wind. He thought of only one thing—of getting the ball into the cup—and he came back in 33. I saw him afterward and asked him in wonder how he had been able to accomplish the remarkable score. He apparently wasn't quite sure himself—just played golf— which, after all, is a pretty fair explanation.

Wind is unquestionably a serious hazard especially because it magnifies errors in hitting and carries to disaster shots which on a calm day would escape without penalty. But because this is true the more accurate hitter a player is, the more his margin of superiority would be increased by a heavy wind. A lifetime of education is not needed to teach a person of ordinary intelligence about how much to allow for the effect of a cross-wind. It isn't a case where a great deal of experience is needed if the player is able to strike the ball accurately.

Golf in Gale Test of Temperament

The fact that this year the Walker cup match will be played over the Royal St. George's links at Sandwich, recalls the instructive though not wholly agreeable day our men spent there in 1926. A competitive golfer has to put up with all sorts of weather and has to ride it through, for to take shelter during a medal round means instant disqualification. Through fourteen years of tournament play I have seen at least my share, but I have never seen anything even remotely approaching that day at Sandwich playing for the St. George's Gold Vase. To the American players a dragon breathing fire, or anything else bearing a promise of warmth, would have been a welcome sight.

I remember my thoughts on awaking that morning and looking out from my window over a very turbulent English Channel and hearing

FIGHTING THE WIND!

the wind whistling under the sash of the window. I had heard of the boisterous weather of the channel coast but somehow I had not pictured it in connection with golf. Now the connection was becoming entirely too close for comfort.

Under ordinary conditions, or rather I should say, under conditions which we Americans regard as ordinary, St. George's is not an unusually difficult course. True, the first nine are tricky and deceiving, and the second nine are rather long, but on the whole, scoring there is not a test of meticulous accuracy. But when the wind blows in true Sandwich fashion the problem is something else entirely.

There were in the field this day all the members of the American team, all the members of the British team, and almost every other amateur of prominence in Great Britain. On the previous day, I myself arriving for a practice round had scored a seventy-three with little difficulty. Yet of the fine field eighty was the low score of the morning round and seventy-eight of the afternoon, Major Charles Hezlett doing both and winning the medal.

A Putt in Reverse

One really amusing thing happened to one of our players—I think it was Jesse Gilford—whose approach to the ninth green had come to rest shakily upon the crest of a ridge which skirted the right edge of the putting surface. Jesse, preparing to putt, placed his putter on the turf behind his ball. The putter blade shut off the wind and the ball starting to roll, continued into the rough. The putter had then to be exchanged for a mashie-niblick, a necessity which added not a bit to Jesse's enjoyment of the day.

I had always regarded with annoyance a wind of sufficient force to back up a tee shot twenty or twenty-five yards. Not only did the Sandwich gale blow the ball back at the player, but it made a problem of standing up long enough to hit the ball. The player was forced to lean against the wind in order to retain his balance, and during the swing he felt that the club would be wrenched from his hands. I recall, as an example of the increased difficulty of playing, that the Sahara hole, which we had all reached the day before with a drive and a number three iron, was played that day with a full drive, a shot up short of the vast bunker, a brassie across, and a chip or run-up to the green.

I mentioned above that the moderate wind provides a fine test of skill, and that the player who displays the best control and the most resourcefulness in overcoming the difficulties opposed by the elements, demonstrates a clean-cut superiority. But I am not sure that the same thing is true when a real gale is blowing. The chief difficulty then is in maintaining a sufficiently good balance to hit the ball truly. If we could play each shot with ourselves and the ball completely sheltered from the wind, the effect upon scoring would be considerably less. This is particularly true in putting where, because of the delicate stroke and loosened grip, there are times when one fears that the club will be torn from his hands.

Wind a Mental Bunker

The main difficulty offered by a strong breeze arises from its effect upon the mind of the player. After mis-hitting a few shots and watching the wind take them yards off the line, one is very apt to become panicky, and thereby spoil any chance of coming through. It should be borne in mind always that the direction of a well-hit shot is not at all affected by a moderate breeze until its force is spent and the ball is coming down, and that this little drift can be easily taken care of by a small allowance in lining up the shot. In driving even the small allowance may be ignored unless the wind is very heavy for the margin of the fairway is sufficiently great.

It seems to me that the real test is of temperament rather than skill. The reward goes to him who plods along unruffled and unexcited, refusing to become angry with himself or the results of his efforts. The man who can appreciate that eighty is a good score under such conditions, is far ahead of the ambitious one who attempts to subjugate the elements and return his low seventies score in spite of them.

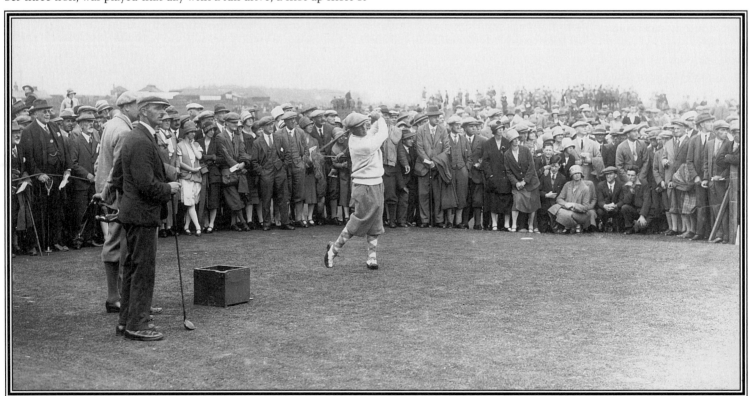

On the 16th tee at St. Andrews in the 1927 British Open Championship. Jones cautions the player to fight tension when the wind blows.

Youngsters Should Play Golf Along With Other Sports

Every golfing father who has a young son coming along entertains hopes more or less ardent that the boy will attain eminence in the royal and ancient game. Not all, of course, are interested in this phase of the youngster's development as the paramount consideration, but nearly everyone is sufficiently interested to give some thought to the best means of encouraging golfing activities. And even those who care little about making champions of their sons would yet like to see them play well enough to enjoy what the fathers think they have missed. I say "think" because I am not sure that the delight of golf is in any way dependent upon the degree of skill with which it is played.

There are two ways of starting a child to learn to play golf, to place him at once under the tutelage of a competent instructor, or to set him free with a few clubs to watch and learn, and work out his own salvation. Which of these is the better depends entirely on the boy and upon his age when he begins to play. Most of our best players began to play at very early ages—5, 6, or 7 years, and most of them started in a sort of haphazard fashion with little idea, I think, that they were doing anything more than amusing themselves.

At nine years young, Bob Jones possessed a full turn and uncommon balance even for a youngster.

It is not even necessary, as a rule, to suggest to the child that he do so. The father's job is merely to interest the boy in the game and to see that he has ample time to potter around with a club and ball in the wake of some one who can really play golf.

A Healthy Exercise

I think that my own experience is indicative of what may happen in the average case. Perry Adair and I began to play golf about the same time-I, a few months before I was six, and Perry, about a year before, when he was nine. Stewart Maiden was the professional at East Lake at the time and Perry and I were turned loose upon the course to play or watch Stewart as we chose. We did quite a lot of both and soon we began to develop fair swings and styles in which even Stewart's mannerisms were evident. Soon, too, we began to play rather decent games, before we had had any instruction whatever. We were, of course, fortunate to have as an example, the graceful, effortless swing of Stewart Maiden, who was at that time as attractive to watch as any man I have ever seen.

Regardless of what ambitions a father may cherish for his boy, he can do far worse than to interest him in playing golf. It keeps him when he is growing, out in the fresh air in about the safest place he can find, and later when he reaches the high school and college age, the game will command a great deal of his spare time which might otherwise be spent in far less profitable pursuits.

Child Will Imitate

I am myself the last person to discourage the free use of professional and expert tuition. For the man who has lost the imitative art of youth, there is nothing that can do his game as much good as competent instruction. But children at the ages when they should begin to play golf are not quite ready for instruction of any kind. At six or seven years they are neither capable of understanding with exactness the things they are told, nor possessed of sufficient patience to practice them if they could understand. I think that any attempt to graft a custom-made swing upon a child of that age would result only in destroying whatever interest he had in the game.

But because the professional is not to have actual charge of the child, and is not to instruct him does not mean that he is not to be responsible for his early development. Fine amateur players are exceedingly rare about the average club, and it is hence to the pro that the child must look for the example which he will imitate if left alone.

A Sport That Can Be Continued

Most boys, when they become old enough to engage in athletics, naturally turn to baseball or football, games which they read about most in the newspapers, and Dad, remembering his days in college, usually encourages them in their ambitions. He immediately begins to picture his boy as a star half-back or second baseman on the team of his Alma Mater, a position which he either played or wished he could play in the old days.

It is a fact though that these football and baseball players when they finish college, unless they gravitate into professional athletics, find themselves suddenly without any means of getting the exercise

YOUNGSTERS SHOULD PLAY GOLF ALONG WITH OTHER SPORTS

and recreation to which they are accustomed. If they are to give any attention to business it is impossible for them to keep in condition to play their favorite games. Baseball and football are far too strenuous to be played on odd afternoons and weekends.

Most of these college athletes turn either to golf or to tennis for their accustomed recreation. But when they take up either game they find that they have a lot to learn. Matured and well-developed muscles are not so easy to mold and train as they were ten years before. Usually these men who have been accustomed to excel on the athletic field are never able to acquire even a fair amount of skill on the golf course. None of them expect or even want to be champions but they all want to rise above the dub class. And the worst of it is that few of them ever do it.

The last thing I should ever do would be to urge a discouragement of football or baseball playing among the younger generation. Aside from other considerations, if there were no college football we should all be deprived of many enjoyable autumn afternoons. But, it is reasonable, I think, to ask that fathers and school teachers try to see to it that the boy's athletic education equips him with an outdoor recreation that he can take through life with him and enjoy. Long after his real athletic days are over he ought to be able to play golf and get a lot of pleasure and real good out of it.

Golf May Soon Be Major Sport in Schools

Preparatory schools throughout the country are taking more and more interest in golf. Some of them employ instructors for the boys and arrange interclass competition to stimulate interest in the game. Many of them have school teams which engage in competition with representatives of other schools.

This is all very fine and should be encouraged, but if the boy plays his first golf after he enters prep school or college, he is still far behind his development in other sports. He has likely played football or baseball for several years and he is not apt to give up any portion of his time to learning a new game. Some effort should be made to interest him in golf or tennis when he begins other sports.

Al Espinosa plays his 294th stroke at the home hole to tie Bob Jones in the 1929 U.S. Open Championship played at Winged Foot G.C. (P&A photos)

The Difference Between British and American Courses

The seventh hole at Pebble Beach in 1929 played by Bob Jones was surrounded by less defined sand hazards than seen today.

The difference between the golf courses of America and of Great Britain can best be expressed by the two words "artificial" and "natural"; and that means a whole lot more than the mere presence or absence of the fabrication of man. The difference begins at the front of the tee and extends to the very back edges of the green, and it is a difference which a player cannot conquer by mechanical proficiency alone. To combat it requires judgment, experience, and as O.B. Keeler would express it, "something between the ears."

To begin with, let us play a round upon the average first-class American course. American architecture allows practically no option as to where the drive shall go. To the expert, there is always the evident desirability of placing the ball on one side or the other of the fairway, but, as a rule, he is much more concerned with avoiding bunkers and long grass along the sides. There is only one safe place for the ball, and it must be put there. The shot is prescribed by the design of the hole–it must be in exactly a certain direction, and, usually, as long as possible.

Suppose, then, that we have made a good drive and our ball is lying nicely in the fairway. From this situation, one of two shots is required–either a long wallop with a brassie with the hope of getting close to the green, or an iron or pitch shot designed to reach the green itself. The brassie shot, being simply an occasion for the application of a strong back, may be dismissed.

The iron shot, like the drive, leaves the player little choice. The green is usually well defined and sloped up toward the rear. Further, it is almost always well-watered, so that any shot with fair height will not go over if it pitches onto the green. The problem is to hit the green, and if that is done, it matters little what spin the ball may have. The soggy green takes the place of the perfect stroke.

Now, let me ask what manner of golfer will be developed by courses of this nature? The answer is–a mechanical shot producer with little initiative and less judgment, and ability only to play the shot as prescribed.

Strategy Required on British Links

Take this man and put him down for the first time on a British seaside links, and watch the result! There the fairways are wide, and the greens are watered only from the skies. The greens are quite unartificial, usually flat or even sloping away from the shot. Bunkers do not surround the green defining the target. In a word, there is no pre-

THE DIFFERENCE BETWEEN BRITISH AND AMERICAN COURSES

Bob Jones driving from the 13th tee at Sunningdale Golf Club in 1926 during perhaps the finest round of golf played in Great Britain comprised of a 66: 33 on the front and 33 on the back, 33 putts and 33 shots.

scription. It is left entirely to the judgment and conscience of the player as to what route he will choose. If the greens are soft, the flag still offers a target, and our shot-making machine will not fare badly. But let there be dry weather for the real show!

I shall never forget how I cursed Hoylake in 1921, and St. Andrews. At that time I regarded as an unpardonable crime, failure to keep the greens sodden, and considered a blind hole an outrage. I wanted everything just right to pitch my iron shots up to the hole. It was the only game I knew, so I blamed the course because I could not play it.

Later, I came to like this seaside golf just as any lover of the game must come to like anything which adds zest to the play. Variable conditions afford ample opportunity for the display of any strategic talent we may possess, and preserve in the most human of games that fascinating personal element which is its chief attraction.

British Courses Need Thought

On an American course we play–indeed, we are forced to play-one stroke at a time. If we played the same hole twice a day for months, we should always be striving to play it in the same manner, usually straight away from tee to cup. We should never change tactics because of wind, rain or dry ground. We should rarely have a choice, or an opportunity to think. Now, British seaside golf cannot be played without thinking. There is always some little favor of wind or terrain waiting for the man who has judgment enough to use it, and there is a little feeling of triumph, a thrill that comes with the knowledge of having done a thing well when a puzzling hole has been conquered by something more than mechanical skill.

And let me say again that our American courses do not require, or foster, that type of golfing skill. Our men have to learn it in England or Scotland, and that is the big reason they cannot play there without experience.

Fascinating St. Andrews

In my humble opinion, St. Andrews is the most fascinating golf course I have ever played. When I first played there–in 1921–I was unable to understand the reverence with which the place was regarded by our British friends. I considered St. Andrews among the very worst courses I had ever seen, and I am afraid I was even disrespectful of its difficulty. The maddening part of the whole thing was that while I was certain the course was easy, I simply could not make a good score. Self-complacently I excused myself by thinking the course was unfair, that the little mounds and undulations should not be there, and because my shots were deflected continually away from the hole, I regarded myself as unlucky.

Yet, I did begin to think a little when a course so unprepossessing forced me to take forty-six to the turn in the third round of the tournament, and finally goaded me into the disgraceful act of picking up my ball after taking a pair of sixes at the tenth and eleventh holes. I must, however, give myself the credit to say that even then I was beginning to know St. Andrews–at least to realize that the Old Course was not to be taken lightly.

In the interim between 1921 and my next visit to Britain in 1926 I heard such a great deal of St. Andrews from Tommy Armour and other Scotsmen who seemed to be convinced that Divine Providence had

No one loved the Old Course at St. Andrews more than Bob Jones. The very fact that the course can be easy when likewise very difficult is a virtue rather than a fault because it is an indication of the variety that can be found there.

had a part in the construction of the course, that I went there determined to make an effort to like it. I really did not have to try very hard. Before I had played two rounds, I loved it and I love it now.

To account for the fascination of the place to one who has not seen it is a very difficult matter. But some little discussion of a few of the holes may show in a measure why I have said it is the finest course I have ever played.

The Famous Road Hole

The seventeenth hole at St. Andrews is the famous Road Hole, and the most historic in golf. It was on that hole that John Henry Taylor, needing only a six and a five, I think, to win the Open Championship, played over into the road and took thirteen strokes!

Watts Gunn and I collaborated at this same hole in one of the most terrifying bits of golf I have ever seen. It was in the Walker Cup matches in 1926 and we were playing Tolley and Jamieson in the Scotch foursomes, which means that each partner plays alternate strokes on the same ball.

Watts and Jamieson were driving. The drive here is supposed to go straight over the middle of a barn, which is out of bounds. Watts just got over, while Jamieson hit the building plump in the middle, and Tolley had to play three off the tee. Cyril, made cautious by his partner's mistake, pulled his drive over into the first fairway.

It was now my turn and I played a conservative spoon shot short of, and in front of, the green. Jamieson topped the fourth for his team and Tolley, in an heroic effort to reach the green, went over into the road. That was five for our opponents, and being in the road, they would do well to go down in eight!

Watts and I looked certain to win the hole. But nothing is ever certain on the seventeenth at St. Andrews. Watts had to play a run-up to the very narrow green between the bunker on one side and the road on the other. He shanked into the road. Now, we were in the road in three, they in five.

Jamieson played a beautiful shot up twelve feet from the hole. That looked bad for us, for our ball was lying in the hard road. The hole was only fifteen or twenty feet away; the green was dry; and the terrible bunker was just beyond the flag. Watts and I put our heads together and indulged in a little mental arithmetic. We finally decided that if I should play down toward the brook behind the green, Watts could pitch back on so that two putts would give us a seven and a half, if Tolley holed his putt. We felt that we would be thankful for anything now.

We did get our seven. Tolley rimmed the long one, and we won the hole, but not until we had used up all our shots and most of the little brains we had.

Always Something New

The Road Hole has carried me farther from my theme than I intended to go. What I started out to say was that at St. Andrews, particularly on this hole and the second and fourteenth, there is untold opportunity to gain or lose a point in the choice of the route to the green. I do not know if I always played the fourteenth to the satisfaction of my Scotch caddie (you know, this is very hard to do), but I pleased myself at any rate. In four rounds I am certain that, depending upon the wind, I took three entirely distinct routes to the hole.

Once with the wind directly behind I drove way out to the left into the fifth fairway, whence I could cut a brassie shot around the mound at the short edge of the green. Next, with the wind directly against, two full wood-shots, as straight as I could hit them, left me an easy run-up from in front of the green. And last, with the wind from right to left, a straight drive, followed by a brassie shot well to the left of the green, left a simple pitch into the wind and down the length of the green.

Of course, it is impossible in limited space to convey any adequate conception of St. Andrews, and to one who has not seen the course, I am afraid my words will mean little. Least of all can one who has never played there appreciate the importance of these little variations made in order to obtain the advantage of the wind or the roll of the ground. Very often it is impossible to hold a pitch to a dry, sloping green unless the ball has been manoeuvered into position where it can be cushioned by a head wind; or if the wind cannot be used, the green must be approached so that a running shot may be employed.

There is always a way at St. Andrews, although it is not always the obvious way, and in trying to find it, there is more to be learned on this Scottish course than in playing a hundred ordinary American golf courses.

Walter Hagen and Bobby Jones playing the third hole at Inwood CC during the 1923 U.S. Open Championship. Jones' score for the day was 71, 73, 144; while Hagen struck heavy weather and finished with a card of 77, 74, 151. (Underwood and Underwood)

Bob Jones sinks a putt on the ninth green during the 1930 U.S. Open contested at Interlachen GC.(P&A Photos)

On the Green!

It is a surprising fact that a golf course may be either made or marred simply by the placing of the holes on the green. This important feature of the play is often entirely neglected by tournament committees and left to some one entirely unacquainted with the conditions of tournament.

The universal tendency is to cut the holes, having regard solely for the ease or difficulty of putting after the green is reached. If the members or the greenkeeper happen to take pride in the fact that par has never been beaten on their course, then very likely all holes will be placed on fast sloping hillsides.

On the Winged Foot course, due to the design of the greens it is possible to place the holes so that no rational being would dare play for the flag. Little narrow promontories projecting between cavernous sandpits are regarded as excellent places for cups, and the hapless player struggles around as best he can, always leaving himself a lot of putting or bunker work to do if he wants to get his pars.

A great deal of pleasure is taken from the game when, hole after hole, one is forced to turn his back upon the flag and endeavor merely to reach a place of safety upon the putting surface, trusting to luck that the ball will stop near the hole.

Holes Should Cater to Well-Hit Drive

I think the placing of the cups at Olympia Fields was very fair. But even there I should disagree with the policy of always seeking the back edge of the green. Where the hole is a scant fifteen or twenty feet from trouble in the rear, bold play is unwarrantably discouraged, for a fine shot if a bit too strong may result in the waste of several strokes.

The hole should be cut to take full advantage of the protecting bunkers—and it is desirable that they should be located so as to confer an advantage upon a well-placed and well-hit drive. But always there should be considered the fact that even the best are not capable of perfect accuracy, and the best likewise abhor bunkers as sincerely as do the veriest duffers.

Suitable Greens a Problem

To one who has played a great deal of golf on courses scattered throughout the country, the need is apparent for developing grasses and modes of treatment which can be made to yield decent putting greens, at a cost which will not be prohibitive for the smaller clubs. Wealthy organizations like Brae Burn in Boston, Old Elm or Chicago Golf Club in Chicago, Oakmont in Pittsburgh, can afford to spend the twenty-five or thirty thousand dollars a year which it costs them to keep their courses in good condition. On these courses and others similarly groomed, the putting greens are excellent and golf is a real pleasure.

But take the little fellows in the smaller cities; they are not able to spend enough money in experimentation, importing soil or sod, and in the many other operations necessary to discover grasses and fertilizers suited to the particular soil conditions of the locality.

The average person playing simply for the enjoyment of the game can tolerate almost any kind of a fairway. It is true bad lies cause him some annoyance. But there is nothing which spoils his game like uncertain or badly-kept putting greens. And the worst of it is that the putting greens offer the real problem to the greenkeeper.

Smaller Clubs To Benefit

The United States Golf Association is progressing rapidly with its work conducted through the Greens Section directed toward solving the greenkeeping problems, particularly of the smaller clubs. The progress already made, if continued, will make this work the most important contribution that has ever been made to the game of golf.

By placing at the disposal of the greenkeeper the scientific knowledge of numbers of experts, derived from experiments with all kinds of grasses and fertilizers in different soils, and by simplifying the eradication of insect pests and the treatment of grass diseases, the ultimate results will be to effect economics which will make it possible to maintain fine putting greens at a cost within reach of nearly everyone. The association is spending nearly thirty thousand dollars each year in this work, and maintains experiment stations in several sections of the country.

The plan is to establish as many of these stations as it is possible to maintain so that a study may be made of the adaptability of certain grasses to certain sections. Naturally, it is not expected that the grass which thrives best in the metropolitan district will do well in Georgia. To be of any value the grasses must be tested under the conditions in which they are to be grown.

In furtherance of this plan, in cities supporting several golf clubs, these clubs are being asked to cooperate with each other in supporting an experiment station to be operated under the direction of the Greens Section. Courses in any one locality have substantially the same greenkeeping problems and by maintaining such a station at their joint expense, valuable information should be available at very small cost to the individual club.

Research Work Necessary

It is impossible to see what very great benefits may result to the game from this work. Our own problems in Atlanta furnish a fair illustration. For years we have been forced to use Bermuda grass on our putting greens during the hot months of summer.

Unable to develop a grass which would thrive in its stead, or to discover a means of refining that which we can grow, mainly because no club has been able to make an outlay sufficient to attack the problem scientifically, we have had to worry along with the best we could get. We are now arranging to put in the experimental plot referred to and while we expect no immediate results, we have every reason to believe that within a few years we shall be able to find something which will give us putting greens as good as those on courses in the North and the West.

California Putting Greens

To date, I have played four golf courses in California, and if these are fair samples, I think I can safely say that the courses on the Pacific coast are the most perfectly groomed and conditioned in the world.

I have played Lakeside, Los Angeles Country, and Riviera in Los Angeles and Pebble Beach in Del Monte. On all of them I have found excellent greens and almost perfect fairways.

The greens everywhere are of bent grass and remarkably free from the "grain" so often found on a sloping surface when the bent grass is not properly cared for.

Strangely enough these beautiful greens offer severe problems to those not accustomed to putting on them. Although it is impossible to detect a flaw in the surface there is something about the color of the grass, or some other thing, which I have not discovered, that makes it awfully hard to see the line. At Riviera we were told to watch the greens carefully because, while almost every green sloped toward the sea, in many cases an optical illusion was created which made it appear that the slope was the other way. We soon found that this was far from an exaggeration.

The splendid condition of the courses in California becomes even more remarkable when one considers the cost of maintenance, which indicates that golf in California must be frightfully expensive. Yet, apparently, the expense has proved no deterrent. Everyone who can, plays the game, and the others talk about it.

Bobby Jones enjoyed playing the "testing qualities" of seaside golf in the British Isles where the greens where hard and unwatered and the fairways and putting surfaces like glass. (Frank Chrisrian photo)

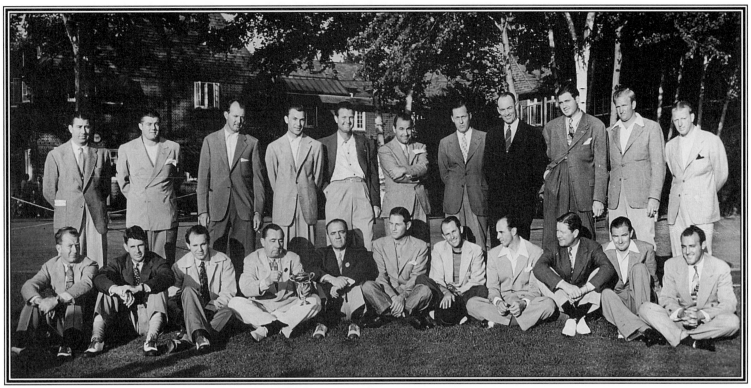

Official Picture of all star match–P.GA.America Ryder Cup Team V.S.Bobby Jones Challenge Team–Played at The Golf Club, Detroit, Michigan, August 23rd and 24th, 1941–Standing, left to right, Fred Corcoran, tournament mgr. P.G.A. of America; Lawson Little, Ed.Dudley, Ben Hogan, Jimmy Demaret, Gene Sarazen, Robert T. Jones, Captain of Challenge Team; Denny Shute, John Bulla, Clayton Haefner, Craig Wood. P.G.A. RYDER CUP TEAM.–Seated left to right, Jimmy Hines, Henry Picard, Ralph Guldahl, Walter Hagen honorary captain, Tom Walsh president P.G.A. of America, Horton Smith, Paul Runyan, Sam Snead, Byron Nelson, Harold McSpaden, Vic. Ghezzi.
THE JONES CHALLENGE TEAM WERE VICTORS, 8½ POINTS TO 6½ POINTS

Bob Jones, left, Captain of successful Challenging Team; Tom Walsh, president P.G.A. of America holding the Ryder Cup and Walter Hagen, honorary captain of the P.G.A. Ryder Cup Team. This match ws played at the Detroit Golf Club, August 23 and 24, 1941 for the benefit of the United Service Organization.

Some Random Thoughts

Winter Tournaments
Stimulate Golf Interest

Beginning some time in October of this past year, away out in Oregon most of the country's leading professionals set out upon a campaign of golf and travel which has carried them through with scarcely a break until now they find themselves in Florida with a little more money to shoot for. To some persons, I am afraid this winter campaign appears of little value save as a means of enlarging the bank accounts of a few of the winners and of providing employment or a vacation for those not so fortunate. But the fact of the matter is, as I see, that this winter schedule is one of the very finest things imaginable for the development of the game of golf. I believe that in future years the effect of it will be seen in an increasing number of star players among the younger generation, and in an increased interest in golf throughout the country.

Golf has always been a game of universal appeal, played by young and old, male and female. Now, even if the northern winter prohibits playing during three or four months of the year, there is never a season in which the golfer does not get news of interest affecting his game. The winter play in climes where golf is a joy even in January stimulates and keeps alive interest which had already been aroused.

But the most important phase of the work done by the winter tournaments is the interest created in places far removed from the competitions of the more formal summer season. During June, July, August, and September when the National and more important sectional championships are played, the tournaments take place all in the East, or at least in the northern part of the country where the weather condition of courses and concentration of population are more favorable. During this period the people of the South or of the far West are unable to see capable players unless they are able to undertake a considerable journey. It is unquestionably a fine thing that at any time of the year or under any pretense the outstanding professionals can be induced to perform at these people's doorsteps.

Playing in Savannah, during every round there were numbers of small boys following the play, and because the tournament represented no important championship they were allowed liberties which

would not have been permitted them at the Open championship. On each tee these little chaps ranged themselves on either side of the players, and made dives after the wooden tees as soon as the player had driven away–often they dove so soon that it seemed they might capture the tee, ball and all. This is not a practice which should be encouraged because it is both dangerous and attended with some little annoyance to the players, especially when some particularly zealous youth comes catapulting between the player's legs just as he is trying to learn in what direction his drive has departed. It is gratifying, however, that the youngsters take that much interest in the play, although their time could be better spent in observing method and style, than in trying to retrieve souvenirs.

A winter layoff impairs the player's sense of timing. It is usually too fast. It is best to remember "no one ever swings too slowly."
(USGA)

I have no doubt that if the winter programs remain as full as they have been, so that the monetary inducement will continue to be sufficient to attract the best players, the benefit to golf in this country will be apparent. It is a vast expanse of territory embraced by these United States, and it is an ambitious program which seeks to cover it all. But the pros have done pretty well so far, and if they receive a few more invitations they will do even better. I should like to see them playing more and more often, missing as few centres and districts as possible in their march.

Some Golf Resolutions To Remember in Spring Practice

And speaking of winter the most trying time of the year for the golfer is always the time when he comes out of hibernation and begins to try to tune his game back to a point where he can again enjoy it. After a long winter layoff, each club feels like a broom-handle and each ball when struck transmits a shock up the shaft which makes the player think he has hit a lump of iron. Golf is not much fun during this period, but it is a thing we must endure to enjoy the pleasures beyond.

Any man would be grateful, I believe, for any hints which would help him to get through this " tuning up" period with as little suffering as possible. While all of us do not have the same troubles and have to apply the same correctives when we are playing more or less regularly, I have noticed that at least the people with whom I play mani-

on the Game

fest much the same tendencies when suffering from lack of practice. Apparently golfing muscles lose a great deal in elasticity and responsiveness when not in use, and these, when unaccustomed to perform such functions, act upon demand in very much the same way for all individuals.

The first failure is in the length of the backswing. It is not hard to detect in any case a tendency to shorten the backward motion and whip the club back to the ball almost before it has reached the shoulder position. This is one way in which lack of assurance is manifested, the player being actually afraid to let himself out as far as he would if extended to midsummer form.

The second failing in part results from the first, although it is attributable also to the fact that the winter layoff impairs the player's sense of timing. This sense is entirely dependent upon practice, and when one fails to practice, he must lose the rhythm of the stroke. But it will be noted that in the spring the error is always on the fast side. No one ever swings too slowly.

The third common tendency is to attempt to lift the ball instead of striking it firmly downward. This, I think, is due to a slack left hand and wrist. The player is not quite certain that he has done everything correctly and he reaches the ball with the feeling that he perhaps ought to turn back to try it over again. He then either slackens his grip or "pulls" the punch and spoils the shot.

These are not all of the sorrows encountered during the first few rounds of spring, but they are those most commonly experienced. If we could start out on the lookout for them and promptly put them away, our days in purgatory would be lessened considerably.

Let us resolve then that in the coming spring we will swing back slowly; that we will swing back far enough–even farther than we think necessary; that we will grip firmly with the left hand; and that we will punch briskly through the ball. If we will do and remember these few things it won't be long before we will find the groove.

My own experience each year is somewhat tantalizing. From the end of the amateur championship until warm weather comes again I usually play only three or four rounds, sometimes with as much as two months intervening between successive attempts. On these occasions I go out relaxed and with very little concern about the results I am able to obtain. Then I play fairly well. But when spring draws near and I begin to play a bit more often, I find myself doing the very things I have mentioned above. The first round, when nothing much is expected is not so bad, but

after that the trouble begins.

An Analogy Between Football and Golf

Mr. Fielding Yost's interesting discussion of the illegal Yale touchdown in the game against the University of Georgia, must strike the golfer as involving certain points which apply with equal force to his own game. Mr. Yost points out that the ruling of the official in permitting a Yale player to recover a fumbled kick-off and run for a touchdown did not merely add six points to Yale's score but actually changed the whole game, quite possibly to Yale's disadvantage. Had the play been ruled properly, it is quite possible that Yale would have succeeded in battering across Georgia's line anyway, and, in doing so, she might have punished the Georgia team sufficiently to prevent Georgia's later scoring her winning margin.

Although a good many spectators fail to appreciate the fact, it is just as impossible to take away any part of a round of golf or of a match without changing the whole of what follows. One often hears that if one competitor had not missed certain short putts he would have won the match. It is always easy to account for a small margin in strokes or holes which might have been saved, yet it is not fair to say that if these had not been lost the subsequent play would have proceeded just the same.

In golf, as in football, the psychological advantage is an important factor. It is always a fine thing to get the jump on the other man or the other team, particularly where the margin enjoyed by either is small. We can all remember matches which have been won or lost in the first few holes of play in which the result was perfectly evident to an experienced observer long before a winning margin was actually established.

I don't know of any physical law which should make it any more difficult to hole a twenty-foot putt after several long ones have gone down than before, but I do know that each one that drops makes the next one just a bit harder than the last. When every putt goes up close to the hole or rims the cup without falling, although the player may be for the moment disappointed, he always feels that sooner or later they will begin to find the hole. But after he sinks three or four he begins to feel more and more doubtful because he knows that he can't keep on indefinitely.

So when a fine putt rims the hole it is fair to say it is bad luck and that a hole or a stroke has been lost that ought not to have been so, but it is not fair to say definitely that if it had gone down, the result of

Those who have played golf understand the stress imposed by our emotions in dealing with adversity. No player ever collapses because he suddenly forgets how to use his clubs.

the match or the tournament would necessarily have been different. The other fellow can always say with truth that if that one had gone down the next one might not have done so.

Furthermore I have seen one putt definitely make a difference of four or five holes, where the turning point was so clearly defined that it could be established with absolute certainty. One long putt tumbling in or one little one staying out is about as potent a means as can be imagined to set the fireworks on the one side or to cause utter despair on the other. And when either happens a close, hard-fought match can be turned into a complete rout.

Miniature Course Golfers Decide Longer Game Is Easier

Even before things began to liven up at Merion prior to the Amateur Championship last year, it was thought that the effect of the Tom Thumb or miniature golf would be seen in the tournament galleries, particularly in the size or number thereof. But exceeding even the best-informed estimate were the pre-tournament galleries, which reached formidable proportions before an important or serious blow was struck. On Saturday a four-ball, composed of Max Marston, Jess Sweetser, Jimmy Johnston and myself was followed by a gallery of not less than three thousand, and on Sunday when Watts Gunn, George Voigt, Dick Jones and I went around together the crowd was fully as large as that which followed the final in 1924. A good part of the increase can be

We have never mastered golf until we realize that our good shots are accidents and our bad shots, good exercise.

ascribed to the more widespread and more intense interest in the game which was evident even before Tom Thumb became a golfer, but it was not hard to see and hear that a good many of the spectators were not entirely familiar with "the long game," as they called it.

This form of entertainment which goes by various names– "shrimp golf" according to Fred Stone, or "premature golf" in the language of Will Rogers–is bound to exert a certain influence upon "the long game." I think and hope that such influence will be beneficial in creating an interest in the Royal and Ancient game among people who might not otherwise come in contact with it. But if comments heard upon the Merion golf course are proper indications of the attitude of the Tom Thumb devotee toward the game of golf, then a lot of poor, unsuspecting, well-meaning citizens are in for a lot of trouble and disappointment before they grow much older.

The following is typical:

"You know, I'm going to take up this 'long game'. These fellows have a cinch. This driving business–there isn't anything to that–all

you've got to do is hit the ball as far as you can down a big wide fairway–anybody could do that. And look at the greens they have to play on–nice and wide and smooth, with no carom shots to make and no pipes to go through and not a thing in the way. Look at that fellow miss that little putt–that's where we'd have them beat."

In a number of ways it is important that a lot of people when they play miniature golf should not think they are really playing golf. As a diverting pastime the little courses are fine, and as a kindergarten for the real game, and as a means of stimulating interest in legitimate golf, I think they are things which a person interested in popularizing the sport would like to see fostered. And likewise they can serve a useful end if they will show to our city officials, mayors, aldermen, councilmen and commissioners, that a lot of people would like to play golf if they had proper facilities at a low enough cost. But I am afraid that the usefulness of these little fellows, at least in conjunction with real golf, will be totally destroyed if the people who play them are allowed to believe that they are playing golf when they do so. Such a belief can only lead to disgust and discouragement once the Tom Thumber acquires the means, and desire, and makes for himself the opportunity, to play golf.

"The long game" very likely looks simple enough when one sees it played by Sweetser, Johnston, Von Elm and the like, but it is a game which breaks the proudest spirit, and one, upon which one must enter humbly.

In one respect particularly, I think the Tom Thumb player gets a very good start in the proper game. He becomes a decent putter before he begins to befog his brain with all the "do's" and "don'ts," straight left arms and flexible wrists of the longer shots. When he begins to play "the long game" he has done what every beginner ought to do–become familiar with the handling of a club for the shorter shots. When the average person takes up golf he becomes so anxious to be a fine, long driver that he completely neglects the shots around the hole. If he can start off a fairly decent performer in this department he has made a good beginning.

Advantages and Disadvantages of Large Galleries

During more recent years, since public interest in golf has become so widespread, a new factor–hazard or aid as the case may be–has been added to tournament play. In the earlier days when the number of spectators at the big championships was comparatively small, the effect of the crowd could be ignored. But now galleries numbering 15,000 people and more are not uncommon and the problems imposed

BOBBY JONES ON GOLF

upon the player by their presence on the links are as real as any placed there by the designer of the course. The fact that the spectators select two or three matches to follow, leaving the rest of the players unattended makes it interesting to learn whether in an open championship the favor of the crowd is a help or a hindrance.

Several times last minute spurts by men who played their last rounds practically unobserved have snatched a victory from the hands of a leader attended by a horde of spectators. Notable instances have been Gene Sarazen's win at Skokie, and Johnny Farrell's victory at Olympia Fields. Neither Johnny nor Gene were followed by more than a dozen people over the stretch of holes in which they won the championship. Yet in these cases the psychology of the situation favors the one behind entirely apart from the effect of the crowd. The leader carries the burden of setting the pace while the other man has a free shot with everything to gain, and this would be true if the entire gallery could be set upon the heels of the trailer.

Although some experience is required to avoid being frightened or annoyed by a large gallery, I think certainly that when this experience has been gained, to be followed about the course by a large number of spectators is a distinct advantage to a competitor. In some ways they may work a hardship, especially if they are unruly, and they may harass the player's nerves, but in the long run the player will do better with them than without. They find his balls for him, they define the greens and bunkers, they make lanes for him to play through, and they inspire him to do his very best, sometimes even a little more.

The only trying times come when the crowd becomes excited and ignores the directions of the marshals. Scurrying and running from one shot to the next they can be a terrible annoyance, and at the same time a real menace to the physical well-being of the player. But as a rule they are neither the one nor the other.

A player certainly tires more quickly when playing before a large crowd. This may be due to the greater competitive strain, for of course the crowd and the strain come together, although strangely enough the crowd is procured by the strain and does not produce it, as might be supposed. If the player is not high enough in the competition to be under tension he will not have to bother much with spectators. Yet playing with a large following is made doubly hard work because it is always necessary to shove and paw a way through to the ball. When this is done on an average of two or three times a hole for thirty-six holes there can be no doubt that a full day's work has been accomplished.

The unfortunate part of the spectator-problem is what it means to the fellows who are struggling on the hole in front, the hole behind, or in some parallel fairway when a well-attended match passes by.

I remember playing the sixteenth hole at St. Andrews in 1921 when Joe Kirkwood, with a large crowd in tow, passed the second green. My partner and I were forced to wait until Joe had holed out before spectators following him could be moved off the green to which we were playing. Roger Wethered, who, it will be remembered, tied with Jock Hutchison that year, had the same experience at the fifteenth for word of Roger's score had not been known sufficiently to direct attention to him.

It might be a fine thing for every man to remember if he loses patience with a gallery that it is better to have it in tow himself rather than tied up to some fellow a hole or so away.

Bob Jones' tee shot on the 6th tee at the no. 2 course in Pinehurst N.C., on March 24, 1938 is the subject of great interest including that of playing partner Ed Dudley. Dudley was the first golf professional at Augusta National Golf Club.

More About the New Golf Ball

On October 1, 1930, all American golf ball manufacturers announced that from that date on only golf balls conforming to the new U.S.G.A. specifications of 1.68 inches and 1.55 ounces would be produced, and simultaneously Prescott S. Bush, Secretary, issued a statement on behalf of the U.S.G.A. declaring that no change in these specifications would be made. This puts the matter in definite form. The change is made and we are embarked upon our course with a ball which has been the subject of discussion and elaborate experimentation for more than four years.

It is of vast importance at the outset for every one of the thousands of golfers in this country to have a perfect understanding that the decision to change the ball and to adopt the new specifications was not made in any haphazard fashion. The executive committee of the U.S.G.A. is composed of men who have been interested in golf all of their lives. They are men of intelligence and of mature and sound judgment. The service which they render by directing to the best of their ability the destinies of the game is one which they perform disinterestedly and at great personal sacrifice. There is not one of these men who would permit a thing to be done which had not been considered carefully and judged to be the proper thing and for the best interests of the game.

New Ball Increases Enjoyment of Game

From the outset, I have been heartily in favor of adopting a ball larger and lighter than the ball in use. Limiting the driving power of the ball was not the most appealing or moving consideration, because such a thing was desirable only from the standpoint of a very small percentage of the great number of people who play the game. What was regarded as of value was the possibility of giving to all golfers a ball which would increase the enjoyment of the game for every one; to give them a more responsive ball and one which would be less taxing upon the powers of the less expert player.

So much has been talked and written about the loss in distance to be suffered by users of the new ball that this feature has been magnified to alarming proportions in the minds of those who think they can ill afford to see precious yards lopped off their drives. This one thing sticks in the golfer's mind and it has almost come to obscure other features which must appeal to all as desirable. Almost everyone to whom I have talked is surprised to learn how very small the loss actually is, that under normal conditions it amounts to only a few yards and only makes a difference of one number in the club used for the second shot.

If everyone would stop to take stock of the situation, to see with the present ball just what difference results from using a mashie-niblick instead of a spade, or a mashie instead of a four, they would see immediately that in actual play five or ten yards can be quite unimportant. The only real trouble will arise on holes where with the present ball the player can just barely get home in two; on these holes, with the new ball, he will just barely fail to get home. Yet let him, in considering the ultimate result, reflect upon how many times on holes where he must extend himself, he finds his ball actually on the putting surface in two shots. I should like to wager that more often than not he plays his third out of a bunker and wishes earnestly that his ball had stopped ten or even twenty yards farther back on the fairway.

Bob Jones and his protege Charlie Yates, also of East Lake GC, who won the 1938 British Amateur Championship. (Wide-World/NYT)

Driving Loss Unimportant

One other reason why the loss of driving power is unimportant: There are a number of courses in America today which are long enough for the new ball. There are a good many more that look silly when attacked by a first rate player with a driver and mashie-niblick. There was good reason to expect that improvement in manufacture and the introduction of new methods and materials might make even our long courses look silly and make jokes of our championships. It was not practical to think of buying more and more expensive ground to keep increasing the length of holes to make them fit for championship play as the ball became more and more powerful, particularly when this increase in power carried no actual advantage to the game in any conceivable form. From the back tees even the small loss of driving power to be noticed in the new ball will restore the testing qualities for championship play to a great many of our courses which are now unfit for it; and all the duffer has to pay for it is to play from the front of the tee instead of the back. We can move all of our tees forward, if we wish, without investing more money in costly land, but we cannot keep on moving them backward.

New Ball Has Better Lie

Prior to the match at Merion last year I had only a passing acquaintance with the new ball because I did not want to confuse my playing instincts during the competitive season. But since that time, I have played several rounds with it and have had opportunities to observe its behavior closely enough to have a true appreciation of what it means.

To me the outstanding delight of the new ball is its ready response to every kind of shot. Not only has it a pleasant feel on the club, but it makes possible shots which simply could not be played with the heavier ball. Everyone appreciates that the heavy ball offers considerable difficulty in the play to the green. If it lies in heavy grass, or on a cuppy lie, it requires a sound blow with a lofted club to give it enough elevation to make it stop on the green, and the player who is not able to hit hard enough is left helpless. With the new ball, the difficulty of a situation of this kind is considerably lessened; first, because the ball, being larger and lighter, sits up higher in the grass; and second, because it does not need to be hit so hard in order to attain sufficient elevation.

I enjoy playing golf on a course and with a ball that does not require slugging. In this respect the new ball is ideal, for while I noted a small loss of distance off the tee, I noted quite definitely also that I could play all the shots with less physical effort. Playing the old ball, full shots and very often forcing shots were necessary. The ball was heavy and it was a good roller. On any shot up to the green, unless it was played against a strong breeze, it had to be hit hard and high to be certain of stopping. But with the new ball, I find that where I used to require a full shot with a number four iron, for example, I can now play a half-shot with a number two. The new ball may require a little better control, but the comfort in striking and the improved lies make such control easy to apply.

Modern golfers have been criticized by the old-timers because of their tendency to neglect the half-shot. The fact of the business has been that the half-shot was made impractical by the heavy ball.

Bob Jones and Walter Hagen were lifelong adversaries and competitors.
They confer on scores during the 1935 Masters.
(USGA)

On Golf Clubs

Golf clubs have changed a lot since the days of young Tom Morris, not only in an improved construction, but in the number of kinds manufactured. The modern golfer can now obtain a club for almost every five or ten yards of distance which he needs to traverse. With a complete set of clubs it is rarely necessary to play a half-shot with any of them, for it is nearly always possible to find one whose normal range is approximately right for the shot to be played.

Most of the better players nowadays carry a bagful of clubs about five irons, three woods, and the putter, but that is the usual allotment. When we think of what a weight these make, it is small wonder that Watts Gunn's St. Andrews' caddy, without consulting his employer, left five of Mr. Gunn's favorite clubs behind when they started out upon an afternoon round. "Ye have no need for so many" was all Watts was able to get out of him!

I must confess that I am particularly guilty in this matter of breaking the caddy's back. In the set which I used at Pebble Beach there were fourteen clubs, all of them full weight as my caddy will testify. There were four woods—driver, brassie, and two spoons, and ten irons—number one, two, mashie-iron, number four, mashie, spade, mashie-niblick, niblick, approach club, and putter. That seems a lot of excess baggage, but the strange thing is that on each round I found use for every club. That, in addition to being some justification for myself, is the highest compliment I could pay Pebble Beach as a testing lay-out. Only a really good course will afford opportunity to use every club in the bag.

An explanation of the reason for the two spoons may be of some interest. It has proved helpful to me, so there may be someone else who will like the idea. The brassie which I use has practically no loft. The head differs little from that of my driver, except that it is not quite so deep. The thinner face makes it easier to loft the ball from a fairway lie. This gives me a very powerful fairway club when the ball is lying well enough to permit its use.

But with a club of this kind it is impossible to play a shot from a cuppy or very close lie. So, next in order, my spoon is lofted very little more than an ordinary brassie. This serves to get the maximum length from unfavorable lies. It was only this season that I added the other spoon—a lofted one. I found that my combination worked well enough within certain limits, but the big spoon which I carried was worse than useless for playing a spared shot. The loft was so little, that hitting even hard enough to assure control sent the ball quite a distance. The more lofted spoon enables me to avoid pressing the number one iron.

Chick Evans is the one first-class golfer who has stuck to what have become old-fashioned ideas. Chick's bag in California contained three woods—the regulation driver, brassie, and spoon—a strong iron, an iron closely resembling a mashie, a niblick, and a putter. Seven clubs in all, and in reality only three irons. How he does it is hard to say, for he never seems to lack the shot called for. Possibly he figures that it is better to know a few clubs well, than to have a slight acquaintance with a great number.

It has been said that the less expert player ought to carry fewer clubs until he can learn to play with those he has. That may be true, but I can't help feeling that the present day assortment makes the game easier for him. He has not the highly sensitive touch of the more experienced man and it ought to be easier to learn to play many clubs in the same way than a few clubs in very many ways. It takes less time to acquaint oneself with a few pieces of wood and iron than it does to acquire the skill of a Chick Evans.

Bob is standing in the porte cochere of the East Lake Golf Clubhouse comparing a "dreadnaught" driver he designed at Harvard with an ordinary driver.

Wooden Clubs

Fads come and go in golf very much as styles in women's clothes, and sometimes with just as little reason. Especially has this been true in the design of wood clubs, various and widely different types having enjoyed their day of popularity and passed on.

Years ago the popular wood models were very small with an amazingly limited hitting area. Some of them appeared to be little larger than the ball, and it must have been disheartening to the player to contemplate the chances of a miss with such a tiny implement. The clubs which I first saw were of this type, although I do not remember taking particular note at the time of their peanut-like appearance. I suppose they were too big for me to handle anyway.

From that time until a few years ago the heads of wood clubs have been continually increasing in size. The so-called "dreadnaught" of fifteen years ago was a rarity but now I doubt if its presence would attract attention among a collection of 1930 models. Almost every driver used today is as ample in horizontal dimensions as the old "dreadnaught", and most of them are deeper in the vertical dimension of the face.

The preference for a deep face is not hard to explain in the case of the expert golfer. The increased power, and hence increased speed of the ball, makes it rise more quickly from a hard, accurate blow. The first-class player's problem is how to keep the ball down rather than to get it up, and the deep face assists him to that end. But the less-accomplished player should have more need for the shallow face than ever before, because, the ball has become heavier and heavier and hence harder to elevate if struck at all inaccurately or without considerable force.

I suppose a deeper face naturally suggests a head larger in all other respects. That may have had something to do with the generous design of present day wood clubs. But there is something else about a large head which is hard to describe or account for. A well-hit shot simply has a more satisfying feel off the large head than off the small one. I have heard numbers of people express the same preference although none could account for it. A big head, of course, means more wood and less lead, which may make some difference in balance or resiliency, although I confess I don't know why it should. But I am sure there is a difference. Often the ball feels heavy off a small club while the large one appears to brush it along quite easily.

The bulged or convex face is another feature of wood club design which has now become universally popular. The purpose supposed to be served by the curve is the correction of small inaccuracies in hitting; the angle of the face at the toe and heel being designed to counteract the hook or slice which would normally result from hitting the ball at those points. It is difficult to see that the bulge accomplishes that purpose, but I believe that it serves another almost equally useful. I have always felt that I could drive farther using a driver with a bulged face.

Driving into Chicago, after the Walker Cup matches at Wheaton two years ago, Francis Ouimet, Gene Homans, Maurice McCarthy, and I discussed this very point. We all confessed to the same feeling, although not too anxious to express an opinion for which we could give no reason. There is only one explanation I could think plausible, and it is purely speculative. This is that the point of the bulge presents a smaller area of contact with the ball than would a plane face, and the force of the blow being the same and concentrated within the smaller area, would penetrate farther beneath the cover and deeper into the resilient center of the ball. The difference, if there is any, is of course, small, but I believe it must exist. If I were the only person who had noted it, I should be prepared to blame my imagination, but seemingly the others had also noted it.

Preference Depends on Player

Nowadays almost the first question asked a player concerning his clubs is whether or not he uses steel shafts. Apparently steel shafts in

Jones played only hickory shafted golf clubs up to his Grand Slam in 1930. In 1932 the first steel shaft clubs bearing Jones' name were introduced.

this country have come to stay, and equally apparently there are numbers of golfers with whom they will never gain favor. The question of the legalization of the steel shaft has been much agitated in England during recent months, with little progress noted by its champions.

Actually there seems to be little reason why the use of steel should not be permitted. Official sentiment was at first opposed to it on the ground that real and substantial advantages would be gained by persons using it. Steel shafts were claimed to produce additional length on the drive, and better direction in all clubs because of the absence of torque.

They were cried down for the same reason that grooved or ribbed-facing was barred, it being the policy of the legislators of the game to discourage the use of any club or device which would tend to assist the player beyond the capabilities of the ordinary club used for years.

But I think it has been demonstrated that it is just as easy to hook and slice with steel shafts as with wood, and that steel does not add appreciably to the length of any drive. It would, therefore, seem that the player might be left to choose for himself as long as he can obtain no illegitimate advantage over his fellows. If he fancies a club with a shaft of steel, I can see no reason why he should not be allowed to have it. I find a more general use of steel among the leading professionals, some of whom had formerly expressed an unalterable affection for wood.

extended use.

In any event, I believe the development of the steel shaft should be encouraged.

Steel Shaft Resembling Wood

There are many men, myself among them, who will never use steel until it can be made to approach more closely the equalities and feel of wood. But there is no reason why in time it cannot be made to behave in exactly the same manner. When that point has been reached, there are many advantages which the steel shaft will enjoy.

An old nineteenth century "rake" iron is compared to the modern sand iron. The "rake" is a popular collectible today. (UPI Photo)

First and foremost is the possibility of uniformity in construction, making possible the replacement of shafts and clubs with others identical in every respect; second, is the greater durability and longer life, the steel being free from the danger of becoming brittle with dryness. There will be no need to oil and rub the steel which is necessary with the woods. And thirdly, the source of supply can never be so limited as the supply of hickory is rumored to be now. I do not know if our hickory has been reduced to as low level as is feared, but I do know that to obtain a real good hickory shaft is sometimes a difficult job.

So whether or not steel or wood shafts are used depends entirely on the player. Many like the feel of steel as it is made today. If you happen to be one of those, then use it by all means. I have learned my

The only objection I have ever had to the steel shaft, is that it has the feeling of being a bit too quick for my swing. The ball seems to get away very quickly, almost before I am conscious of striking it, and it never flies with the arching trajectory which I like. Off steel the ball appears to rise rapidly and descend precipitously, reaching the ground without roll. Of course, that is probably due to the peculiarities of my swing, and might be overcome after a little more

game with the wood shafts, and until I become unable to procure good hickory, or until steel shafts are made which act and feel like wood, I shall continue to use wood.

Bobby Jones on Golf

Club with Flexible Handle

A short while ago, I played in a four-ball match which included Mr. Charles Stone of Schenectady, New York, who was in Atlanta on a short visit. On the way to the course, Mr. Stone invited me to try a novel type of driver which he had with him. Being out of practice, I was not at all certain what I would do with my own clubs so it was with some hesitation that I consented to drive with the curiosity which Mr. Stone described.

When we arrived at the first tee, I was handed a driver which had every appearance of an ordinary golf club. I thought I might get away with that. But on taking the thing in my hands, I discovered that instead of a wood or steel shaft, it was fitted with a shaft which was nothing more nor less than a section–and a very limber section, too–of an ordinary buggy-whip! When waggled in the ordinary manner of address the head flapped about aimlessly as though it were on the end of a stiff rope. The shaft had not even enough rigidity to support the head which caused it to bend in various directions according to the position it occupied in the hands.

The first fairway on the Druid Hills course is very narrow, closely restricted on either side by dense forests. I figured that my chances of finishing the hole would be very slight if I should drive with Mr. Stone's club, so I begged to be excused until the third tee where I would have ample room.

Arriving there I teed a ball and without consciously varying my swing in the least degree, with this queer club I hit a drive which was certainly the straightest one I hit all afternoon, and which may have been the longest. At any rate, the ball was found in about the usual situation after a good drive.

This is not in any sense an effort to gain business for the whip manufacturers by recommending that good hickory be displaced by buggy-whips for use in golf clubs. But the experience does make one wonder if we do not lay too much stress upon the strength and steely qualities so much sought after in the hickory shafts. Most people have been in the habit of discarding old clubs when the shafts become the least bit shaky. Yet no hickory shaft could possibly become as soft or as lifeless as this whip affair which propelled the ball as well as any club I ever used.

I have been told by men versed in the laws of mechanics that no force is actually transmitted through the shaft to the clubhead–that is, no force which for transmission would require a rigid connection. The shaft is simply a means of transmitting motion and of building up velocity, the force of the blow depending upon how fast the clubhead is moving at the instant of impact. Apparently then all that is needed is a shaft of sufficient rigidity to keep the clubhead in a given path.

The amazing thing about the buggy-whip shaft is that except for a perceptible tug on the hands when the swing changes direction at the top the player is conscious of no strange feeling. Evidently centrifugal force keeps the shaft taut and prevents the head from lagging.

I doubt if a person could ever gain sufficient confidence in a wobbly contrivance such as the buggy-whip club described, to make regular use of it. It is only of value as a curiosity although its use may prove enlightening in the selection of hickory and steel. After my experience with it I determined that I should never again part with an old favorite simply because the shaft had softened a bit with use. Apparently that does no harm.

I don't believe it possible that the thing would work in the clubs for the shorter shots, because the force of the swing would not be sufficient to keep the club-head pulling at the end of the shaft. But here again I may be wrong. When I first saw the driver it did not occur to me that it was actually possible to use it.

Freak Club Seldom Practical

In the clubhouse of the Royal and Ancient Golf Club at St. Andrews there is a rather spacious room where walls are lined with cases containing a marvelous collection of golf clubs. Some of them are very old and of much historical value. Others are interesting as oddities or freak design intended to overcome some particular difficulty which the golfer encounters. Examining the old clubs one is impressed by their clumsy construction compared to the modern implements of the game. Monstrous grips, very soft shafts, and long, ungainly heads are characteristic. But there is not a very radical difference in fundamental design. The refinements are not there, but the difference is scarcely as great as that between the gutta-percha and the rubber-cored balls.

The freak clubs, on the other hand, are astonishing. As you look at them you wonder how any person could have conceived half of them to be of any practical value. For example, one is a small niblick with a hole of about the size of a quarter in the center of the blade–the idea being to facilitate the passage of the club through the sand of the bunker and so make easier the extrications of a buried ball. Another, a mid-iron this time, is equipped with a broad sole with ribs over a quarter of an inch high. These ribs were intended to grip the ground and prevent any turn of the face as the club came into contact with the ball.

I have mentioned only two of the collection. There are many, many more, all the result of a continuous effort to find some method of accomplishing what the golfer cannot accomplish for himself. A good many similar clubs have been designed which are not represented in the Royal and Ancient Collection. Yet not one of them has ever met with any particular favor, either because they serve only one purpose, or because–and this is usually the case–they are not good for anything. Until someone finds a club which will swing itself, even the rankest duffer will be better off to accept the well-constructed conventional clubs and try to learn to use them.

This effort to improve the player's score by mechanical means has found expression in another way. It is possible now to procure some sort of equipment which will prevent almost any known fault. There is a sort of glove affair which insures a proper grip; a sleeve which will keep the left arm perfectly straight, a harness which prevents lifting the head, and so on. Conceivably, by wearing them all, a person could not fail to play perfect golf. But the trouble is the thing just won't work that way. The golf stroke has not yet become so standardized that it is possible to lay it out upon an exact plot, without making some allowances for physical difference between this man and the next.

Whatever improvement has been wrought in golf clubs, and it has been considerable, has been done by a careful and sensible improvement in the methods of the construction. This is only natural, as experience was added to the skill of the manufacturer, this material or type of construction was found to be superior to the old. But no innovation or freakish design has been accepted as a part of a standard golf club. The change in the ball made necessary certain differences in the size of the grip, the material of the face, and the strength of the shaft. But aside from these features and the gradual refinements which have been made, the golf club of today is substantially what it was fifty years ago.

The player who relies upon a freakish club to do something for him or who expects to find a key to golfing success in some sort of appliance to strap on his body, is doomed to disappointment. He will make much more rapid progress if he will procure a good set of ordinary clubs and go to his pro for instruction.

Naturally, this resorting to freak clubs is due to the fact that the average golf enthusiast is continually on the lookout for some means of improving his game. If he despairs of being able to make better scores by increasing the skill with which he handles his clubs, he will likely assemble an astonishing collection of odd-looking implements claimed by the manufacturers to be almost capable of playing the shot for him. Drivers which can neither hook nor slice, iron clubs without a socket to prevent shanking, and putters which, of themselves, roll the ball into the hole, are some of the clubs which many men will buy hoping rather than believing that some improvement may be effected.

Of course, some of these clubs in a measure produce the effect claimed for them. It is conceivable that wind resistance may be decreased by design, or that a certain method of facing or of distributing weight may tend

Clubs play an important part in every golfer's play. Deprived of a favorite he is temporarily lost. Here are Bobby's favorites.

to correct minor inaccuracies of hitting. But the effect is never so great as the player has hoped it would be, for he invariably discovers that he still must play the shot.

In the field of legitimate design, putters perhaps vary more than any other clubs. Iron, aluminum, wood, goose-neck, straight socket, and center-shaft, are all widely different types, and the golfer cannot resist trying a new one if he has one or two bad days with the old.

The putting department of the game requires more delicacy and control than any other. That elusive thing we call "touch" is born only of a complete mastery of the club, and a feeling of comfort, ease and confidence in its use. A man can never know his putter too well. I should always prefer a familiar club to a good one.

Nine times out of ten a change from one putter to another will effect no lasting good. The new one may work better on occasions, but consistency would be better served by sticking to the old one and

by making friends with it.

It is, of course, up to the individual to choose the kind of putter he wants. The design makes little difference. So long as the balance is good the club is easily handled, and the face is true. Generally speaking, whether the head be of aluminum, wood, or iron, is a matter of little consequence, although it has been the experience of most good putters that certain kinds of clubs are more reliable under certain conditions.

For instance, the iron putter of medium weight seems to be more effective on fast, keen greens, for with it the ball can be struck a firmer blow. For the same reason it is more reliable on putts of ten feet or less. This type is certainly the most popular today in America where greens are small and very long approach putts are rare.

Putters of wood and aluminum are splendid implements for rolling a long putt up close to the hole. With either it is practically impossible to impart sidespin or underspin to the

ball and hence the putt always runs freely and easily over the green. This is a splendid feature when the surface is rough, or heavily grassed, and slow. These putters are treacherous on very short putts for then it is difficult to hit both firmly and gently.

The center-shaft putter is usually of an upright lie. It is amazingly effective from short distances. When the ball lies two yards or less from the hole, it is comparatively easy to keep the putter swinging on line with the hole. But this upright position is sometimes embarrassing to the free swing of a long approach putt. It is this difficulty I believe which has been largely responsible for the almost complete disappearance of the Schenectady and Travis models.

Rust Sometimes a Help

Many times during the Open at Winged Foot, as I walked to my ball where my caddy was waiting for me, I heard remarks from those close by evidencing some amazement that a man who thought enough of golf to worry about Open championships should play with such terrible-looking clubs. My clubs are really not terrible but it must be admitted than when covered with a generous coat of rust their appearance is not prepossessing. And whenever I play in the North, away from Atlanta's Bermuda grass fairways, my clubs are never polished.

The golfer who fails to care for his clubs, is in the same class with the fisherman who neglects his tackle, or the rifleman who never cleans his guns. But sometimes things are not exactly what they seem.

It was at Merion in 1924 that I first found the difficulties that a highly-polished iron club might bring about. In that year the grass on the Merion fairways was abundant, and a little too long. Unlike our southern Bermuda grass it was not strong enough to support the weight of a golf ball, and the result was that most of the lies were heavy. Added to this, there was always a heavy dew which lasted on the grass until after ten in the morning. This combination of circumstances made the polished surfaces of my irons as slippery as any greased surface could possibly be. I found it absolutely impossible to control or apply backspin to the ball.

I complained about my troubles and someone suggested that I let my clubs rust. I followed the suggestion and noted a considerable improvement, the rust roughening the face enough to insure a better grip on the ball. About the same purpose is served, and at the same time a more dressy appearance given the clubs by polishing all except the space between the markings on the face. I think Walter Hagen was the first golfer I ever saw keep his clubs in this way. In my opinion, it is desirable to keep the hitting surface of the clubs as dry and rough as possible in order to take care of the heavy lies which are bound to be found on any course.

Punched-Faced Clubs Aided Good Golfer

The old punched-faced clubs which were ruled out of the game about 1922 were marvelous aids when playing from wet grass or clover. From a dry, clean lie a properly hit shot is in no need of assistance from any source. There is no trouble about a clean, gripping contact. But these punchings on the face, driven in at an angle and leaving a small burr at the edge of each hole, are the only means which I have seen of controlling a shot out of clover. I was a little sorry to see them ruled out for while they did enable the player to stop the ball more quickly, still he could not do so unless he hit the shot properly, and the punchings did minimize the clover hazard, a thing which has no place on a golf course.

Hard To Replace Favorites

Have you ever stopped to think how peculiar and individual are the characteristics of a golf club, how difficult it is to replace an old favorite, or how silly you are to keep on acquiring and using new clubs when the old one still remains in serviceable condition?

A golf club in the hands of its owner is one of the most delicately sensitized implements in sport. It is fairly bristling with individual characteristics which are incapable of reproduction. The displacement of the balance by so much as a scant half inch, or even an infinitesimal reduction in the size of the handle, will make all the difference in the world in the "feel" of the club.

Yet how many times do we make allowance for these factors? Often a new club has such a friendly feel that we cannot resist trying it out. But rarely do we take accurate note of its construction to see if it is suited to the use we intend to put it to.

The main thing to be considered in the club is the shaft, whether the amount of "spring" is proper for the capabilities and habits of the purchaser. Timing which is proper for one shaft will

not be so for another no matter how nearly the same weight and lie of the clubs may be.

Last September, I motored from Atlanta to Montreal with an organized automobile tour, and thinking that opportunities for playing golf might be forthcoming, I carefully forgot to take my clubs along. But on the road I discovered that I was not really as sick of the game as I had thought, and at two or three stops I borrowed a club and hit a few balls.

Stance and Swing for Each Club

To drive reasonably straight and reasonably far is not impossible with any sort of club but I was struck with the fact that I actually had to alter my swing and timing with each club, and in every case it was necessary to hit with a good deal less than full power. In other words, I had to control the club consciously rather than lash away with the assurance that I knew what would happen.

Now that is exactly the burden which a man puts upon himself when he discards an old club in favor of a new one. Golf clubs are like human beings in that no two are exactly alike. It is rare indeed when a new club functions well from the very first shot, simply because, as we say, we must get used to it, which means that we must adapt our timing to the new implement.

To develop a new swing for every new club is quite a task in itself, especially for the business man golfer who has rarely time enough to perfect one swing. If he can get consistent results from the club he has he is doing very well.

The balance and feel of the club are of paramount importance, but I should advise never to try to use a club which does not appeal to the eye. A little clumsiness in the head or an improper line in the face is enough to ruin a club for me. I always find myself eyeing the defect in the club rather than looking at the ball.

Probably I have been prompted to write all this by a desire to unburden my soul of all the grief that is in it. Recently, while I was in the locker room changing my shoes, an officious caddie either tried a swing with my pet driver or banged it over the head of one of his brothers, and succeeded in smashing the head clean off the shaft. That I could not discover who was responsible prevented a first-class funeral, but even that could have given me only momentary relief. It is odd, indeed, that a club which I have cared for like no other should be the very one to meet disaster in this fashion.

Clubs Part of Golfer's Game

The point of all this is that a golfer should be immensely careful with the implements of his trade. They are as much a part of his game as his knee action or his follow through. And when he finds a club that suits him, let him remember that no human hand can fashion another exactly like it. I have had eight copies of a defunct driver, a favorite of a few years ago, some made in this country and some in England, and have never found one I could use, although the original undoubtedly suited me better than any club I have ever owned.

The purpose which should be within view of us all when we practice is that we may reduce the swing as near as possible to a mechanical perfection which will enable us to reproduce it every time. To gain this end is, or course, impossible, but we may at least eliminate some variable factors. And the easiest constant quantity to fix is the club. We can, by continued use, eliminate the necessity of compensating for the action of strange clubs and thereby take one difficulty from those which are already too many.

Handicap in Golf Makes Game Popular

There are many things about golf which cause me to delight that it is the game which was given to play and enjoy. And I think its greatest charm lies in the fact that no matter what the difference in age or ability of two players may be, there can always be found a handicap which will put them on an equal basis. We can enjoy a round of golf in a detached sort of way, keeping our own score and allowing an opponent to keep his, but it is much better if we can have a friendly match for caddy fare or a ball, or for just the fun of the thing.

Tennis is a splendid game. I love it and should like to play it more. But no decent player could give me a handicap which would make an even game. Any player of more than average ability could concede me forty-love and I should scarcely ever get a game, simply because his ability would prevent my playing at all.

But golf is different. In Atlanta, I play regularly with my friends who play in the neighborhood of eighty and eighty-five, I give them from six to twelve strokes and we have some great matches.

Only recently I visited Mr. H. M. Atkinson of Atlanta, in North Hatley, Quebec. Mr. Atkinson, a retired business man, plays a very nice game, but naturally for one who has played little, his scores usually run around ninety. But we had a most enjoyable match with a handicap of a stroke a hole, Mr. Atkinson winning two of the last three to beat me one up. I can truthfully say that I got more pleasure out of that game than any championship match I have ever played.

hitters so the professionals' side of the match looked to be a certainty. But the handicap was taken at the other end and every ball within twenty yards was counted in the hole. Of course, Abe and George took a very bad beating.

Another man, whose name I did know but have forgotten, once persuaded a professional to give him one stroke in the round to be taken any way he pleased. To the consternation of the professional, after halving the first hole in a good four, the clever one announced that he would take one-eighteenth of his stroke there. The result does not need to be told!

Many Joke Handicaps

I remember at East Lake one day in our regular Wednesday afternoon game, after considerable argument, one member of the match agreed to give another six strokes if he took them where the donor should designate. On the second hole, after the one giving the strokes had taken a bad six he announced that all the strokes should count on that hole.

HANDICAPS of "woofs"–when you are allowed to shout a certain number of times while your opponent is playing–and the like are well known among members of most clubs.

Players nowadays especially in America, like to carry a great many clubs, and from this many heated arguments have arisen. Once after discussing what could be done without the more modern clubs like the spade mashie, mashie niblick, number three iron, etc., one enthusiast offered to bet a friend that he could beat him with any five clubs of his friend's selection. He had to play with five niblicks!

Bob Jones and George Duncan pose for this photo before teeing off in the 1920 U.S. Open at Inverness GC in Toledo, Ohio.

A Laugh Plus a Handicap on Duncan and Mitchell

And there are a lot of stories about handicaps which were not asked or given with the intention of making a close game–little tricks which have led to considerable amusement in our great golfing family.

One of the best of these was pulled on George Duncan and Abe Mitchell, if the remarkable yarn is to be believed. The story goes that two ordinary players in England made a wager that they could beat Duncan and Mitchell in a best-ball match if that pair would concede them twenty yards on each hole. Both of the challengers were short

But there are perfectly legitimate handicaps for nearly every occasion, and everything possible should be done to encourage this kind of friendly competition. In golf it is by no means necessary to limit one's golfing companions to those of nearly the same accomplishment. The object of handicapping is to make an even game and it can achieve its purpose if properly applied. Fortunately, not many of us are like the fellow who proclaimed, as a true sportsman, that all he wanted was a reasonable advantage.

The Unfairness of Furrowed Bunkers

After the Open Championship at Oakmont a few years ago, there was a general explosion among newspapermen and contestants alike, concerning the furrows which had been carefully and diabolically raked in all the bunkers. This method of preparing a hazard for the unwary was rather much of an innovation at that time, although it had been used once before in 1925. Now it is unfortunately alarmingly close to becoming a vogue on very nearly all of the championship courses throughout the country.

I was afraid, after Oakmont, that any criticism I might make of the sand hazards there would be interpreted as an ill-natured grumbling against the course, because I had made such a miserable showing in the tournament. But now, I feel that I may say something which I believe to be for the good of the game, without fear of being misunderstood.

Indeed, I have never conceived that playing conditions offered the least excuse to any man for his failing to win a championship, for the whole field has to play the same course at approximately the same time, and no man deserves to win who cannot win under existing conditions, whatever they may be.

I have no wish to criticize anything, or anyone, unfairly, but I believe that the only way to promote the interests of golf as a competitive sport is to discuss openly and fairly the problems which arise in playing the game.

The idea behind the furrowed bunker, unless I am mistaken, was to encourage and reward a superlative excellence in the play through the green. The thought was, I am sure, that the man who drove straight, and who played his irons accurately, would be doubly rewarded because his opponent, less accurate than himself, would be engulfed in a trouble from which he could not even miraculously extricate himself. At Oakmont, and at Minikahda where they also have furrowed bunkers, a shot into a bunker meant simply and positively a lost stroke unless a long putt happened to go down. There was no amount of skill in bunker play which would avail.

The only fault in the theory is to be found in the regrettable circumstance that on even our very best days, we are all intensely human, and no matter how well we may play, we must make a few bad shots. And no matter how hard we may strive for perfection, we cannot eliminate from the game that part of it which is played within the confines of the sand traps. It may be all very well to determine that skill with the tee and fairway clubs is the highest type and that such skill should reap the greatest reward, but the fact remains that when the element of skill is eliminated from a necessary department

of the game, the very game itself is thereby weakened by just so much.

It would be just as reasonable for those who contend that the premium on putting is too great to enlarge the hole to a diameter of a couple of feet or more, so that all would be equal on the green. The Oakmont furrows seemed to say, "Well, here you are in a bunker, and it doesn't matter how good you are, or how much nerve you have, the only thing you can do now is blast."

In the chapter dealing with bunker shots, I discussed three types –the chip, the cut-shot, and the blast. Of these three shots the least ambitious and the one in reach of more players is unquestionably the blast, and I am sure any professional will agree with me that this shot requires far less skill than the other two.

Yet, a furrowed bunker, supposing to reward the skillful player, absolutely precludes the use of a recovery shot requiring more than the application of a strong back and a willing heart!

The sense of justice of those who like to rake furrows in bunkers may be offended when some gifted person, braving disaster, is able to recover from a sand-pit and reach a green nearly two hundred yards away. But when a person is able to combine skill and nerve sufficient to bring off a shot of that kind, he is entitled to everything he can get out of it. No man of mean ability can do it, and because he can't I see no reason for bringing the expert down to his level simply because both happen to be in a sand-trap.

Skill Helps But Little

One favorite argument in support of the stymie has always been that it was a golf shot and skill could be acquired in its execution. The same argument may be advanced in favor of the ridges. And possibly such is the case. But if it is, then I am sure the standards of golf will have to advance considerably, for I saw no one in the fine representative field at Oakmont and at Minikahda who displayed the least bit of assurance in the bunkers.

I should never care to argue for anything which would lessen the difficulty of the game, for its difficulty is its greatest charm. But when, in spite of the vast improvement in the ball, in seeking to preserve the difficulty and to make scoring as hard as it was in the old days, we make the mistake of destroying the effect of skill and judgment in an important department, I cannot help protesting.

I am, of course, open to be convinced that a ball can be played as artistically from a furrow as from wind-blown sand, and if the raking is to continue, I should very much like to be so convinced. But until then I cannot help thinking that the practice is hurting the game.

It is surprising with how little effort a ball may be extracted from a nasty looking place if the clubhead is allowed to do the work.
(Ralph Miller Library)

If Golf Is Worth Playing, It Is Worth Playing Right

Bob Jones holes his putt on the ninth green at Winged Foot GC during the 1929 U.S. Open Championship won by Jones in a playoff against Al Espinosa.

When playing friendly games, golfers are too prone, I think, to a lax observance of the rules of golf. In any sort of a match no one likes to take a hole upon a technicality. But a disregard for the rules in every-day play is apt to encourage an ignorance which may be costly at a crucial moment, when the generosity of an opponent has nothing to do with it.

In a great number of places I have been told that the local rules entitle a player to lift without penalty, if he drives into a certain ditch or stream upon the course. The idea is, of course, that the hazard is unfair, and if a ball is driven far enough to go into it, the player driving it should not be penalized. That, of course, is a very charitable viewpoint. No one enjoys getting into trouble, especially after hitting a splendid shot, and in more or less informal games the free lift granted by the rules is very welcome.

But however discouraging may be the penalty, it is not the spirit of the game that a man may plunge headlong into trouble and be allowed to escape unhurt merely because he has had to cover a lot of ground to reach the untoward position. When he stands on the teeing ground he knows, or can find out, what is before him. The golfer plays his shots according to the design of the hole and the location of hazards. If a creek crosses the fairway at a point too far distant to be

played over with safety, it is the player's duty to avoid it. There is no requirement that a driver be used off the tee. A spoon or an iron will do just as well. If either is demanded for the sake of safety, the player should be made to use it. We may condemn the location of the hazard, but we should not encourage the player to wholly disregard its existence.

In tournament play, especially in medal competition, it is the duty of every competitor to call attention to infractions of the rules and to see that the proper penalty is imposed. Nearly everyone must hesitate to call a penalty upon an opponent, and usually the embarrassment is relieved by the presence of an official referee whose duty it is to take cognizance of a breach by either competitor. But in medal play, there should be no such hesitation, for every player, as regards what happens within his ken, is the representative of every other player. He might be willing to waive the penalty in a personal encounter, but he has no right to waive it for the hundred odd men against whom his playing partner is competing. If he does so, he is liable to disqualification.

I do not recall that I have ever seen what appeared to be an intentional breach of the rules. I do not profess to be an expert upon the rules of golf, for I have not made a very serious study of them. But I should never think of entering an important competition without a fair understanding of the questions which are apt to come up. Time and again, in watching national championship competitions, you will see displayed an ignorance of the rules which is really surprising.

In Atlanta several years ago, Tom Prescott and Louis Jacoby met in the final of an important tournament at Druid Hills. Coming to the seventeenth the match was even. Jacoby was on the green with his tee shot and Tom was bunkered beyond. For some unaccountable reason, Tom took a practice swing a few inches from his ball, knocking up a double handful of sand. Now, the penalty for grounding the club in a bunker before a player strikes at the ball is loss of the hole in match play. Immediately realizing what he had done, Tom picked up his ball and conceded the hole, eventually losing the match one up. No one yet, not even Tom, knows why he took that swing.

Also Reggie Lewis at the thirty-sixth green of the historic match at Engineer's when Chick Evans beat him on the forty-second hole, committed a breach of the rules which should have lost him the hole, without the excitement of Chick holing a long putt, and of Reggie missing a short one.

Reggie's ball lay on a grassy slope beyond the green and fully forty yards from the hole. He was, therefore, not within the twenty yard radius which is defined as the putting green. In that position Reggie had the right to remove only those loose impediments in his line which were within twenty yards of the hole or within a club-length of his ball. But he went carefully down the slope, picking up dead leaves all along the line to the hole! And very properly, no one said anything about it, for Reggie was perfectly innocent, and it couldn't help anyway.

Of course, Chick was right in not calling the penalty. He could not want to win the hole because of a purely unintentional lapse

Bob Jones led an amateur team of challengers to victory in 1941 at Detroit over Walter Hagen's Ryder Cup Team.

on Reggie's part which gave him no advantage whatsoever. The referee's position was equally difficult. He knew Reggie well enough to know that he would never have thought of infringing the rules if he had known what he was doing.

One must be very careful in removing obstructions on the putting surface. Particularly is this true in Great Britain, for there the greens are much larger than ours, and a ball may be far onto the green and still be over twenty yards from the hole. Many people have the idea that the putting green comprises all the closely cropped and rolled surface around the hole, but it certainly does not. If your ball is on the putting surface but more than twenty yards from the hole, you have no more right to remove obstructions than you would have if you were in the fairway two hundred yards from the green.

I saw one instance where ignorance of the rules caused a player to lose a valuable right to which he was in all good conscience entitled. It was in the qualifying round of the Amateur Championship at Merion in 1924. This man's ball was buried in the white, fluffy sand

of the bunker in front of the thirteenth green and had disappeared completely from sight. The caddie preceded his player to the ball, and pointing to a depression in the sand bank, he said, "It went in there." Whereupon the player took two or three vicious wallops at the sand. Nothing emerging, he discovered that his ball was not there, but some eight or ten feet away from his point of attack. Of course, he had to count the strokes and barely failed to qualify. He did not know that he had the right to remove enough sand so that he could see the top of the ball. Had he attempted to do so, he would soon have discovered that his ball was not beneath the first depression.

Several years ago I played with Jock Hutchison over the course of some small town in Indiana or Ohio, I cannot recall which. On one hole of the course there was a cross-bunker some 250 yards from the tee. The local rule provided that in case a ball was driven into the bunker on the first stroke it might be thrown out without penalty. Jack having driven into the bunker, picked up his ball and to the consternation of the spectators, threw it as far as possible in the direction of the green. "Well," he said, "there is nothing in the rule saying in which direction I should throw it."

Winter Rules

So called "Winter Rules" are also subject to queer interpretations. A prevalent idea seems to be that the permission to improve the lie of the ball is given for the sole purpose of enabling the player to make a good score. On that principle, there are countless players who do not hesitate to make use of wooden pegs, sand, rubber tees, or anything else that may be handy; or to exchange a position on an uncomfortable slope for one yards away on level ground.

"Winter Rules" are employed only to prevent undue damage to the course resulting from hacking balls from bad lies. They are in effect usually during the period of the year when replaced divots will not take hold and when the fairways do not afford good lies. The player's convenience or his score is no part of the consideration for the existence of "Winter Rules." As near as possible, the ball should always be played where and as it lies. Rules which permit liberties to be taken with the established regulations of the game should positively be discouraged, and, when found absolutely necessary, confined within the narrowest limits.

Henry Cotton, the young English professional, while visiting America last year to take part in the winter tournaments, mildly scored the purely American habit of providing so-called "Winter Rules" for tournament play. Under these rules the player has the right to lift and clean his ball upon the putting green.

The U.S.G.A. has long looked with disfavor upon any concessions in this direction. The rules of golf require that except in a few rare situations, the ball must be played as and where it lies unless a penalty be incurred for moving it. Allowing the ball to be lifted opens the door to anyone who might be minded to take advantage of the rule to improve his lie. I admit that I have never seen the rule abused in this

If Golf Is Worth Playing, It Is Worth Playing Right

way, and it may be that the more serious aspect is the responsibility placed upon the player to be certain that he replaces the ball exactly as he found it. Whatever the effect may be, it is certain that the game is not helped by permitting a ball once in play to be lifted for any purpose. Mud on the ball, bad lies, and soggy greens are circumstances and conditions which have to be met, and they can be met and overcome by one who possesses sufficient skill.

When Willie Hunter beat me in the National Amateur at St. Louis in 1921, I was impressed with the necessity of adapting one's game to existing conditions. The course was very wet that day and, as the turf on the putting greens was not heavy, a ball pitched with backspin invariably picked up a big chunk of mud. Before the rain on the previous day I had played about as well as I could wish, so I expected to beat Willie without too much difficulty. But after the soaking rain, though the iron shots and pitches, which had continually left me holeable putts for birdies the day before, stopped no farther from the hole, the putts ceased to be holeable. It was like putting with an egg. Naturally, I didn't like it, but there was nothing I could do about it.

A Bit of Headwork

But Willie knew something which could be done and that something made enough difference to win the match for him. Instead of steep, quick-stopping shots he played every shot to the green on a low trajectory designed to roll several yards across the wet turf. The advantages of that type of shot where twofold—first, it was not so likely to pick up mud as it hit the ground; and, second, whatever mud did adhere to the ball was dissolved by the roll over the sodden grass.

I remember particularly the fourteenth hole of the second round, the thirty-second of the match, which really was the final turning point. I was one up at the time, and both second shots stopped less than ten feet from the hole. Willie, putting a clean ball, holed his putt, a task which I found impossible with my mud-covered sphere. It was then that I realized that it was no freak of fortune which was giving my opponent the advantage on the green. Certainly the lesson should have sunk in by that time.

That is golf. The test should never be standardized. If it becomes so the game loses its fascination to a great extent. If we had been

allowed to lift the balls and clean them that day, Hunter would have been deprived of an advantage to which he was entitled by reason of superior skill and better headwork.

An Involuntary Action

In stroke competition it is impossible to avoid some amount of lifting and replacing. The man nearer the hole does not always want to hole the short one and move out of the way. He may feel that to do so would endanger the stroke. In that case there is nothing to do but mark the other ball. But sitting behind the ninth green at Olympia Fields I could not help noticing that almost every player who marked his ball rubbed it clean either in his hand or upon his knickers before replacing it. In nine cases out of ten, the action was evidently involuntary, done unthinkingly or prompted by nervousness; in the tenth case, no doubt, it was done in ignorance of the rules. In no case was there any attempt at concealment.

Apparently insignificant though the matter may be, those who have attempted to putt a mud-laden ball will appreciate the value of a clean one. After playing in tournament after tournament where cleaning is permitted, it is hard for the player to realize that it is not an absolute right. It is very hard indeed to call a person on a thing of that kind, but the practice ought to be discouraged.

If the course is in playable condition, the likelihood of picking up mud is a hazard of the game just as much as bunkers or anything else. If a ball may be lifted on the putting green, why not in the fairway? If the course is not playable, then the competition should be postponed until it is.

And if you are going to play golf, you should play by the rules of the game. If you don't, call the game by another name.

Bob Jones putting on the third green at Inwood GC in the playoff with Bobby Cruickshank
after playing out of the bunker where his bold second had placed him.

Sportsmanship and Golf

Some time ago I saw and read things which caused me to think more than ever about what we call sportsmanship as applied to competition in sports. Like everyone else I suppose I am most interested in those affairs which concern myself, and after reading in the English papers that I was more intent upon winning than most British golfers, and in American papers that I was taking golf so seriously that I was spoiling the fun of it, I began to wonder if I was all wrong, and if the composure and concentration I had worked so hard to achieve were, after all, only qualities which we should like to see only in those who make a living out of their sport. And please don't understand me here as taking a crack at professionalism, for nobody knows better than I what glorious sportsmen professional golfers are. If you want to hear alibis and excuses don't go to the pros because they don't make them.

Recently I made a statement to one of my friends which I am willing to back with all my heart. It was that no professional golfer ever gave a thought to any pecuniary advantage to be gained by victory in a golf tournament. These men who live eat, and sleep golf are out to win, but if they don't they are the most generous of losers.

What Is a Sportsman?

And that last phrase brings me to the point of my story. What is a generous loser? What is a sportsman? Is a man a good loser or a sportsman who says, "Well, I was playing for the fun of the thing, anyway." Isn't that taking something from the winner which he rightfully has earned? Wouldn't it be better to say, "Old man, you beat me in spite of all I could do. I congratulate you."?

I do not like an ill-natured loser. No one does. But I object equally to a winner or loser who makes light of the contest. Whether he has won or whether he has lost, a man owes it to his opponent to make him feel that the match has been a serious one.

Naturally, I have respected the giants of the past, and I have tried to mold my golfing technique and my attitude toward the game after the fashion of what I have known about my heroes.

In America we admire above all other amateur golfers, Walter Travis, and Jerry Travers. From what I have heard and read of these men, nothing could have been more cold and determined than their demeanor upon the golf course in a championship or other important match. Both had what I have always regarded as the ideal competitive temperament: a desire to win exceeded by nothing except a determination to play fair.

Ouimet Has Right Idea

Francis Ouimet, one of the gentlest, kindest boys in the world, is what the Scotch call a dour golfer in championships. I have played against Francis in many important matches, and I have also been lucky enough to play with him when no one was watching and when nothing depended on the result.

Bob Jones shares the tee with Francis Ouimet who defeated Harry Vardon and Ted Ray in a playoff for the 1913 U.S. Open.

And there is the difference. The friendly round to me is the place and time for levity. That is the place for camaraderie and all that sort of thing. And we can play friendly rounds fifty weeks in the year. But when we stand on the first tee in a national championship our only purpose should be to play the best golf we know. The championship is popularly supposed to be a competition to determine the best golfer and it cannot be such if every man entered is not prepared to give the best he has. To this end concentration and fixity of purpose are indispensable.

That is the code of sportsmanship on which I have built all my life, and if it is wrong, I should like to know. But I must say here to every man who has beaten me in the past, and to every one who will beat me in the future, that their victories have not or will not come from want of effort on my part. If I find that I cannot concentrate on the game and work my hardest to win, I shall join the gallery and cheer for the men who have a better right than I to their place in the field.

An Unjust Epithet

It is truly astonishing how often we hear it said, "Oh, So-and-So is a fine golfer, but he'll never win because he's yellow."

SPORTSMANSHIP AND GOLF

"Yellow!" What do we mean by "yellow"? The term has always been used to reflect upon a man's physical courage, to imply that he is a coward, and unable to bear a man's burden. It is one of the most disagreeable epithets in the American vocabulary. I wonder if we realize how often we apply it unjustly to a golfer.

Golf is not like football or baseball. Golf does not require the least degree of physical courage. A man is walking into no danger when he ventures upon a golf course. Nothing will bite him and even his opponent is usually civil and considerate. Why, then, call him "yellow" if he misses a putt or flukes a pitch at a crucial stage?

A Break of the Game

Four years ago, when the open championship wasplayed at Worcester, Leo Diegel came to the seventy-second tee with a three to tie Johnny Farrell, who, at the time, was leading. As the hole is an easy drive and pitch affair, a three there was by no means unlikely for a player of Leo's caliber.

But the way he played the hole was the most pitiful thing imaginable. His drive was long and although in the rough, he was left with a very wee niblick pitch to the plateau green. Leo consumed worlds of time studying the shot. Carefully he addressed it and swung. Up came his head and he knocked the ball a bare five yards. On the next try the same thing happened, leaving him in the bunker short of the green in three. His fourth he played over the green, his fifth back on, and three putts for an eight. "Yellow," you say. Some one, perhaps, but not Leo.

Diegel, before he became prominent in golf, was one of the best basketball players around Detroit, and a splendid all-around athlete. Any man who plays basketball can not be said to have any "yellow" inclinations on the golf course.

Concentrate on Shot

Often you see men who do not last to the final ditch. There are many players who score miracle rounds in practice, but are helpless in competition. These players have been able to thrust from their playing consciousness the fear of bunkers and hazards confronting them, but their concentration cannot bear the added burden of being in a competition. Every shot in golf carries a responsibility. The greatest value of some hazards is the mental effect upon the players. When the bunker you see in front of you may not only cause you to lose a shot, but may also cost you a championship, it becomes so much harder to concentrate upon hitting the ball.

I have always thought that possibly the amateur golfer was at a distinct advantage in competing against a professional in an important championship. I remember someone once said of Walter Hagen, "Why shouldn't he have courage? He has enough contracts already to put him in the rich man's class. A championship does not mean a fortune to him."

Glory, or Glory and Money?

That's it. A big championship to a young pro like Cruickshank in 1923, or like Turnesa in 1926 meant fortune as well as glory. To me it meant only glory. Why shouldn't the strain of the finish bear down harder upon them than upon me? And yet I don't quite know if these fine sporting boys give a thought, when they're playing, to the money involved. They love the game, and they love to win. I don't know if that doesn't overshadow the other.

There is only one sort of golfer who can properly be called "yellow," and he deserves every implication the term carries with it. I mean the fellow who quits when he is down; the man who does not give out his very best until the last putt is holed. That golfer is "yellow" and he ought not to pursue a sportsman's game.

But don't blame the man who misses a shot because the strain is too great. Just stop a moment and remember that we are all human and that golf is a cruel game. And in it there are no chances to overlook responsibilities. They must all be faced and borne, and yet not thought of. Quite an assignment, isn't it?

Don't blame the man who misses a shot because the strain is too great. Remember we are all human and golf is a cruel game. (Ralph Miller Library)